DONE INTO *Dance*

DONE INTO

Isadora Duncan IN AMERICA

ANN DALY

Indiana University Press   Bloomington & Indianapolis

Dance

The paper used in this publicaion meets the minimum
requirements of American National Standard for
Information Sciences—Permanence of Paper for Printed
Library Materials, ANSI Z39.48-1984.

∞ TM

Manufactured in the United States of America

Library of Congress Cataloging-in-Publication Data

Daly, Ann, date

    Done into dance : Isadora Duncan in America /
Ann Daly.

        p.   cm.

    Includes index.

    ISBN 0-253-32924-8 (cl : acid-free paper). —
ISBN 0-253-20989-7

(pa: acid-free paper)

    1. Duncan, Isadora, 1877–1927.   2. Dancers—
United States—Biography. I. Title

GV1785.D8D35 1995

792.8 '028'092—dc20

                                  95-11633

1 2 3 4 5 00 99 98 97 96 95

FOR MY PARENTS,

Edwin and Claire Daly

Contents

Preface ix   Acknowledgments xv

1. PROLOGUE: DONE INTO *Dance* 2

2. THE *Dancing* BODY 22

3. THE *Natural* BODY 88

4. THE *Expressive* BODY 118

5. THE *Female* BODY 156

6. THE BODY *Politic* 178

7. EPILOGUE:
TWILIGHT OF AN AMERICAN *Goddess* 206

Notes 221   Index 261

PREFACE

Practically everybody knows at least *something* about Isadora Duncan. Probably not that she read Plato or that she considered her development of successive movement a significant artistic achievement. More likely, they know that she died in a sports car, her neck snapped by her own trailing scarf. Or that she was one of the original "liberated" women. Or that Vanessa Redgrave played her in the movie.[1]

Books are still written about Duncan with outdated information. Plays are still produced, exploiting the sensational aspects of her personal life. Scholarly references are made to her as though she never moved beyond her lyrical Chopin years. New scholarship inconsistent with the old anecdotal history is met with indignation.[2]

"Isadora"[3] is a product of our own personal and collective projections.

And, indeed, that is the way she wanted it, from the very beginning. Duncan insisted on mythologizing herself, because she longed to be noticed and remembered. That is why she refused to be filmed, because she wanted to become a legend: an absence rendered perpetually present.[4] The sense of longing that was so much a part of Duncan's dancing reproduces itself in our always thwarted but never-ceasing desire to see her dance, if not in the flesh or on celluloid, then at least in the mind's eye. Any cultural historian operates out of some degree of such longing, but the cultural historian of the body—and especially of the *dancing* body, which is, fundamentally, but a trace, even in its own moment—seems to emblematize this seductive (because impossible) task of reconstruction.

Duncan's career was an immensely grand gesture, spacious enough to accommodate a range of cultural needs and fantasies. My purpose with this book is to reconstruct, as it were, the body of Duncan's vanished practice— its processes, structures, and techniques,[5] its origins, its effects—as it developed in her native America. An expatriate most of her adult life, Duncan is usually considered more a product of Europe, but I see her exile as heightening rather than minimizing her relationship with her homeland and have situated her specifically within that American context. In doing so, I hope to demonstrate the complex and powerful ways in which the dancing body participates in the production of cultural identity.

Duncan was an unlikely subject of study for me, as a former journalist who has spent much of my career searching the new and avoiding the sentimental. I worked my way backward to Duncan, beginning with postmodern dance, backtracking to early modern dance, and then singling out Duncan. She was, it seemed, a major source of it all. She set the agenda for modern dance in America, defining the terms and literally setting the practice in motion. But the Duncan of whom I had seen glimpses, in history books and didactic performances, was perplexing. Was she a great dancer, a great mime, or merely a clever frolicker? Was she all intuition? Typically "female"? Was she a mere discoverer, driven by romantic notions of self-importance and even self-indulgence? Or did she forge, invent, create? As much as had been written about Duncan, none of the literature sufficiently answered these questions.

Then, in 1988, I saw the Elgin marbles. Suddenly this murky figure out of dance history came clearer, as I could feel in the sculptures of the pediment that Duncanesque sense of weight undercut by grace and buoyancy. In the next room, the Nereid trio seemed even nearer to the dancer. With their legs lifted—feet arched but not pointed—their airy mime seemed to resurrect Duncan's dancing body. I may have been no closer to the answers, but I was hooked on the questions. What had her audiences seen on stage? What dreams and fears of theirs did she play out? What was the logic of their fascination? Why, in short, was Duncan's dancing so compelling?

Recognizing the limits of historical knowledge, I decided to look at least a little more closely and a little more widely at the existing evidence, at least to try to fantasize what it was about her dancing that drew her body into the American imagination in the first place. I never had found the naive, instinctual Duncan very laudable, let alone interesting. As I read, and as I looked, and as I imagined, a much more complex Duncan emerged—one who was certainly inclined toward the instinctual, but far from naive.

Here, then, is yet another book on Isadora Duncan, but one distinguished, I believe, by its focused attempt to articulate the meanings of Duncan's dancing for her American audiences and the ways those meanings were produced. To my mind, such an interpretive project demands attention to the negotiation between text and context: only by reading each one through the other could the fullest possible account be attempted.

My research, then, involved three levels of inquiry. The first was descriptive and analytical: What did Duncan do and say, and what were her spectators' responses? I was eager to revisit primary sources in an effort to identify the apocryphal or distorted stories that have sedimented in the Duncan literature. In synthesizing Duncan's theory of dance and tracing its sources, I have built, gratefully, on the sturdy foundation provided by biographers and scholars such as Fredrika Blair, Deborah Jowitt, Elizabeth Kendall, Allan Ross Macdougall, and Nancy Chalfa Ruyter.[6]

The second, central level of inquiry was interpretive: What did Duncan's practice mean to her audiences? While most studies of Duncan deal with the dancer's significance in very broad geographical and historical terms, I was interested specifically in the potency of Duncan for her American audiences during her lifetime. To that end, and informed by the work of philosopher Mark Johnson and sociologist Pierre Bourdieu, I conceptualized Duncan's body as a practice through which a variety of cultural issues such as self, race, Woman, art, democracy, and America were being negotiated.

The third level of inquiry was critical: What were the ideological implications of Duncan's practice? I assumed her ideas and principles—such as "Nature" and "Beauty"—to be constructions and sought to unpack their origins and effects. Bourdieu's concept of cultural "distinction" as a reproduction of class difference and Toni Morrison's work on the creation of an "American" literature as the response to a projected Africanism provided points of departure for considering the construction of Duncan's practice in terms of class and race. Because I have found Julia Kristeva's semiotics, as outlined in *Revolution in Poetic Language*, very enabling, insofar as it theorizes a space for the marginal to be culturally productive, I used it as a ground for my reading of Duncan's dancing as a feminist practice. Although these and other theories fundamentally informed my choice of questions, the structure of my inquiry, and the shape of my arguments, this book is not *about* theory. Instead, I have deployed theory instrumentally: it is rarely given center stage.

In my research, I worked from Duncan outward, progressing in general from the descriptive/analytic to the interpretive to the critical. Of course, certain questions—primarily about Duncan's representation of Woman—framed and thus produced my descriptive and analytic research, but I spent so much time wading through the vast amount of primary data that it took me several subsequent readings of that material, finally organized chronologically and contextually, to articulate with any clarity or coherence my interpretive and critical axes.

These descriptive/analytical, interpretive, and critical modes of inquiry were neither discrete nor linear, and in my writing I have chosen not to uncoil the looping shape of the project. This book, from the very start, was conceived of architecturally. The contextualizing prologue and the critical epilogue, like pillars at either end, support the thematic chapters in between. I think of these central essays, each one winding through the Duncan corpus at a different angle, through a different bodily trope, as a spiraling progression, sometimes doubling back around itself in order to move forward. I organized the book in multiple thematic spirals rather than in a single chronological line because it was important to me, first, to make the writing move and, second, to amplify, rather than to simplify, Duncan's shifting, multiple negotiations of and with American culture.

Duncan's project was not just to produce art but to legitimize dance as a "high" art. In an albeit oblique manner, this is the story I am telling—only one of many that can be told about Duncan. My project, similarly, is one of legitimacy, of reinscribing Duncan into American history, that is to say, into historical time and discursive space. I want to reconnect Duncan with her spectators, identifying the dancing body, in both its material and its symbolic aspects, as the point of contact, or medium of discourse, between Duncan and her American audiences.

Not only do I want to trace the webs enmeshing Duncan and her spectators within American culture, but I also want to situate those webs in their specific historical moments. Duncan's life (1877–1927) spanned a swiftly changing period in American history, from late Victorianism, through the fin de siècle, through progressivism and the Greenwich Village radicals, through World War I to the Red Scare, and to modern art. The interpretive milieu when Duncan arrived back in the United States in 1908 was different from when she danced the "Marseillaise" during World War I or when she returned from Moscow in 1922. As Duncan aged and as American culture changed, the body enacted on stage metamorphosed, too. I want to represent the complexity of Duncan's lifelong practice, in both its textual and its contextual dimensions.

To that end, I chose not to foreground the global, overarching, theoretical aspects of the work, but rather, following Clifford Geertz's long-ago (but still echoing) call to "thick description" and "local knowledge," to concentrate on the local, the particular, the specific. "Cultural analysis," according to Geertz, "is (or should be) guessing at meanings, assessing the guesses, and drawing explanatory conclusions from the better guesses, not discovering the Continent of Meaning and mapping out its bodiless landscape."[7] When Geertz wrote that twenty years ago, he was refuting the tenets of structuralism, arguing against the construction of master narratives (the Continent) at the expense of local complexities (the landscape). Poststructuralism has taught us well to beware the master narrative, but, paradoxically, in many ways poststructuralism has calcified into another master narrative and has produced a voracious appetite for more of the same. As a scholar who was constructed within that paradigm, and who still works within that paradigm, I invoke Geertz's approach to cultural analysis as a necessary intervention. I do not extrapolate from the case of Duncan to the universal; I do not generate from her particulars any grand theories of art, culture, or feminism. I do, however, aim to reconstruct the bodies in the landscape

ACKNOWLEDGMENTS

To many people I owe my gratitude.

First, to my dissertation advisor at New York University's Department of Performance Studies, Marcia B. Siegel, and to the rest of the committee: Lynn Garafola, Barbara Kirshenblatt-Gimblett, Peggy Phelan, and Richard Schechner.

To Robert Crunden, Susan Foster, Peter Jelavich, Deborah Jowitt, and Susan Manning, who read the book manuscript with such care. To Hans Gumbrecht, Amy Koritz, and Bill Worthen, who made salient suggestions on particular chapters.

To Duncan dancers Lori Belilove, Julia Levien, and Hortense Kooluris (who generously loaned her videotapes to me); to Duncan historian Margaretta Mitchell; to Gordon Craig scholar Arnold Rood; and to Dalcroze scholar Selma Landen Odom.

To dance scholars Barbara Barker and Deborah Jowitt, for their help with photo research.

To friends who generously offered their translation skills: Neda Doany, Judy Sebesta, and Jurgen Streeck.

To research assistants Kamy Bolson, Christia Osborn, and Cathy Tubb.

To the librarians, archivists, and administrators who have assisted me, including Madeleine Nichols, Monica Moseley, Rita Waldron, Richard Buck, and Heidi Stock, the New York Public Library for the Performing Arts Dance Collection; John Kirkpatrick, Ken Craven, Pat Fox, and Melissa Miller, the Harry Ransom Humanities Research Center, University of Texas at Austin; Claire Hudson, Theatre Museum, the Victoria and Albert Museum; Verna Curtis, Mary Ison, and Eveline Overmiller, the Library of Congress; Vicki Wulff, Performing Arts Library, the Library of Congress; Anne Caiger, the University Research Library, University of California, Los Angeles; Barbara R. Geisler, the San Francisco Performing Arts Library and Museum; Nicole L. Bouché, the Bancroft Library, University of California, Berkeley; Harold L. Miller, the State Historical Society of Wisconsin; Roger B. Berry, the University of California, Irvine, Library; Richard L. Popp, the University of Chicago Library; Lauren Bufferd, the Chicago Public Library; Sibylle Zemitis, the California State Library; Craig Marley and Constance Olds, the Metropolitan Museum of Art; Philip N. Cronenwett, the Dartmouth College Library; Faye Phillips, Louisiana State University; Melissa Dalziel, the Bodleian Library, University of Oxford; E. M. C. van Houts, Archivist, Newnham College, Cambridge University; Elizabeth Fuller, the Rosenbach Museum and Library; Teresa A. McGill, the Chicago Historical Society; Kathryn Mets and Tony Pisani, the Museum of the City of New York; and Hélène Pinet, Musée Rodin.

To my colleagues at the University of Texas at Austin, especially Jon Whitmore, dean of the College of Fine Arts; Sharon Vasquez, former head of dance and current chair of the Department of Theatre and Dance; and Coleman Jennings, former chair of the Department of Theatre and Dance.

And, finally, to my extraordinary parents, Edwin and Claire Daly.

The weaknesses of this book, however, I claim as my very own.

***

Support for travel, research, and writing was provided by the University of Texas at Austin in the forms of a University Research Institute Summer Research Award, a College of Fine Arts Summer Research/Creativity Award, and grants from the Morton Brown Fund of the Department of Theatre and Dance.

A portion of chapter 2 originally appeared as "Isadora Duncan's Dance Theory," *Dance Research Journal* 26, no. 2 (Fall 1994): 24–31.

Portions of chapters 2, 3, and 7 originally appeared as "Isadora Duncan and the Distinction of Dance," *American Studies* 35, no. 1 (Spring 1994): 5–23.

Excerpts from the manuscripts and letters of Isadora Duncan reprinted courtesy of Mr. Angus Duncan, the New York Public Library for the Performing Arts, the Theatre Museum of the Victoria & Albert Museum, the Bodleian Library at the University of Oxford, the Harry Ransom Humanities Research Center at the University of Texas at Austin, the Museum of the City of New York, Shirley H. Steegmuller, and Theater Arts Books and Routledge, NY.

Excerpts from *My Life* by Isadora Duncan reprinted courtesy of Mr. Angus Duncan and Liveright Publishing Corporation. Copyright 1927 by Boni & Liveright, Inc. Copyright renewed 1955 by Liveright Publishing Corporation.

Excerpts from the manuscripts and letters of Irma Duncan reprinted courtesy of the New York Public Library for the Performing Arts.

Excerpt from *The Letters of Hart Crane 1916–1932*, edited by Brom Weber, reprinted courtesy of Brom Weber.

Excerpts from *"Your Isadora": The Love Story of Isadora Duncan and Gordon Craig*, edited by Francis Steegmuller, reprinted courtesy of Shirley H. Steegmuller.

DONE INTO *Dance*

1.

One of Isadora Duncan's earliest programs, performed in September 1898 in Newport, Rhode Island, was titled "Done into Dance." She had designed three such programs, each of which translated into a dance either a musical score (Ethelbert Nevin's "The Water Scenes" and "A Shepherd's Tale"; Felix Mendelssohn's "A Midsummer Night's Dream") or a poetic text (Omar Khayyám's *Rubáiyát*). This aesthetically elaborated process of embodiment—of being "done into dance"—provides the framework for this book. What was "done into dance," however, was more than just music or poetry. Indeed, the major discourses of American culture during Duncan's lifetime (1877–1927), a period of complex and significant change, were engaged through her dancing body. Some choreographers are masters of structure, others of symbolism or the innovative step. In Duncan's case, she reinvented the fundamental of her art: the body.

PROLOGUE: DONE INTO *Dance*

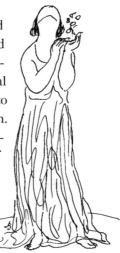

The body is that curious place where nature and culture—what anthropologist Mary Douglas called the "physical" and "social" bodies—somehow inter-penetrate.[1] It is the most obvious of our cultural symbols (the place where gender and race are said to originate), and yet it is, curiously, the most hidden. It is undeniable and yet, in our logocentrism, con-stantly denied. As both a source and a product of culture, the body is just as resistant to change as it is subject to change. Our collective fears and our collective dreams are produced and reproduced within the body; culture, as sociologist Pierre Bourdieu has explained it, is "not a 'state of mind,' still less a kind of arbitrary adherence to a set of instituted dogmas and doctrines ('beliefs'), but rather a state of the body."[2] And yet the body's extraordinary ideological power historically has been produced by a communal denial of its sociality, in the belief that it resides above culture, in the realm of "Truth." As the contingent nature of the body's meanings is covered over, as Duncan did, the body is endowed with the authority of the "natural," the "universal," the "timeless," and the "God-given."

"The beauty of the human body is a myth," wrote poet Shaemas O'Sheel in 1910, "and it needs a priestess to point us [to] the truth of it."[3] For O'Sheel, and many of his contemporaries, Duncan was that priestess. She believed that the body was the prime reality, the template of life, the source of all knowledge. The body was inseparable from the mind; when she talked about the body, she was talking also about the soul, about the "self." The "Truth" of the body as she constructed it lay in its depth and in its harmony with "Nature." It was about "Beauty," and about moral force.

Today, the body is a battleground, where the naturalized, privileged contingencies of a white, male, heterosexual body are challenged daily, in the streets, in the arts, and in the universities. In Duncan's day, the body was more like a meeting ground, where discourses of science,[4] nature, art, and metaphysics were happy to find themselves not-so-distant relations. Walt Whitman's body electric, psychologist William James's expressive body, evolutionist Ernst Haeckel's monist body, and photographer Annie Brigman's female nudes were not considered incompatible.

If today we fixate on the technological mastery of the body—through laboratory reproductive techniques, cosmetic surgery, and death-defying medical machinery—Americans around the last turn of the century were interested in fathoming the depths of the bodily container, and were conflicted about the release or control of its inner forces. Delsartean expression manuals (widespread in the 1880s) explained how internal emotions were encoded in external behavior. The resurrected Olympic Games (which debuted in 1896) asked how fast, high, and far the body was capable of projecting itself. X-rays (discovered in 1895) penetrated the very sheath of the body, objectifying its invisible depths into an external image. The birth control movement (which gained initial momentum in the 1910s) advocated the social virtue of containing rather than reproducing the female body.

In this era, not so far removed from the implosion of a civil war, America was reconstituting itself, self-conscious about the creation and

imprinting of national identity. The country was generating unprecedented wealth, industrializing and urbanizing at great speed, and gaining large numbers of immigrants. In the midst of this leap from the
nineteenth to the twentieth century, bodily practices were, as always, a
potent barometer of cultural transition. The dancing body, however,
whether on stage or in the ballroom, never had been considered much
more than a social diversion, at best, or an evil distraction, at worst. But
with Duncan, the dancing body became a conspicuous participant in
America's social, cultural, and political life. It became a place where
contested ground—nation, Woman, culture, self, race, art—was negotiated quite explicitly.

To speak of "the body," of course, is a verbal deception. There is not
one body, but many. And what is especially interesting about Duncan is
that she enacted so many of them: the dancing body, the natural body, the
expressive body, the female body, and the body politic, to name the ones
I will explore in this book. What they all share is movement, or, to be more
exact, what philosopher Mark Johnson calls the image schemata of
"force."

Johnson argues that the world is not divined objectively but is grasped
imaginatively, by means of, among other things, metaphors generated by
embodied experience. Perception—that is to say, meaning-making—is
structured by bodily based image schematas such as containment, balance,
and force. An "image schemata" is not a static template or visual image;
rather, it is "a recurring, dynamic pattern of our perceptual interactions and
motor programs that gives coherence and structure to our experience."[5]
These patterns are constrained by the logic of bodily experience (which
refers not just to perception, manipulation of objects, and body movement,
but also to the body's embeddedness in history, culture, and language) and
are projected metaphorically across various domains of experience, connecting up art and mathematics, for example, or science and religion.
Metaphor thus becomes a basic mode of understanding, not just expressive of knowledge but constitutive of knowledge. "Through metaphor,"
Johnson writes, "we make use of patterns that obtain in our physical
experience to organize our more abstract understanding."[6]

We first grasp the meaning of force, according to Johnson, when we are
born, as we are subject to external and internal forces. Then we begin to
realize that we ourselves can be sources of force on our bodies and on external objects—we learn how to move our bodies and manipulate objects and
interact with the environment. The meaning of force gradually is extended

and modified and conceptualized, and we realize that forces are not just physical but can be moral or logical or social as well.[7]

The general components of force are also those of Duncan's dancing: interaction, motion, directionality, and intensity.[8] Duncan's solos—a single body struggling against, shrinking from, floating on, and thrusting into space—were enactments of agency, the self in the process of engagement with the external world, whether that meant love or fate, oppression or death. The way she enacted this force changed over time: from the lyrical manipulation of space and time in her early years, to the allegorical trajectories during the war years, to the dynamic force within utter stillness that she strived for in her later years. When Duncan proclaimed that she had "never once danced a solo,"[9] she was, I think, referring not just to herself as the collective Chorus but also to the interaction, or "duet," so to speak, of her body on/by/with its surrounding space, which she rendered not just visible but palpable. At root, Duncan's dances, recalling her readings of Schopenhauer and Nietzsche, exemplified the striving and struggling of human Will.

Duncan essentially played out the drama of the self yearning for somebody, or something—an Ideal, really—that continually obsessed her. "I realize in my philosophy," she wrote in her early twenties, "that a desire for the unattainable is perhaps the happiest of states."[10] She was dogged all her life by the inability to integrate all the different aspects of herself, and her early choreography repeatedly embodied a person yearning and searching, and in that process finding beauty and pleasure. The little *Prelude* from her earliest Chopin program (c. 1904), described by Julia Levien, a leading second-generation Duncan dancer, provides an example:

> The dance begins with three simple steps on half-toe, the arms moving outwards from the side (second position to en couronne), on the second phrase of music. On the next musical phrase the dancer runs into corner right with a questioning lift of the body and head as the hands move to the center of the chest and up, with an imploring gesture to the upper corner of the space. As the line of the music ascends, the dancer turns to the rear of the stage, continuing her exploration of space, from side to side. As she moves, her back to the audience, her body sways against her momentum and her arms, raised above her head, describe a curve in the upper sky. She turns again to the audience, repeats the first figure of "hold and run," to the opposite corner, with larger gestures as befits the stronger chords of the music. The dance ends with one more searching gesture to the back of the stage and then a final turn forward and a gesture to earth, to sky; the arms circle up and down, the hands fall forward, the head turns slowly from side to side, as if waiting for the answer to the question implied in the opening phrase of the dance.[11]

Even today, the choreography is taught not as a series of steps but as a narrative of force: of someone moving forward but being pushed backward by an unseen but nevertheless powerful entity, for example, or of someone repeatedly searching here and there for something beyond reach. These were the virtual forces that drove the choreography, formally and narratologically. At a time when Americans were concerned with finding for themselves a national selfhood, a cultural identity, and a means of individual self-expression, spectators were primed to participate in this force, in this dancing "subject-in-process," to borrow a term from French theorist Julia Kristeva.[12]

And, too, the force of Duncan's dancing body implied the transgression of the body as a container: a transgression of bodily and, by extension, cultural boundaries.[13] In her dancing, the wavelike energy of the self's inner, individual life burst through its container, flowing outward into space, into culture. On the one hand, the fluidity between inside and outside did permit Duncan's spectators to imagine themselves as subjects of ideal social potentialities. On the other hand, she did respect the boundary, with all its ideological implications, between harmony and chaos. In her later writings, she saw the *controlled* and thus harmonious fluidity of her own dancing as prayerful liberation, while she regarded what she saw as the spastic chaos of ragtime and jazz dancing as a reversion to "African primitivism." The "distinction," to borrow Bourdieu's phrase,[14] of Duncan's seemingly spontaneous, expressive, liberated body was produced in explicit opposition to a stereotypical Africanism defined as uncivilized, sexual, and profane.[15]

The vitality of a breathing, moving work of art enthralled Duncan's audiences (mostly white, and members of the economic, intellectual, or cultural elite), who were desperately seeking a way out of the moribund nineteenth century. "A strange and dark century, the nineteenth!" wrote socialist writer Floyd Dell, an editor of Greenwich Village's radical monthly, *The Masses*. "When they thought of creating beauty, they thought of creating it by means of colored paints and stone and words. The human body as the medium of high artistic expression did not seem to occur to them."[16] To Dell, and many other Americans, Duncan's body symbolized the promise of the twentieth century, of a "living life."

Duncan's powerful resonance with her American audiences can be explained by the consonance between text and context: between the force of her dance practice and its cultural moment, self-consciously defined in all its aspects by the "forces of progress."[17] Duncan represented a concrete bodily experience of force—read as progress, change, liberation—that was metaphorically projected by her various American audiences into abstract domains ranging from art to politics. In other words, the image schemata of force was the logic of Duncan's appeal to her various American audiences. Progressivists and radicals, modernists and realists alike constructed the significance of her practice through the metaphorical projection of force from her dancing to their own particular artistic, intellectual, social, or political projects. She "was our symbol," recalled one writer, "the symbol of a new art, a new literature, a new national polity, a new life."[18]

* * *

In Europe, Duncan's "Americanness" delighted her admirers (the German Karl Federn lauded "her sure, free, and youthful Americanism")[19] and her lovers (Gordon Craig was charmed by her "American *push*").[20] Her outspokenness, her expansiveness, her ambition, her grit, all marked her as "American." So did her expatriate mentality (as much as she raged bitterly against the iniquities of modern America, she seemed unable to let it go) and her claim to the invention of a "new" dance. She was seen as a "pioneer," that romanticized emblem of initiative and vision, supposedly born of a brief history (since the native Americans had been written out of it) and aversion to tradition. As the Franco-Russian critic André Levinson commented (not quite approvingly, from his classical, European perspective), "She was the product of a race that had no past."[21]

Duncan, a California girl, had the sort of long and loose stride from the hips that seemed to echo the west's wide-open landscapes. Her emphasis on "evolutionary" dance motion—her insistence that each movement give birth to the next and to the next in organic succession—was in itself indicative of a peculiarly American love of motion that was giving rise to Eadweard Muybridge's sequential photographs of the human figure in motion and Thomas Alva Edison's moving pictures. Historian Howard Mumford Jones sees this as the "Age of Energy," whose twin images were that of the mobile (images of movement such as immigrants pouring into cities, railways stretching westward, and the automobile) and of the motor (images of machines that incite motion, such as the steam engine and the dynamo).[22] Cultural historian Hillel Schwartz points also to the escalator, the assembly-line conveyor belt, the roller coaster, and the zipper as symptoms of a "new quality of motion"[23] and argues persuasively that, from dance to penmanship to prosthetic legs, torque was the "new kinaesthetic" of the twentieth century.[24] "Migration and movement, mobility and motion," writes historian Thomas J. Schlereth, characterized identity during this period, when "[a] country in transition was also in transit."[25] As Gertrude Stein observed, "It is something strictly American to conceive a space that is filled with moving, a space of time that is filled always filled with moving."[26] It seemed peculiarly modern, too, this love of movement, which suggested the forward motion of American culture, into a new century, and a new world.

The years roughly between 1890 and 1914 were watershed years, when both Duncan and her homeland came of age. This was the era of progressivism: not just a politics but an ethos, stressing moral values and spiritual reform, that permeated every sphere of culture.[27] It was a great industrial age, which witnessed the woman movement and the development of modern art, and it was a time of intellectual optimism. In these decades Duncan emerged, alongside modern America. As architectural historian and cultural critic Lewis Mumford observed, "What mattered in Isadora's Hellenic dances and dramatic presentations was not the Greek themes or the gauzy costumes but the uninhibited vitality, the sense of a glorious nakedness about to be affirmed, not only in the rituals of lovers but in every part of life."[28]

And yet, the progressivists embraced many traditional values. Progressivism, which culminated in the election of Woodrow Wilson in 1912, was as much a response to the social and political changes wrought by the city and factory as it was a response to the enervating spirit of the Gilded Age. Rooted in Protestantism, it was ultimately less an innovative than a conservative force, seeking to restate old-fashioned American ideals of morality.[29] Although often portrayed as a flagrant iconoclast, Duncan at the same time embodied the forces of moral and spiritual righteousness. For the woman who bared her flesh knew that in order for dance to be accepted in America as a legitimate art, as "Culture," it had to be accepted as moral.

Americans looked askance at "Culture," at the same time that they longed for it. On the one hand, it appealed to their desire for respectability, but on the other hand, it smacked of European pretentiousness. This ambivalence is evident enough in the early reportage on Duncan: a mixture of admiration and skepticism, alternately poetic and derisive. But by carefully defining her relationship to class, race, and gender, she eventually managed to institutionalize the opera house dance concert: it became as unapologetically American as vaudeville and yet as tasteful as

Shakespeare or Mozart. As Duncan packaged her performances, and as her audiences understood them, her dancing offered all the vigor of the West, tempered with the refinement of a Greek goddess. Her dancing appealed to a growing upper-middle-class desire for social prestige.

Duncan claimed dancing as moral—and thus as eligible to be considered part of "Culture"—on the grounds that it served an ideal of harmony; as such, it was a religious practice—a prayer. She saw herself as a goddess, or prophet, like Nietzsche's Zarathustra, spreading the gospel of a utopia of beauty built from love and art. "If artists," she wrote, "would realize that true art is the revelation of highest truth, that they are the high priests of the religion of beauty, . . . Utopia would probably come true."[30] Thus she shifted the drive for perfection—considered a necessary condition of "Art" in her day—from physical perfection to spiritual perfection. Her movement vocabulary may have been mundane (stepping, walking, skipping, leaping), but the music (Beethoven, Bach, Schubert) was noble. Her body may have thickened over the years, but her intentions always remained pure: to dance a sacred dance that reached beyond the mere sensual to the spiritual. Her schools, she always emphasized, were not meant to train professional dancers; they were meant to release and maintain the child's love for beautiful and moral living. As one who was seen as "preach[ing] and liv[ing] an aesthetic gospel,"[31] Duncan both anticipated and reiterated the progressivist impulse toward the remoralization of American society.

Duncan had a lifelong love-hate relationship with "America." She brandished the term, as she did others, such as "Nature," "Woman," "Truth," and "Beauty," with willful certainty, as if they were eternal constants with intrinsic meaning and inherent truth.[32] In Duncan's discourse, from beginning to end aimed at legitimizing dance as a respectable, "high" art, "America" served as a kind of compensatory myth. Her vision of "America" was an elite, white, Europeanized monolith without a hint of the social, racial, and economic diversity that immigration and the northern migration had intensified by the 1910s. Despite—or because of— her self-imposed exile (she left for Europe in 1899, at the age of twenty-two), Duncan was fundamentally informed by the idea, if not the reality, of her homeland.

The "America" that Duncan loved was one that she constructed primarily from two sources: first, her rather unsupervised childhood spent amid the natural splendors of the San Francisco Bay area, and, second, the poetry of Walt Whitman. Duncan routinely was compared to Whitman;

they were seen as twin prophets of the "American" body—its exuberance, its physicality, and its spirituality—as they felt the Puritans had refused to acknowledge it.[33] Like Whitman's writing, Duncan's dancing was admired for its seeming transparency. He using vernacular language and she using basic ambulatory movements, they aimed at a seeming artlessness, without obvious form or conventional content to separate the artists from their art. ("The words of my book nothing," Whitman wrote, "the drift of it every thing.")[34] Like Whitman, Duncan claimed "Nature" as her inspiration and mimed its grand simplicity. They both glorified the human body, finding in it the very soul of being; they both paid homage to the majesty of "Woman"; they both affirmed the splendor of the self, the ego, the personality. Yet at the same time, they had great affection for the masses. For in the end, they believed, we are all linked in a great cosmic chain, humankind and "Nature." Not members of any organized religion, Whitman and Duncan still participated in a pantheistic religion of the self and created an art of intensely personal expression. They consciously birthed a new art form, free, they wanted us to believe, of any artificial European precedents.[35]

Raised as a Californian, whose typically heroic sense of self seemed induced by the landscape's wide-open spaces,[36] Duncan conceived of "America" in the mythic terms of the frontier and its pioneers—as spacious and youthful, ambitious and heroic. Duncan explicitly returned to this "America," if only in her rhetoric, at the end of her life. In her autobiography, *My Life*, completed shortly before her death in 1927, she denied (years of Hellenic references notwithstanding) that her art was ever anything other than "American."

The "America" that Duncan hated she constructed from a vague utopian vision of "freedom and justice for all." This was an America repressed by Puritan propriety and guilt, corrupted by materialism, and blinded by hypocrisy. Spawned by the progressive discourse of reform at the turn of the century, Duncan's cultural criticism developed into a more radical vision of personal liberation during the teens, and then later into a critique of capitalist wealth.

Whether loved or hated, Duncan's "America" began and ended with California. She was born there, in San Francisco, on 26 May 1877, to Joseph C. and Mary Dora Gray Duncan, who apparently divorced shortly after the birth of their fourth child, Angela Isadora.[37] And as was the custom in California, where divorce was not an uncommon occurrence, women who were found innocent in the proceedings gained custody of the children.[38]

Without support, the thirty-year-old divorceé had to eke out a living for herself and her children by selling knitted goods and giving music lessons. Perhaps because she was the youngest and thus would garner the most sympathy, "Dora" (as Isadora was then called) was the one sent to charm the credit from the baker. (It required a measure of confidence beyond her years—a confidence that eventually grew large enough to fill an empty stage for hours on end.) It was thus very early that Duncan acquired an immense sense of entitlement; later on, over several decades and several continents, she would continue to appeal indignantly for her just deserts: full governmental funding for a school of dance. Even when the family did come into money, it was spent quickly and lavishly—another habit the dancer never relinquished.[39] As an adult, Duncan would cling to the vagaries of her largely lower-class childhood, justifying its nobility on the grounds of "Nature" and "Art" and overcompensating for its self-conscious poverty.

At first in almost constant financial straits, the Duncans kept moving from one set of rented rooms to another. Sometime in 1878, after the family's breakup, Mrs. Duncan first moved the family out of San Francisco, where rents for working-class families were among the highest in the nation.[40] Except for a six-month period in 1880, when they retreated to a Napa farm, and their last two years in California, when they moved into a fine house in San Francisco courtesy of their errant patriarch's newfound fortune, the Duncans lived in Oakland, across the Bay. Its population a little above ten thousand in the 1870s, Oakland was a city of spire-topped churches, homes both modest and elegant, and schools ranging from kindergartens to the nearby University of California in Berkeley. Perhaps partly because of the university, the city attracted a fair number of writers and poets, including Ina Coolbrith, who later would become poet laureate of California, who served as librarian for the Oakland Free Library. Duncan recalled making her way to the library, no matter the distance, where Coolbrith "encouraged my reading and I thought she always looked pleased when I asked for fine books."[41]

Many San Franciscans moved across the Bay, building tall, roomy frame houses, planting gardens, and commuting to the city by ferry. Oakland boasted paved roads, "as smooth and symmetrical as those of Paris," which "stretch away for miles in every direction, leading to the hill side and the mountain top, to groves and gardens, to lake and seaside, to valley and plain." It offered its citizens wide sidewalks, serviceable sewers, beautiful parks, and picturesque Lake Merritt. A wooded city, filled with oak, poplar, eucalyptus, and other magnificent trees, Oakland was surrounded by fruit orchards.[42]

Although absent, Joseph C. Duncan—a poet, an art connoisseur, and a cunning businessman—did indeed play a part in Isadora's story. The suave and cultured man reappeared at his former family's home at some point during her childhood, and she alone was willing, even eager, to meet with him. It inspired her to discover that he was a lifelong poet and an accomplished journalist. Early on, he had published Coolbrith's poetry.[43] For a time Duncan had run an auction house, and then he became an art dealer, traveling to Europe to purchase his goods. A private art collector and one of the first presidents of the San Francisco Art Association, he was a leading force in establishing the fine arts there. Unfortunately, art dealing was not consistently profitable, so he turned to real estate, back to journalism, and then on to banking. Given the wildly erratic economy, the tapering off of the silver mines, and hence the failure or suspension of other, more established, banks, it is no surprise that Duncan ran into trouble. He attempted to keep his bank afloat by selling off the family's assets (he claimed to have melted down their table silver)[44] and through some shady dealings, but it collapsed nevertheless in October 1877. Accused of forgery, embezzlement, and grand larceny, Duncan ignominiously fled the charges but was eventually found. After four inconclusive trials, the charges finally were dismissed, on a technicality, in January 1882. All in all, according to *My Life*, Joseph C. Duncan earned and lost four fortunes. Isadora's own fortunes would prove just as erratic.[45]

Although Duncan usually is claimed as a daughter of bohemian San Francisco, she had no direct contact with that world. And neither did she engage with the kind of "aggressive luxury" that characterized upper-class San Francisco, which was known for its love of theater, cuisine, and books.[46] Her aesthetic was much more the product of her clannish upbringing—unsupervised romping in the out-of-doors, dime novels, barn theater productions, an Irish grandmother who urged her grandchildren to resist the commonplace,[47] and salon-like evenings of Shakespeare and Chopin. Actually, her childhood literary and musical excursions were quite conventional. Even the agnostic Robert Ingersoll, whom Mrs. Duncan read aloud, was a relatively mild social radical who, in the age of Darwinism, used scientific reason to confront outmoded conservative thought. (Duncan's adult sources were less than revolutionary, too. Ernst Haeckel, the American press's favorite European scientist, failed to shock, because his ideas were overtly moral and religious.)

When the Duncans moved back to San Francisco to live in Castle Mansion from 1893 to 1895, young Dora found the place unwelcoming. For as much as San Franciscans may have defined themselves as a people liberated from the Puritan past, they still lived by Puritan codes, such as strict limits on the public behavior of "respectable" women. "San Francisco is par excellence the city of extremes," wrote native son Gelett Burgess in 1897. "Romantic in situation and in the complexity of its population—cosmopolitan, picturesque, radiant with local color—it has, besides, the unloveliness of youth and crudity with the sordid and dreary aspect of the Philistine as well."[48]

The first, unselfconscious wave of frontier bohemianism in San Francisco had passed before Duncan's birth, and the second wave was just crystallizing when she bailed out for points east. ("The high noon of culture and repose has not yet come," wrote one impatient aesthete in 1892. "The unwelcome truth is: California is young, and does not understand art.")[49] It is questionable, anyway, how readily, if at all, the young artistic coterie of writers and painters, catalyzed by Burgess and Bruce Porter, would have taken such a naive eighteen-year-old dancer into their fold.[50] If we heed novelist Gertrude Atherton, a San Francisco native, Duncan was lucky to get out of the seductive climate and lifestyle so soon. "Never was such a high percentage of brains in any one city," explained one of Atherton's artist-characters in the 1907 novel *Ancestors*. "But they must get out. And if they don't go young they don't go at all. San Francisco is a disease."[51]

Duncan did leave young. She was eighteen in 1895, when she and her mother left for Chicago, then New York City, then London. They made their way to Paris, which found the young dancer a novel salon item, and, on later trips, to Vienna, and Budapest, which acknowledged her talent, and then Munich and Berlin, where she came to fame. Her subsequent career would take her across western Europe, through the expanse of the Soviet Union, to South America and North Africa and, on occasion, back to the U.S. Duncan's American career can be divided into three clusters of tours, each of which corresponds to a different phase of her dance practice and to a distinct cultural milieu.

The first period (twice in 1908, 1909, 1911) featured the Duncan who has persisted in history: the young, gamboling nymph, joyful and graceful. The native daughter, returned from her European triumphs, was enormously successful, billed as the "celebrated Greek dancer." During these years, when a wave of cultural nationalism yoked art and politics with unprecedented intensity, she was admired by radicals, artists, and intellectuals for the "naturalness" of her appearance and for the depth of her expression. Her dancing, which was based on physical release, seemed to materialize her spectators' inner longings and impulses. This fluid self freely circulating—an image of "becoming"—appealed to a wide variety of spectators, who saw in her the embodiment of their own desire for social, political, and artistic change. She was, for them, a symbol of spontaneity and freedom. Not only did she appeal to those modernists who wanted to overthrow the old genteel tradition, but she also appealed to antimodernists, who read her "naturalness" through their own longing for a return to something authentic, simple, and pure.

The second period (1914–1915, 1916–1918) saw a more mature Duncan, taking on more heroic, even patriotic, postures. She took to heart the example of the Greek chorus, and she endeavored to fuse the arts of music, drama, and dance with her monumental productions of *Orpheus* (1900–1915), *Oedipus Rex* (1915), and *Iphigenia* (1905–1915), but what drew the most attention was her rendition of the "Marseillaise" (1914). During World War I and after the much-publicized deaths of her children, she came to symbolize Lady Liberty, a combination of motherhood and nationalistic pride. If her radical supporters, now taking an antiwar position, were disappointed in her pro-Allied stance, she drew widespread praise for her wartime allegories, which depicted a self triumphantly mastered through adversity and oppression.

The third period, during her final tour launched from her base in the Soviet Union, in 1922/23, saw a monumental Isadora who barely moved, striving for the ultimate: to harness the force of dynamic movement in utter stillness. Her solos, sculptural and increasingly independent of their musical accompaniment, became more a matter of tragic acting—the expression of epic gesture—than dancing. Although most of her repertoire (a lot of Wagner and Tchaikovsky) was familiar, she was read as a traitor because of her Soviet connections. Questioned about her politics at Ellis Island before she was even permitted to enter the country, Duncan was held responsible for the evils of communism, through her dancing, through her marriage to the Soviet poet Sergei Esenin, and through the color (red) of her costumes and hair. In the aftermath of the Red Scare, to be an idealistic "revolutionary" was no longer tenable. Where Americans once had seen freedom in Duncan's dancing body, now they saw sedition. The tour ended prematurely, as city after city threatened to shut down the "Bolshevik hussy."

Duncan found herself, for the first time, out of step with her native culture. The twenties proved to be the twilight of an American goddess—a social utopian at a time of Red-bashing, a voluptuary in the age of the flapper, a neoromantic in the first flush of modernism, an individualist in an era of mass culture. She voiced her bitterness loudly when she left, on 3 February 1923; as a result, her citizenship was called into question and deemed lapsed, on a technicality, shortly thereafter. Despite her exile, explained Max Eastman, editor of the radical Village monthly *The Masses*, she remained recalcitrantly American:

> The great big way in which she conceived things, and undertook them, and the way she succeeded with them, was American.
> Even her faults were American—her passion for pulling off stunts—"gestures" is the refined way to say it—was American. She made a grand sport of her public position and character. She played with publicity like a humorous Barnum. Even her extravagant and really bad irresponsibility, which went almost to the point of madness in late years, was in the reverse sense an American trait. It was an exaggerated reaction against America's "righteousness." *Wrongtiousness* is what it was. . . .
> America fighting the battle against Americanism—that was Isadora.[52]

***

How did Duncan manage to insert such a previously marginal practice as dance into the center of a cultural vortex? By consistently aligning her dancing with upper-class, WASP America. Dancing was considered cheap, so she associated herself with the great Greeks, who deemed the art noble, and she associated herself with upper-class audiences by carefully courting her patrons and selecting her performance venues. Dancing was considered mindless, so she invoked a pantheon of great minds, from Darwin to Whitman and Plato to Nietzsche, to prove otherwise. Dancing was considered feminine, and thus trivial, so she chose well her liaisons and mentors—men whose cultural or economic power accrued, by association, to her. Dancing was considered profane, so she elevated her own practice by contrasting it to that of "African primitives." The fundamental strategy of Duncan's project to gain cultural legitimacy for dancing was one of exclusion. In order to reinvent the idea of the "dancer," that is to say, to make dancing (but specifically her kind of dancing) a matter of good "taste" within the existing cultural order, Duncan employed the dominant logic of difference along a number of axes, and used it to cultivate "distinction." Effectively, she elevated dancing from low to high, from sexual to spiritual, from black to white, from profane to sacred, from woman to goddess, from entertainment to "Art."

Thus Duncan spent much of her career, on-stage and off, staging her origins. Unlike the modern avant-garde, which touts its iconoclasm, whose legitimacy depends upon its perceived break from the past, Duncan needed to "invent" a pedigreed past (which shifted over time) in order to justify her innovations. She did this by appropriating the dominant discourses of the 1880s and 1890s—evolutionary theory, Hellenism, and physical culture, to name a few. Duncan always showcased the famous names from whom she had gleaned an idea (or in whom she found support for her own ideas), and in doing so she acquired credibility, or, in Bourdieu's terms, "capital," for herself. In 1914 she made transparent this strategy, by publishing a small booklet consisting solely of brief quotations by herself and by her admirers (such as Auguste Rodin, Robert Henri, and John Collier), as well as by those who had inspired her (including the Bible, Friedrich Nietzsche, Walt Whitman, and Percy Bysshe Shelley).[53] Out of these scientific, intellectual, social, aesthetic, and political discourses Duncan constructed various bodies, each one intricately and variously linked with the others: the dancing body, the natural body, the expressive body, the female body, and the body politic.

The body, as the ground of discourse between Duncan and her American audiences, has served as a thematic structuring device for my project. On an obvious level, it only makes sense to navigate a study of dance through the body. But on a deeper level, this strategy enabled me to more accurately locate the meanings of Duncan's dance practice, because I conceive of the body not as a surface, or even as an object, but as a space, a site of discursive intercourse—a place where Nietzsche meets Whitman meets Lenin. By thus charting the discursive complexities of Duncan's body, as it was constructed dialogically by her and her audiences, I hope to further our understanding of Duncan's significance to her American contemporaries.

In this project, I was greatly benefited by Duncan's penchant for the written and spoken word. A writer's daughter, who herself started up a neighborhood newspaper as a youngster, Duncan spoke and wrote a great deal about her art. She left behind a book's worth of essays and articles and letters to the editor (*The Art of the Dance*); a partial autobiography (*My Life*); and another book's worth of love letters to Gordon Craig ("*Your Isadora*"). In addition, there were literally hundreds of newspaper and magazine interviews, and almost that many more letters (some collected into *Isadora Speaks*, and the rest in archives).[54]

Describing and analyzing what Duncan wrote and said is easier than describing and analyzing what she did. Despite all the artifacts that remain of Duncan's life and art, at the center of her practice persists a massive void: her dancing body.[55] Without any substantive filmic record, we must be satisfied with the moving picture, in our mind's eye, that we can construct from the iconography, the reviews, the reconstructed dances, and the memoirs. Marie Theresa Duncan (one of the six student-performers known as the "Isadorables"), for example, recalled that "when she danced the moods of music, how quick-footed, nimble, and feline were her movements then. They became supple and strong, alternating with undulating motions as she lifted her legs in a perfect curve, to bring them down with a strong stamp of the foot."[56]

The overabundance of primary and secondary sources on Duncan is both a blessing and a curse. There are gaps, discrepancies, and contradictions, but those are the obvious limits of historical evidence. The point is, to reconstruct Duncan's dance practice is not a matter of fact-finding but an act of imagination. For me, there is no better suggestion of the dancer's performative powers than a story told by Irma Duncan, another of the Isadorables. The incident took place in Egypt in 1912, at the Kom Ombo temple overlooking the Nile. Irma was a child then, and quite unexpectedly, Duncan asked her to perform solo in the temple, in front of the entire entourage. Irma complied, reluctantly and, ultimately, unsuccessfully. Disappointed, Duncan proceeded to lecture Irma and her guests on the importance of the connection between gesture and its surroundings. Then she herself demonstrated:

> Adjusting her flowing white shawl, she strode across the court and disappeared into the shadows in the background. . . .
> Presently, as we peered into the background, we saw her emerge from the deep shadows cast by a peristyle of such massive proportions that it dwarfed her white-clad figure. But as soon as she started to move in and out of the tall lotus columns she seemed to grow in stature. The long shadows cast by the columns on the floor of the court formed a symmetrical pattern. And each time she stepped in her stately dance from the shadows into the strip of bright moonlight in between, there was a sudden flash created by her appearance. Alternating in this manner the entire length of the colonnade, slowly in one direction and faster coming back, she created a striking rhythm of brilliant flashes, which in a strange way suggested the beat of music.[57]

Here, I can see Duncan composing her way up and down the colonnade, materializing human drama out of the immaterial—light, color, line, rhythm, speed, space, and scale.

As for identifying the responses of her audiences, there are plenty of reviews, articles, and memoirs. The exact makeup of Duncan's concert audiences is impossible to determine, given the wholesale lack of documentation, but there are clues enough to suggest that women—upper-class women with a desire for "Culture"—made up the bulk of her early audiences. Rather quickly she began attracting artists, intellectuals, and radicals of both sexes. Given the fact that she appeared only in concert halls and opera houses and that she commanded premium ticket prices, her spectators were of the upper or at least upper-middle class. (On the rare occasion, as with her 1915 season at the Century Opera House, which she produced herself, she included a category of cheap ticket prices.) It needs to be realized, however, that the dancer's "audience" extended beyond those who actually saw her dance. In fact, she did not tour beyond the major cities of the Northeast very often. Only once, for example, did she return to California. But from her first successes in Paris, in 1901, she was reported on in the American press. Her ideas, her life, her photograph, if not her dancing, were made available to the general public.

In the chapters to follow, I will identify and contextualize Duncan's five major bodily practices: the dancing body, the natural body, the expressive body, the female body, and the body politic. I am interested in the discursive and historical specificity of these bodies, which Duncan herself presented as transcendent. Although I take up a different body in each chapter, examining it as a negotiation between Duncan and American culture, I do not mean to imply that these bodies were discrete; they were, of course, interconnected. But their relative importance shifted across different periods of Duncan's American career, so different bodies are sometimes identified with different points in the Duncan chronology. My analysis shifts across the literal and the metaphorical bodies, for where, and how, does a line separate them?

As new as Duncan's dancing body was, it was forged out of existing discourses and practices, which she either seized or rejected, according to her artistic needs and desire for cultural legitimacy. She very carefully framed the dancing body (chapter 2) as a moral practice, reconstructing and privileging it as the nexus of science, nature, art, and metaphysics. As for her technique and performance practices, she offered to her audiences the illusion of spontaneous freedom, where there was actually conscious craft and, indeed, considerable labor. Invoking "Nature" as the ultimate origin of her natural body (chapter 3), Duncan appropriated the authority of the classical nude in an effort to legitimize dancing as "Culture."

The expressive body (chapter 4)—that which makes externally visible its invisible depths—already had been established by American Delsartism as a means of self-improvement and upward mobility, although, really, it seemed to have served as a technique of channeling and, ultimately, controlling the force of the female body, both physically and socially. Often disparaged for opening the dam of dilettantish "self-expression" into American dance, Duncan's theory of dance—which changed significantly over time—was not one of mere *self*-expression, but rather a more complex semiotics of representation.

As for the female body (chapter 5), put in historical context, Duncan's feminist leanings are both less and more radical than usually portrayed. Her "feminism" (our word represents neither the terminology nor the thinking of her day) was not the American brand of suffragism. Instead it was rooted in the German "mother protection" movement. On the one hand, Duncan emphasized the traditional role of woman as mother, but on the other hand, she supported such radical ideas as voluntary motherhood. In the effort to redefine dance from a "leg business" to "Art," she hoped to dismantle the sets of opposition (sexual/religious, whore/virgin, physical/metaphysical) that structured the image of the female dancer. Duncan took advantage of the female body as a marginalized site of expression in order to make of it a symbol of cultural subversion.

Duncan's dancing body became an explicit body politic (chapter 6) when she directly played out on stage the nationalism that accompanied the Great War, and later on, in the early 1920s, when she served as a ground for the projection of anticommunist paranoia. The epilogue (chapter 7) expands upon Duncan's career in the 1920s, the twilight of this American "goddess." Rejected and exiled from America for political, aesthetic, and social reasons, Duncan returned to her homeland—if only in her rhetoric—shortly before her death in 1927. In her now-famous "I See America Dancing" essay, Duncan performed her origin for the last time, now resituating herself from ancient Greece to pioneer America. My reading of this essay offers a final critique of Duncan's American dance practice as a process of distinction, sustained in her final years by a nativist construction of the "African primitive" against which she defined her own dance as high, white American "Art."

2.

I

In turn-of-the-century America, Edith Wharton
wrote in her autobiography, "Only two kinds of
dancing were familiar . . . : waltzing in the ball-room and
pirouetting on the stage."[1] Wharton missed her earliest opportunity to see Duncan, in 1899, when a
Boston philanthropist and Newport hostess featured the young dancer at a garden party:

> "Isadora Duncan?" People repeated the
> unknown name, wondering why it had been
> used to bait Miss Mason's invitation. . . . I
> hated pirouetting, and did not go to Miss

THE *Dancing* BODY

No doubt the young Duncan's earliest performances must have looked peculiar. She neither waltzed nor pirouetted. She did not kick up her legs; she manipulated no skirts; she rarely portrayed any specific character. Legend even has it (though not quite accurately) that she was maverick enough at a very tender age to disavow her toe dancing lessons. In her more semantically polemical moments, Duncan rejected the label "dancer" altogether, in order to dissociate herself from the questionable antics of her colleagues.[3] Instead, she set herself apart as an "artiste." That is what she listed as her occupation on the birth certificate for her second child, Patrick Augustus Duncan, in 1910.[4]

Duncan's dancing was something very new. And yet it did not spring whole from the head of Zeus, as she preferred people to think.[5] Rather, she emerged into—and appropriated—discourses and practices that already had been established by American and European intellectuals, who had begun to make quite serious inquiries into the nature and status of dancing. "How has dancing [as a social institution] reached its present recognition as an important function of civilised life," inquired one such writer, "and can that position be justified on rational, moral, or aesthetic grounds?"[6] From the 1860s to the turn of the century, and especially around 1890, dancing became a legitimate topic of consideration in respected journals and books. Authors criticized the current state of the art: acrobatic entertainment, ta-ra-ra-boom-de-ay skirt dancing,[7] and the ballet, with its ever-shortening tutu. Although it was generally agreed that dancing was in serious decline ("This first-born and eldest sister of the arts has fallen upon evil times in this old age of the world"),[8] authors recounted its past glories and called for its "renaissance."

Even before Duncan ever trod the boards, cultural and intellectual leaders were interested in reclaiming dancing as something more than mere "amusement," which implied a lack of social import or, worse, moral degeneracy. By 1894, according to a presentation at the World's Congress of Representative Women, social dancing was taught in primary schools, enjoyed in "modern girls' clubs" and at parties, and even sanctioned as church recreation. In New York, there were more than four hundred dancing schools.[9] "The ethical value of the dance," observed Lady Battersea, "must depend upon the wholesome exercises it entails, upon the fine spirits it engenders, and upon the healthy social tone it imparts."[10]

Furthermore, dancing became an appropriate subject of legitimate scholarly study, not under the aegis of the arts but in the spirit of scientific inquiry, whose desire for causality and classification lent respectability to the study of dancing, both historically and anthropologically. One writer laid out the necessities of such a discipline: "Why do people dance? How have they danced? What (if any) is the essential difference between the dancing of the South Sea Islands and the dancing of Queen's Gate? . . . These are the essential problems of the virgin study of comparative chorology, a science which is still, in 1885, awaiting its exponent."[11]

Evolution theory, in particular, gave new impetus to the study of dance in "primitive" cultures, whose dancing was seen as a way of distinguishing their distance from present-day civilization. Herbert Spencer, the leading social Darwinist of the mid- to late nineteenth century, wrote about the evolution and professionalization of dance and music in the *Contemporary Review* and the *Popular Science Monthly*.[12] In 1895, Mrs. Lilly Grove, influenced by the work of late Victorian anthropologists such as E. B. Tylor (author of *Primitive Culture*) and James George Frazer (author of *The Golden Bough* and Grove's second husband), authored a detailed accounting of dance through history and across cultures. In addition to covering the traditional story of dance history, *Dancing: A Handbook of the Terpsichorean Arts in Diverse Places and Times, Savage and Civilized* also included sections on the dances of "savages," ritual dance, and the dances of the East.[13]

Serious studies—historical, anthropological, and philosophical—were published in reputable journals such as the *Popular Science Monthly*, *Eclectic Magazine*, and *Lippincott's*.[14] Throughout these articles runs a still-familiar story. Told largely through the writings of figures such as Lucian, Soame Jenyns, Thoinot Arbeau, Sir John Davies, and Jean-Georges Noverre, the history of dance traversed from the glory of religious and military dance of the ancient Greeks to the Romans and the Christians; to the flowering of ballet in Italy; and through to its development in the French court. Curtain drawn, the stage was readied for a new act.

***

The "new dance," as Duncan referred to it, was forged, practically and discursively, out of three American movement traditions: social dance, physical culture, and ballet.

From social dance she inherited the tradition of dance as a model of social, sexual, and moral behavior and as a means of promoting healthy exercise and achieving graceful refinement. Manuals such as the distinguished New York dance teacher Allen Dodworth's (1885) stressed the importance of ballroom dancing as a means of modeling social intercourse. "With children," he wrote, "the effort to move gracefully produces a desire also to be gracious in manner, and this is one of the best influences of a dancing-school."[15]

Dancing, then, was a matter of manners, or etiquette—a body "technique," both physical and social, which, by disciplining the range and repertoire of body movement, marked a person's class and, thus, suitability for courtship.[16] Dodworth himself made the connection, defining manners as "morality of motion." He believed that dancing—if taught correctly—could encourage moral, healthy living. Of the many popular "do-it-yourself" dance manuals available at the end of the nineteenth century, Judson Sause's *The Art of Dancing*, published in Chicago, was typical. It cited the benefits of dancing as physical development, freedom and grace of motion, social culture, morality, recreation, and, at the end of the list, enjoyment.[17]

From the physical culture movement, Duncan appropriated an upper- and upper-middle-class interest in behavior as the visible expression of the inner self. Physical culture, a blending of Delsartean practices with the fields of elocution and gymnastics, emphasized not only the fitness of the body in motion, but also the expressive and social implications of that body in motion. It displaced the notion of the self's essential (and thus unchangeable) "character" with that of the self's malleable "personality." The message of physical culture—that by changing your outward behavior, you could improve your inner being (and thus your worldly standing as well)— was extremely important for Duncan, who conceived of dance not as entertainment but as social betterment. It was a matter not simply of what dance should be, but of what it should do—what it should accomplish within the social sphere.

While social dance and physical culture contributed the positive arguments of Duncan's discourse, she used ballet to construct her negative argument. By the late nineteenth century, ballet outside Russia was chiefly a form of spectacle entertainment and a staple of the music-hall stage,[18] and Duncan was by no means alone in her disdain for the form. Philip Hayman, in the May 1891 issue of *Theatre*, articulated the growing disillusionment with the art near the turn of the century:

> Now is there anything rhythmic, expressive, or descriptive about the movements of the ballerina? I harden my heart to say "certainly not." When on the tips of her toes she palpitates from the footlights to the fringe of *coryphées*, and whirls down again in a series of lightning pirouettes; when she springs into the air making her heels vibrate to each other; when she is held head downwards with one limb extended in the air; when she finishes in an astounding whirl of pink tights and tulle frills—in all these postures and motions she may be active, agile, athletic, gymnastic, acrobatic, but *not* expressive, *not* descriptive, and certainly *not* rhythmic.[19]

To Duncan, and many of her admirers, ballet was the old order that needed to be overthrown, an embodied symbol of all that was wrong with overcivilized nineteenth-century living. Americans had lost their connection with the earth, and that loss was enacted onstage by ballerinas on point. Americans had lost their connection with their own bodies, and that loss was enacted onstage by ballerinas in corsets. The question of ballet vs. the new dance went beyond aesthetics, for, as Duncan wrote in her "Dance of the Future" manifesto, echoing the rhetoric of eugenics, "It is a question of the development of perfect mothers and the birth of healthy and beautiful children."[20]

***

As Duncan's experience at Miss Mason's must have taught her, merely demonstrating her novel art form was not enough. Somehow her audiences must be convinced otherwise of the worthiness of her new dance. And eventually they were, as Duncan's verbal discourse began running alongside her nonverbal one. Although the young dancer's Newport appearances stirred no significant enthusiasm, her New York performances in the homes of society women and at theaters such as the Lyceum did garner modest attention from the press. She spoke eloquently to her interviewer from the *New York Herald*, for example, of the importance of dancing as a means of "character formation" for children.[21] This term she perhaps learned from the kindergarten proponents back in San Francisco, who were spreading the work of Friedrich Froebel, which was, as he described it, a "means of emancipating the bound up forces of the body and the soul."[22]

Duncan proposed dancing as the connective tissue between mind and body, which had been yoked together by evolution theory.[23] By sharpening the skills of the young body, Duncan argued, dancing would concomitantly sharpen the skills of the mind. "The dance," she wrote, "is a series of movements being the expression of connected thought, and is in its higher exercises a concentration of mind and body on the understanding of a form or emotion, thus being a means of supporting the mind with the strength of the body, and thereby obtaining greater understanding."[24]

At a performance at Mrs. Arthur Dodge's in February 1898, reported by the *New York Times*, it was Duncan's sister, Elizabeth, who lectured on these same ideas: dance as movement expressive of thought, dance as an exercise that increases the support of the mind from the body, and dance as an autonomous expression.[25] Elizabeth had learned about the "dance of life," she told an interviewer many years later, "from nature in California . . . —partly from the giant redwoods, seen on Sunday walks; from sea lions at San Francisco, from the graceful movements of horses."[26] Five and a half years Isadora's senior, she was herself a dance teacher from an early age, with experience in some private San Francisco girls' schools.[27] She helped teach Isadora to dance, accompanied her to New York and London, and later directed Isadora's first school in Grunewald, Germany. Elizabeth was the real teacher of the two; she continued teaching, mostly in Europe, until her death in 1948. Elizabeth's and Isadora's philosophies remained much the same, with a continuing emphasis on the character formation of children.

As the younger sister's career progressed, she never neglected to seize the opportunity to render her theories of dance verbally. Second only to Duncan's talent for movement was her uncanny instinct for appropriating the discourses of her day as a way to lead people to her dancing. She displayed a much greater interest in working out her theory on paper than most other choreographers of her stature. Her writing is unsurprisingly florid and high-minded: "Beauty," "Rhythm," "Dance," and like terms are reverently capitalized. Her notebook drafts indicate that she wrote swiftly, without much revising. Her words ebb and flow one into the next, as do her sentences, with punctuation clearly implied but not always indicated. In both early and final forms, her essays dart quickly from topic to topic, often threading back and again to important themes. Like her dancing, her writing does not find its power through linear logic. (On the rare occasion when assertion opens into a modestly extended argument, it tends to beat a circular path.) Rather, the power of Duncan's writing lay in its sheer force of belief—a kind of ingenuous, sometimes breathless force rather than a sharply insistent one. As Whitman wrote in "Song of the Open Road": "I and mine do not convince by arguments, similes, rhymes, / We convince by our presence."[28]

Duncan may have quit school at about age twelve, but she was a voracious reader, whose choices (other than the dime novels) were guided at an early age by poet-librarian Ina Coolbrith. There is also indication that she received sporadic private instruction in French, German, and English at the Anna Head School.[29] But, in fact, only a small percentage of the women of Duncan's generation gained a college education. Instead, they did as Duncan did: they taught themselves. Women's clubs, large and small, flourished across America during the late nineteenth century. Having been largely excluded from higher education and public opportunities for self-improvement, the clubwomen turned to the private drawing room. They took turns giving reports on various social and intellectual subjects, as well as inviting in guest speakers.[30]

Unlike most clubwomen, however, Duncan soon became an artist-celebrity of great personal charm who could gain access to some of the great minds and imaginations of her time—Auguste Rodin, Ernst Haeckel, and Edward Gordon Craig, for example. She may not have systematically understood their thinking ("It is not for us to arrive at knowledge," she wrote, "we know, as we love, by instinct, faith, emotion"),[31] but she was smart enough to know what would be of use to her, and how to make it useful. A selective learner, Duncan did not need to master the depth and breadth and nuances of an aesthetic theory or scientific principle; she needed only to discover that which helped to articulate and legitimize her dancing.

Despite this lack of rigor in her arguments, Duncan's writings yield a consistent theoretical framework that dates back to those early interviews and lectures in New York. The theory is stated most comprehensively in her 1903 manifesto, "The Dance of the Future," a published essay which was originally a speech delivered to the Berlin Press Club, invited as a response to the clash of opinions surrounding her performances. Afterward, she wrote to her young British poet-friend Douglas Ainslie that she was received with "much sympathy & the journals write about it as seriously as if I were a Member of Parliament."[32] It was here that she learned firsthand about the power of intellectual discourse as an aid to her dancing.

"The Dance of the Future," written in a blue copybook amid quotes from Descartes's studies of mind in relation to body and Rousseau's ideas on education and notes on ballet history, touched on all the main points of her dance theory, which she would spend a lifetime repeating and elaborating. Most significant, Duncan used this opportunity to build upon a compelling, but largely imaginary, past—specifically, the ancient splendors of the Greeks—to create a foundation for the "Dance of the Future." Beginning with a tribute to Darwin and Haeckel, Duncan immediately tapped into the power of the evolutionist discourse in order to invent a pedigree, so to speak, for her dancing: "If we seek the real source of the dance, if we go to nature, we find that the dance of the future is the dance of the past, the dance of eternity and has been and will always be the same."[33]

While "The Dance of the Future" pays its obvious debt to Wagner's "The Artwork of the Future," and to the evolutionist premise that life will progress to higher levels of development, much of her optimistic infatuation with this "dancer of the future" is also attributable to Nietzsche's concept of the Superman.[34] Like an entire generation of American radicals, Duncan embraced the iconoclastic philosopher's exhortation to break with the narrow, bankrupt morals and values of a Christian civilization and to harness the expansive, life-affirming creativity of the Superman.[35] This dancing body that Duncan constructed—"The highest intelligence in the freest body!"[36]—was, essentially, her version of Nietzsche's Zarathustra, the philosopher-dancer who bitterly chastised the "despisers of the body" for their failure to recognize its wisdom and will. Dancing was far more than a physical activity, for the body is the self incarnate; it is reason, soul, and spirit; it is the self's means of creating beyond itself. Like laughter, the upward bounding of the dancing body is a symbol of all that resists death and affirms life.[37]

Duncan defined dance as "not only the art that gives expression to the human soul through movement, but also the foundation of a complete conception of life."[38] This theory—both aesthetic and social—was based on the following seven tenets.

1. Our first conception of beauty is gained from the human body.

The body, according to Duncan, is the first principle of any aesthetics, for our fundamental understanding of proportion and symmetry arises from our experience of embodiment. She wrote in an early, unpublished notebook entry that without this bodily consciousness,

> [man] could have no consciousness of the Beauty surrounding him—his knowledge of the beauty of Earth forms—& from that his conception of architure painting sculpture and all art comes originally from his first consciousness of the nobility & Beauty in the lines of his own body— And when we study accurately the proportion & symmetry of a noble form—we see how from this form as first idea all noble forms follow as natural sequence.[39]

It is as a corollary to this first principle that Duncan addresses the issue of dress reform. The body is an eternal constant, subject to change only through evolution, not through fashion. Not only are the disfiguring properties of the corset physically and morally degenerate, but they are also aesthetically distasteful. Again, from the same early notebook entry:

> I have before me on my desk the correct drawing of a woman's skeleton—The form of the skeleton is beautiful & its chief beauty rests in the fact that the ribs rest *lightly* & far separated—This gives to the [form] its lightness & strength. I look from this beautiful design of a woman's skeleton on my desk to the dummy forms accross the way [in a dressmaker's shop] on which the girls are fitting the dresses—and I can not find any analogy between the form of this woman's skeleton & those dummy forms whose ribs are pressed tightly together. But if I am bewildered at the complete difference of these dummy figures to the

skeleton what is my complete astonishment when I further regard another chart on which is represented the muscles—which clothe this skeleton and the organs which are protected within it—Then it appears to me plainly that there is no analogy of woman's form with the dummy forms accross the way without the deformation of the beautiful skeleton—the displacing of the internal organs—and the decadence of at least a part of the muscles of the woman's body—[40]

The body, in its extraordinarily rich relationships with nature and art and Will and movement, is the centerpiece of Duncan's aesthetic. From the body, she connects with the entire universe. She creates religion. She harnesses "Nature." She participates in the forces of evolution. As Whitman wrote, in a poem called "Kosmos": "Who, out of the theory of the earth and of his or her body understands by subtle analogies all other theories, / The theory of a city, a poem, and of the large politics of these States."[41]

2. The source of dance is "Nature."

Up until Duncan, the only alternative to technical mastery as the defining characteristic of theatrical dance was, at best, amateurism and, at worst, incompetency. Duncan challenged the paradigm of technique with that of the "Natural." That is not to say that there was no technique to her dancing, but that she ennobled an "artless" aesthetic, transforming it from defect to virtue. According to Duncan, the true dancer—whether amateur or professional—participates in "Nature," thereby engaging in a universal rhythm that embraces the entire cosmos.

For Duncan, only the movement of the naked body can be perfectly "Natural." Although Duncan used the words "naked" and "nude," she never danced that way and probably never intended complete undress, as we understand those words today. A "naked" dancer here means an unsheathed, unshod dancer, whose bodily *form* is clearly visible but whose details are modestly veiled, as were the fifth-century Greek statues she so admired.

3. Dancing should be the natural language of the "soul."

Duncan stared into the face of a long, strong Puritan belief that the spirit is sacred and the body profane. Cartesian dualism and Christian denial of the body had disqualified dance a priori as a legitimate form of significant expression. But Duncan looked to another precedent, to Nietzsche, who wrote that "body am I entirely, and nothing else; and soul is only a word for something about the body."[42] Duncan understood the

American temperament—after all, she had spent her formative years here trying to gain recognition for her dancing, without much encouragement, even from fellow artists. She realized that dancing would never be considered more than an "amusement" unless people were made to understand that it was religious: "Art which is not religious is not art," she wrote, "is mere merchandise."[43]

Since 1899, Duncan had been asserting the intimate connection between body and soul as a fundamental basis from which to legitimize the body in motion as an artistic means of expression. Duncan made this idea acceptable by retaining the conventional distinction between moral and immoral but displacing the terms: the dancing body is sacred when it aspires to express the spiritual, but it is profane when it remains at the level of sensuality.[44] As an outward expression of the soul—of its upward yearning toward the good and the beautiful—the dancing body thus gained acceptance *within* the existing moral code.[45]

Dance was Duncan's religion, and it was the gospel that she preached. Through dance, as either dancer or spectator, each soul could partake in divine unity with "Nature." Each soul could participate in the harmonious "Beauty" that merged self with God through the medium of "Nature." Thus Duncan endeavored to guide the world back to "Nature," whose evolutionary process, if we permit it, would deliver us to God.

4. The Will of the individual is expressed through the dancer's use of gravity.

Duncan cohered body and soul into one entity: that inner mechanism called "Will," which she explicitly adapted from Nietszche and Schopenhauer, who conceived of the body as objectified Will. She used the term and concept as the German philosophers generally outlined it: as the essence of being—an endless striving. Just as the soul yearns upward, so does the body. "Upward goes our way, from genus to over-genus," spoke Zarathustra. "Upward flies our sense: thus it is a parable of our body, a parable of elevation."[46]

Yet the Will could not aspire heavenward without a solid basis on the earth, that is to say, within the stabilizing force of gravity. Duncan's theory echoed Schopenhauer's assertion that the pull of gravitation is the simplest form of the objectification of Will. Rejecting the extreme and unvarying lightness of ballet, she instead emphasized groundedness as its necessary complement and foundation. Though her upper body soared, her lower body was resiliently strong and well rooted, giving the appearance of a "Will"—or, in other words, an inner force—very present in, responding to, and acting upon the world. And, furthermore, since Schopenhauer posited the Will as a unifying universal and the body as the objectification of the Will, Duncan used this underlying connection between the dancing body and the cosmos to reinforce her vision of dance as originating in "Nature." The natural gravitation of the dancer's movement, or Will, she explained, was ultimately a human translation of the universe's gravitation, or Will.[47]

5. Movement should correspond to the form of the mover.

The natural correspondence between form and movement was part of the bedrock of Duncan's theory and practice. Besides discussion of this principle in a number of essays, Duncan entitled one of her notebook essays, an unusually lengthy one, "Form and Movement" (c. 1915). Mimicking the tone and empirical logic of scientific inquiry, she aimed to discover the true nature of dance movement. She began:

> In my pamphlet *The Dance of the Future* I have endeavored to touch on the subject of form and movement in their relation to the Dance. That is that the form of an organism and the movement of an organism are one and grow together—The study of this subject is most beautifully illustrated in Charles Darwins Movements of Plants—where he shows how the movement and form of the plant are one manifestation Any one who has watched the movements of fishes must have noticed how the long & light fish move in long & light undulating lines just the lines of their form. how the round stodgy fish move in short thick curves—The porpoise describes a curve through the air which is exactly conforming to the curve of the line of its back—The whale moves in great pondrous lines—[48]

From there she launched into a further litany of impressionistic thumbnail sketches of various birds, throwing in a kitten for good domestic measure. She then continued:

> In other words Form and Movement are one—Now through this sequence of the form & movement of spheres—plants—fishes Birds and animals we come in sequence to consider the form & movement of Man—What the form & movement of man has been—what it is—is the study for the scientist The movement & form of man kind in general in its real state is the study of the scientist—in its ideal state the study of the Artist—That particular real ideal form in its realism to Harmonious movement is the study of the Dancer The True dance would be to find the Harmonious rhythmetic movement to the ideal form—[49]

Duncan turned to the tradition of art for further clues, but really she succeeded only in asserting her prior assumption:

> All this is so well known I would hesitate to repeat it if it were not for the fact that I am endeavoring to prove that the study of the Beautiful in form & movement which is considered as a knowledge a priori in all art should also be considered on the basis of the art of the Dance. We have seen through all Nature that form & movement are one in line & character—There fore may we not say that we should take this as our foundation text of the School of the Dance[50]

So, taking her "evidence" from Darwin's study of the natural kingdom, and secondarily from visual art, Duncan "proved" that the movement of a dancer must correspond harmoniously and naturally to the line, proportion, and symmetry of the human form. Reacting against ballet, whose artificial movements Duncan found an offense against the "Natural beauty" of the human body, she aimed to discover movements so suited to the human form that they would be rendered virtually transparent on the body. "In my dance," she wrote in an early notebook, "I search those movements which are in direct proportion to the human form—so that the form & movement shall be *one* harmony."[51] This seeming transparency, itself the product of work and study, paradoxically facilitated the myth that Duncan's dancing was spontaneous, her body independent of technique.

Two corollaries follow. First, since individual human bodies vary greatly within the general form, therefore every person will move differently. Duncan did not envision dancers duplicating her style (although in reality this is what happened with her students, the Isadorables); rather, she imagined a multiplicity of forms of dance, based on each dancer's own form and vision. This ethos of the body-as-originary persisted, as the fundamental aesthetic of modern dance as a genre. Second, since the form of the body changes over the course of a person's lifetime, movements will change accordingly. To Duncan, only movement that corresponds with the individual's particular stage of development could be properly termed "Natural." Duncan used this precept in her work with children, and she embodied it in her own career, modifying her vocabulary, style, and choreography to suit her aging body.

6. Dancing must be successive, consisting of constantly evolving movements.

During Duncan's youth, stage dance consisted of a display of steps rather loosely strung together. Within that context, her idea that the dancer's every movement should be born from its predecessor, obvious as it seems today, was quite new to the American theater. She herself felt that this was her most important innovation as an artist.[52]

With the term "successive," Duncan implied two things: first, that movement should spread seamlessly throughout adjacent body parts; second, that each action should evolve seamlessly into the next. This was contrary to the ballet, Duncan argued, whose geometrical figures were based on straight lines. Its energy ended at the extremities of the limbs, and the rhythm constantly stopped and started, without a continuously rising and falling pulse.

Duncan's paradigm of successive movement was the wave, which, she argued, is the basic movement pattern of "Nature." It is the alternate attraction and resistance to gravity that creates this wave movement, in "Nature" both visible and invisible: "All energy expresses itself through this wave movement. For does not sound travel in waves, and light also?"[53] The waters, the winds, the plants, the living creatures, and the particles of matter all obey this controlling rhythm, and thus should the dancer:

> He starts with one slow movement and mounts from that gradually, following the rising curve of his inspiration, up to those gestures that exteriorize his fullness of feeling, spreading ever wider the impulse that has swayed him, fixing it in another expression.
> The movements should follow the rhythm of the waves: the rhythm that rises, penetrates, holding in itself the impulse and the after-movement; call and response, bound endlessly in one cadence.[54]

Besides its roots in "Nature" and science and its significance as a formal principle of dancing, the wave also held spiritual connotations for Duncan, as it did for the romantics. Unlike the ballet, whose stop-and-start motion is "an expression of degeneration, of living death," the continuing line of the wave symbolizes eternal life: the conquest of death through perpetual rebirth.[55] At a time of considerable cultural instability, the wave privileged continuity over discontinuity.

7. Dancing must express humankind's most moral, beautiful, and healthful ideals.

From beginning to end, Duncan worked through the characteristically progressivist discourses of her day (health, morality, womanhood and motherhood, and education), through which social, political, and religious leaders sought to reform the ills that had been wrought upon American society by modernization. Duncan's was a quintessentially progressivist program; she wanted nothing less than to "make over human life, down to its least details of costume, of morals, of way of living."[56]

Hers was not a material program, however; like many modern artists of her day, Duncan brought to her program a strong transcendental belief. Dancing was socially progressive because it could create "Beauty," both in the dancer and in the spectator. By "Beauty" she meant not just outward appearance but essential human goodness—a state of being in harmony with self, others, and the cosmos. Irma Duncan, the Isadorable who stayed with Isadora the longest, recalled in her autobiography, "I had learned my first English words at Isadora's knee when she taught her pupils to recite Keats' immortal lines: 'Beauty is Truth, Truth Beauty,—that is all / Ye know on earth, and all ye need to know.' "[57]

Because she claimed the improvement of humankind's lot as the basis of her dancing, Duncan was able to gain the approval of the educated, the radicals, and the upper classes during the first two decades of this century. She succeeded where no other American dancer ever had: By aiming to establish dancing as a social and not just aesthetic necessity, she managed to gain its public acceptance as a legitimate art form.

II

Dance educator and critic Lucile Marsh, a contemporary of Duncan's, described her as having "soft, gently rounded but deeply molded contours." With a small head and a long, flexible neck, she possessed delicate shoulders, sloping down and back. Her "back was flat, her chest deep and high." Her arms, Marsh continued, "were soft and plump with tiny wrists and hands of child-like delicacy and sweetness." Small-waisted (at least in her youth), she had an abdomen that lifted up and in with the rise of her chest.[58]

Duncan (figure 1) was not a particularly beautiful woman. Along with her luminous cheeks and large, expressive eyes framed by dramatically arched brows, she also possessed a pursed little mouth, an upturned nose, and a dimpled, weak chin that sagged with age. (One acquaintance conjectured that she assumed her characteristic stance—with head slightly inclined to one side and chin tilted upward—in order to minimize her double chin.)[59] Her figure was pleasing enough but by no means classically exemplary, and over the years it rounded considerably. Her manner could be charming, full of Irish humor. But she was also capricious and sometimes willfully contrary, even exasperating.

Figure 1. Along with her luminous cheeks and large, expressive eyes, Duncan also possessed a pursed little mouth, an upturned nose, and a dimpled chin. Photo: Jacob Schloss. Courtesy of the Dance Collection of the New York Public Library for the Performing Arts, Astor, Lenox and Tilden Foundations.

It was in performance that she transfigured herself, that she became a generation's vision of "Beauty," with all its transcendent implications. Even in her final year, in a makeshift studio, she still performed magnificently. Witnessing that evening, Sewell Stokes wrote:

> Nothing mattered, when Isadora danced, except her dance. She herself did not matter much. One forgot, watching her move very slowly, that she was there at all. She drove out of the mind, with one slight movement of her foot, or of her hand, the impression one had had a short time before of a large red-haired woman drinking lager beer. Her largeness, with everything else about her, disappeared. In its place was a spiritual vitality that defied the body it animated.[60]

This is one of the tamer contemporary descriptions of Duncan dancing, less ecstatic than most. No matter the extravagance of the language of her critics and admirers over the years, it is clear that Duncan possessed in abundance what today is called "presence."

Presence—the magnetic sense of fullness that certain dancers possess—is as difficult to define as it is to overlook. It is something that cannot be taught per se; it is not contingent on technique, but it is tied up with some discernible physical/mental skills. It has to do with focus, with concentration, with one's saturated attention to everything surrounding and everything within. It has to do with a quality of bodily listening as well as bodily singing. It has to do with skin as well as muscle. It has to do with filling every moment as if it were eternity.

Duncan learned about "divine presence" from the Italian actress Eleonora Duse, whose performance in *The Second Mrs. Tanqueray* the dancer recalled as an epiphany:

> The play goes through two acts of utter vulgarity and banality and I was shocked to see the divine Duse lending herself to such commonplace characterization. At the end of the third act, where Mrs. Tanqueray is driven to the wall by her enemies and, overcome with ennui, resolves to commit suicide, there was a moment when the Duse stood quite still, alone on the stage. Suddenly, without any special outward movement, she seemed to grow and grow until her head appeared to touch the roof of the theater, like the moment when Demeter appeared before the house of Metaneira and disclosed herself as a Goddess. In that supreme gesture Duse was no longer the second Mrs. Tanqueray, but some wonderful goddess of all ages, and her growth before the eyes of the audience into that divine presence was one of the greatest artistic achievements I have ever witnessed. I remember that I went home dazed with the wonder of it. I said to myself, when I can come on the stage and stand as still as Eleonora Duse did tonight, and, at the same time, create that tremendous force of dynamic movement, then I shall be the greatest dancer in the world.[61]

Today, we do not necessarily attribute anything spiritual to a performer of great presence. We choose to savor the phenomenon for its compelling pleasure. (Presence, by its nature, draws us forth. It demands our participation.) But in Duncan's day, such invisible power—like light waves and X-rays—was accorded divine dimensions.

It is difficult to "reconstruct" Duncan's dancing without a filmic record. And for someone so famous, there were relatively few stage photographs of her. Those few photographic dance images that do exist are all posed, according to the demands of convention and the limits of technology. Consequently, the most familiar, and useful, images of Duncan in performance are artists' renderings, but their quality and reliability range widely.[62] "It is very difficult to draw her," wrote the American artist Robert Henri, leader of the Ashcan School and one of many artists who were enthralled by Duncan. "Noted artists abroad have tried to do her—and failed."[63]

There was, however, one who succeeded, in Duncan's estimation. The now-famous photographs of Duncan by Arnold Genthe—some head-and-shoulder shots, more of them heroic poses from her dances of the teens, such as the *Marseillaise*—are important indicators not of how she danced but of how she wanted to be perceived: as the philosopher-dancer, after Zarathustra (figures 2 and 3). A classical scholar, Genthe came in 1895 from Germany to San Francisco, where he took up photography, and then in 1911 he moved to New York. There he met Duncan, as she was opening her studio, the Dionysion, at Fourth Avenue and Twenty-third Street. Both romantics in their quests for "Beauty" and "expression," they shared an artistic emphasis on transcendence over appearance. From 1915 to 1918, Genthe made a series of portraits of Duncan, and his pictorialist aesthetic, with its idealized soft-edged focus and dramatic chiaroscuro, was well suited to the dancer's goddess persona.[64] In the photographs, her actual body is engulfed in murky darkness; instead, what has been made "visible," literally and metaphorically, is the dancer's radiance, haloed around her triumphant arms or her downward-cast face. The prophet's aura is mysterious yet palpable. "He has taken many pictures of me which are not representations of my physical being but representations of conditions of my soul," she wrote in *My Life*, "and one of them is my very soul indeed."[65]

Probably the most famous Duncan images are the roughly five thousand Abraham Walkowitz drawings and watercolors, which he continued to produce even after her death. Walkowitz, an experimental artist associated with Alfred Stieglitz and his Gallery of the Photo-Secession, began to draw

Figures 2–3. Arnold Genthe's soft-edged, dramatically shadowed photographs suggest how Duncan wanted to be perceived: as the philosopher-dancer, after Nietzsche's Zarathustra. Photos: Arnold Genthe. Courtesy of the Museum of the City of New York and the Dance Collection of the New York Public Library for the Performing Arts, Astor, Lenox and Tilden Foundations.

Duncan in 1906, the year he met her in Rodin's studio and then saw her perform, in a private salon, for the first time. He attended later performances in 1908, 1909, 1915, and 1916 in New York, and after her death he spent a summer at her sister Elizabeth's school in Salzburg.[66]

Walkowitz had absorbed the lessons of Rodin and Matisse; he declared himself fully aligned with the "great tradition of art that . . . envisaged the human form in terms of energy and counterpoise."[67] He had a distinct feeling for form, movement, sheer weight, and force; critic Charles Caffin described his drawings as "the products of memorized knowledge, translated . . . into realized sensation."[68] Walkowitz continued drawing Duncan throughout the various phases of his career: first he drew her as a woman whose solid flesh was veiled in a semitransparent Greek gown; next she was a muse described through gesture; later she was depicted with geometric lines and then with fluid ones, these last two abstract phases influenced by the work of Wassily Kandinsky.[69]

The early Duncan images are minimal, simple, and fluid, the broad, undifferentiated body shape sometimes tending toward caricature. What is telling, however, is the way that the face, throat, and chest open up into a single broad expressive plane (figure 4). And like most of the graphic art of Duncan, they tell us a lot about the evolving design of her body—how she curled her spine, tossed back her head, and unfolded her limbs, all in endless combinations. Walkowitz was particularly adept at capturing the way that Duncan kneaded through her doughy center of gravity.

Drawings and watercolors by Rodin (or previously misattributed to him) are almost too highly stylized to be informational. One watercolor in particular, however, reveals Duncan's enormous lift from the rib cage. Valentine Lecomte's pencil drawings depict her use of gravity, the oppositional pull between her upper and lower torso, as well as her off-center configurations (figure 5), and the works by Jules Grandjouan clearly show her body shape and her distinct lines of force (figure 6).

José Clará's crosshatched drawings are the most telling for me, because they contain so much movement (figures 7–9). They convey a strong sense of the diagonal twist and force of Duncan's torso, and of the spatial tension between upward and downward, forward and backward. In them we can see the deeply arched feet and the single, flowing line she created from fingertip to toe, against which the mere curving of her back or the drawing in of a knee becomes an emotional event. Clará captures the way she moves through her torso, with all of her frontal surfaces—throat, chest, midriff, abdomen, thighs—rushing forward at once, accentuated by the con-

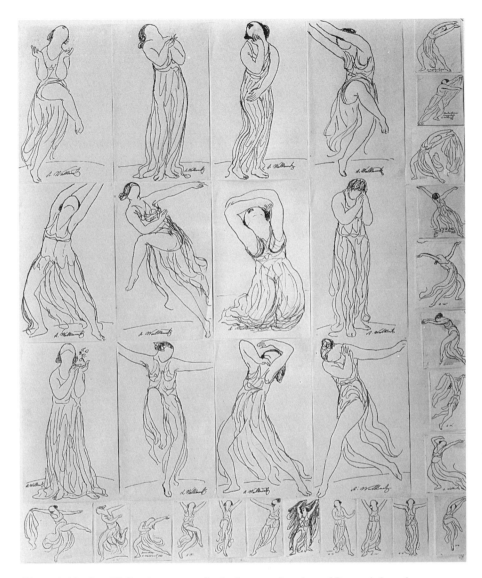

Figure 4. Abraham Walkowitz captures the single, expressive plane of Duncan's face, throat, and chest, as well as the constantly evolving design of her body. Courtesy of the Dance Collection of the New York Public Library for the Performing Arts, Astor, Lenox and Tilden Foundations.

trasting effect of her thrown-back head. The mass of her body is heroic, yet curvaceous enough to remain conventionally "womanly."

Of all the visual artifacts available, there is one set that tells us most about Duncan the dancer (figure 10). It is an unlikely source, of a very young

27 JUIN 1903

Figure 5. Valentine Lecomte depicts Duncan's use of gravity (especially by deploying a single bent leg), the oppositional pull between her upper and lower torso, as well as her off-center configurations. Courtesy of the Dance Collection of the New York Public Library for the Performing Arts, Astor, Lenox and Tilden Foundations.

Figure 6. Jules Grandjouan indicates the spatial complexity of Duncan's body shape, emphasizing its lines of force through the use of pencil shading. Courtesy of the Dance Collection of the New York Public Library for the Performing Arts, Astor, Lenox and Tilden Foundations.

*Figures 7–9. José Clará suggests the
way that Duncan moved through her
entire torso, her throat, chest, midriff,
abdomen, and thighs all rushing forward at once as a single surface, accentuated by the contrasting effect of her
thrown-back head. He conveys the
strong diagonal twist of Duncan's body
even when kneeling, its line twisting
from knee to forehead, and he indicates
the various ways she used one lunging
leg in dynamic tension with arms and
opposing leg. Courtesy of the Dance
Collection of the New York Public
Library for the Performing Arts, Astor,
Lenox and Tilden Foundations.*

Duncan, still wearing tights and ballet slippers, starting out her career in New York in 1898. There are the strained, even awkward poses (according to convention, she sometimes used the back wall for support during the considerable exposure time), but she seems to have hit her stride by the last six frames. This series of cabinet cards, taken by longtime theatrical portrait photographer Jacob Schloss, reveals her flexible back, double-jointed arms, and expressive hands (figures 11–20).

They are quiet images, in which an averted face or inflected neck, a lifted chest or loosely curled hand communicates subtle emotion. The

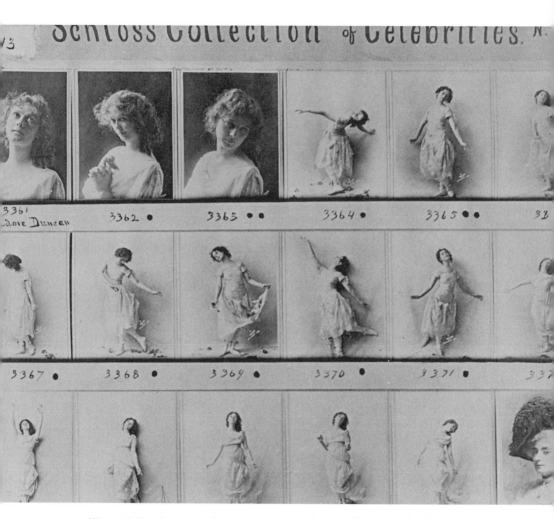

Figure 10. Despite some awkward poses, a young Duncan displays her flexible back, double-jointed arms, and expressive hands. Photo: Jacob Schloss. Courtesy of the Theatre Arts Collection, Harry Ransom Humanities Research Center, the University of Texas at Austin.

dancer does not play to the viewer, but neither is she withdrawn. Something keeps the images from appearing isolated: the subtle distinction between her outward visual gaze and her more restrained bodily focus, which clings to the surfaces of her flesh. I imagine that she can feel the brush of air along her gently curving neck or the creamy underside of her arms. Those Récamier-length arms seem boneless. They do not take flight on their own; they claim their connection to body—and to "soul." Their line is broken at the wrist, setting off the extraordinary expressiveness of her hands, whose power lay not in mimicry but in suggestiveness. There

Figures 11–20. In the following 1898 series of photographs, subtle emotion is communicated through an averted face or inflected neck, a lifted chest or loosely curled hand. The line of Duncan's long, seemingly boneless arms is broken at the wrist, setting off the expressiveness of her hands. Duncan never missed the opportunity to expose her long, pliable neck, which always gave her an aura of vulnerability. Photos: Jacob Schloss. Courtesy of the Dance Collection of the New York Public Library for the Performing Arts, Astor, Lenox and Tilden Foundations.

THE *Dancing* BODY

THE *Dancing* BODY

THE *Dancing* BODY

SCHLOSS
N. Y.

THE *Dancing* BODY

THE *Dancing* BODY

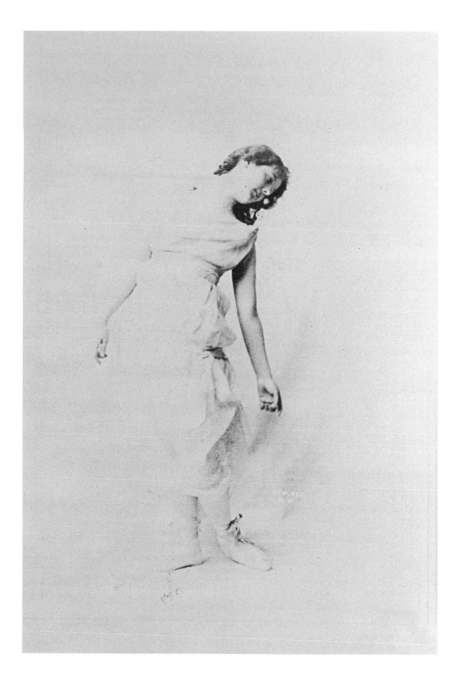

is poignance in how the hand is cupped, or stretched, or half-closed, and in how the fingers curl or spread. Duncan rarely misses the opportunity to expose her long, pliable neck, which gives her always an aura of vulnerability. She never stands squarely on both feet, but neither does she sink into *contrapposto*. Void of apparent tension, the dancer is oriented toward her body; she is not interested in conquering space. The only thing she projects is calmness.

Duncan's images are unique among Schloss's portraits, in which the actors and dancers are given over completely to the stiff convention of the period (figure 21). Interestingly enough, Duncan shares one of her most awkward poses with another Schloss subject, Annie St. Tel. Despite the awkwardness of Duncan's configuration, bending backward from the wall to smile at the camera, her back is by far the more flexible and extended; her head is more relaxed, and her extended arm is noticeably double-jointed. The personas of dancers such as Mabel Clark and Eunice Hill are mature, as their figures are corseted into hourglass shapes and their faces are sharply chiseled with makeup and framed by formal hairdos. They usually pose before an embroidered curtain and atop a carpeted mound of a pedestal. The only spatial variation is a bend at the waist diagonally forward; the most common pose adds to this a pointed foot forward. Some dancers manipulate their skirts coyly; others stand on one leg with the other leg grazing an ear. The more spectacularly acrobatic dancers manage to touch the backs of their heads with a foot, or to smile from atop a split on the floor.

Duncan, in contrast, looks pleasantly soft and youthful in bare face and gauzy dress. Her *mise-en-scène* is simple, with plain curtains, and she remains on the ground, which is strewn with flowers. Her hair and her draping skirt are soft, her body supple. She appears searching, evasive, anticipatory, all at once. The suggestion is that something is stirring inside, beyond the decorative arrangement of a leg or a costume.

***

Duncan left America in May 1899, not long after the Schloss photographs were taken. When she returned to tour the United States in 1908, 1909, and 1911, her reputation as the "Barefoot Classic Dancer" had preceded her from Europe, through newspaper accounts that had reported on her rise to fame and on her colorful lifestyle ever since her first Parisian appearances in 1900. Broadway producer Charles Frohman initially

Figure 21. Duncan's images are unique among Schloss's studio portraits, in which dancers such as Annie St. Tel stiffly execute their acrobatic poses and coyly manipulate their skirts. Photo: Jacob Schloss. Courtesy of the Theatre Arts Collection, Harry Ransom Humanities Research Center, the University of Texas at Austin.

imported the dancer as a novelty in late summer 1908, pushing up the original September debut in order to preempt the appearance of Duncan-style dancer Maud Allan, whose *Salome* was wildly successful in London (figure 22). When Duncan fared poorly both at the Criterion Theatre and in

Figure 22. Duncan was deemed "chaste" in comparison to the sensational Salome dance, made wildly successful by Maud Allan in London and widely imitated in New York vaudeville. Photo: Foulsham & Banfield. Courtesy of the Dance Collection of the New York Public Library for the Performing Arts, Astor, Lenox and Tilden Foundations.

her subsequent tour, she parted ways with Frohman. She soon began work with the esteemed conductor Walter Damrosch and the New York Symphony Orchestra, making her second American "debut" in November, this time at an eminently upscale venue, the Metropolitan Opera House.

The Duncan/Damrosch tour was a success, as were her subsequent American appearances, when she traveled primarily to large northeastern cities. Duncan's repertoire included the dance interludes from Gluck's *Iphigenia in Tauris* (c. 1914–1915) and *Iphigenia in Aulis* (1905–1915), scenes from Gluck's *Orpheus*, Beethoven's Symphony no. 7 (1904), a Bach/Wagner program, and selections from Chopin and Tchaikovsky. Her encores included Schubert's *Moment Musicale* (1908) and the popular *Blue Danube Waltz* (1902). It is the lyrical, innocent youth of these early tours, rather than the Amazon of the war years or the dramatic actress of 1922/23, who dominates the Duncan legacy. It is that dancing body that I will examine here.

Even before her actual appearances, it was clear that Duncan offered something different, for the simple reason that no one else, besides Loie Fuller, had ever devoted an entire evening to dancing solo, without respite of song, skit, or recitation. Furthermore, she performed in legitimate theaters and concert halls rather than vaudeville houses. These fundamental changes of format reframed the event, from an anonymous mass spectacle to a seemingly more intimate communication between performer and spectator and from a low to a "high" art. Before the public even set foot in the theater, it was predisposed to accept Duncan on legitimately artistic terms, for two main reasons. First, she placed herself within the Hellenistic tradition, which then was considered the pinnacle of genuine artistry. Second, she had been acclaimed by European royalty, artists, and intellectuals. At a time when America was struggling to develop a cultural tradition of its own and claimed to eschew imported European high culture, its imprimatur nevertheless held great authority. It did not hurt, either, that this high priestess of the terpsichorean art could be claimed as one of America's own daughters.

That is not to say, however, that Duncan's reputation as a barefoot dancer was not in some cases a drawing card for the merely curious. But no matter what her audience's expectations were, they were confounded by the dancer's actual performance. Duncan's dancing was different from anything that had hit the American stage before. She did not construct herself as a visual spectacle, as her contemporaries did, performing a string of steps in routine time in some thematic costume, complete with backdrop and props. Ballet girls and vaudeville dancers were step dancers; their legs were their stock in trade, and not much of interest arose from the rest of their bodies. They operated in a pictorial mode, striking pose after pose or performing trick after trick. This was entertainment, whose appeal lay in the shapeliness of the female form, the successful (maybe even graceful) achievement of physical feats, and the novelty of the *mise-en-scène*.

Duncan's dancing did not conform to these conventions, and many of her reviewers—mostly music critics—found themselves at a loss for words. (Dance criticism was only in its infancy: it would be two more decades before the first full-time newspaper dance critic would be appointed.) The critics spent a lot more space rhapsodizing than describing, analyzing, or even interpreting. Although they did not know exactly what she was intending in some of her dances, they assured their readers that it was a "poetic" experience nevertheless. Others voiced that same feeling in stronger terms, declaring outright that the exquisiteness and depth of Duncan's expression defied being put into words. Clearly she was revealing something about the powers of the dancing body that they had not seen on stage before, and neither her audience nor the critics had discovered the vocabulary to articulate what seemed to them a strangely ephemeral, transcendent, elusive vision.

Duncan made it a rule never to perform in vaudeville houses or music halls, where dancing was considered only a diversion. This was no insignificant decision; even the Danish-British ballerina Adeline Genée, who experienced overwhelming success in her American tours from 1908 to 1914, was packaged as a vaudeville-type number, in musical revues and a Ziegfeld show.[70] Duncan played in legitimate theaters, concert halls, and opera houses, where she transformed the stage into a mythic space. She effectively metamorphosed the stage, paradoxically, by not attempting to make it into something other than itself. There were no conventional sets or props. A simple set of tall, voluminous, blue-gray curtains surrounded the stage on three sides, and there was a similarly colored carpet underfoot. Having dispensed with the harsh glare of the footlights, Duncan placed the light sources in either wing. They were soft tones—ambers and pinks, violets and rosy hues, but never, ever stark white—that gently mottled the stage in shadow and light.

Into this awaiting space, unmoored from any particular time and place, flooded the sound of the orchestra. It always played for a while first, sometimes as much as the first movement of a symphony. Only after the space had been enshrouded in melody and rhythm would the dancer slip through the shadows into the audience's awareness. In this dim radiance Duncan surged and floated, gathering her limbs inward and spreading them outward, without a hint of self-consciousness. Every time she moved, "she gives you a wonderful majesty of pose, an abundance, a completeness of gesture," wrote Robert Henri. "You always feel that she is very full, very plastic, very solid."[71] Duncan seemed to her spectators a vision of freedom, her tunic as alive as her body, the garment's light silk catching the force of her curving, swaying, onrushing motion. The chiton-like costumes, which ranged from knee-length Liberty silks to heavier, floor-length fabrics, helped to visually unify her body. The loose fabric riding along the skin, as if the two were organically connected, also communicated a feeling of tactile pleasure—a pleasure that conventional heavy, tailored clothing rarely afforded men or women.[72] "I took off my clothes to dance," she wrote, "because I felt the rhythm and freedom of my body better that way."[73]

Unlike ballet, her dancing was not vocabulary-intensive. The basic ambulatory steps, founded on simply a shift of weight, were adapted from the social dances of her childhood and implied in the S-curve stance of classical sculpture. There were variations on a skip, or a waltz turn, or a run, explains second-generation Duncan dancer Hortense Kooluris. A run could be Olympian, or it could skim the floor with loose steps, or it could be horse-like, with the knees raised high for a prancing effect.[74] The steps were, however, deceptive in their simplicity. The stepping, skipping, and leaping were only what she did to get from here to there. Like her curtains, her vocabulary served as a kind of neutral backdrop for the dynamic coloring of her movement. For it was how she moved—and sometimes how she stood still—that distinguished her dancing.

Duncan's body was always moving of a single piece, the torso and the limbs integrated seemingly without any effort. Motion and gesture (she was a very talented mime) were never isolated; they were always woven together into the line and flow of the dance. Her gestures could be very evocative, or rather explicit. She suggested literal actions by finding their essential impulse, and she could conjure up a companion, real but invisible, in the same way. She produced the most dramatic impact out of a minimum of means. And she modulated the scale of her gesture to the scale of her surroundings. Robert Henri testified that he had "seen her often enough to know that she makes a new and wonderful adjustment of gestures to space every time she dances."[75]

There was a strong oppositional pull in her movement—her torso twisting to the left while her arms motioned to the right, for example—which always kept the movement going. But no matter the flush and urgency, she never rushed. The impulse of her movements visibly originated from the center of her body (what she identified as the solar plexus), and that energy flowed freely outward, through her head, arms, and legs and into the furthest reaches of space. She achieved a kind of groundedness at the same time that her arms floated—that mixture of strength and grace seeded by the Delsarteans. While the ballet girl's arms etched static geometrical lines, Duncan's were always carving out sculptural space in three dimensions.[76] Duncan's arms were far from stiff—they were supple and sinuous (qualities inspired very early by the Japanese actress-dancer Sada Yacco, in appearances that Duncan saw at the 1900 Exposition Universelle in Paris). And unlike the movements of the typical dancer of her day, who went statically from pose to pose, Duncan's melted one into the next into the next into the next.

She was extraordinarily sensitive to the dynamic qualities of movement. In fact, much of her effect was communicated through her extraordinary ability for choreographing the drama of kinesthetic force—the sense of intentionality communicated through activated weight, the attentiveness signaled through spatial awareness, the impression of decisiveness or indecisiveness gained through the manipulation of time, and the degree of resolve suggested by relaxed or tensed musculature. Particularly important was her attitude toward the space surrounding her; rather than continually focusing on a narrow, distant point, she approached her environment with great flexibility. Not that she was scattered; quite the contrary, she was all-embracing.

The essence of Duncan's dancing was what she called "the profound rhythm of inner emotion."[77] Rhythm was the controlling matrix within which time, space, dynamics, gesture, and vocabulary were all embedded. The force of her movement—outward/inward, forward/backward, upward/downward, side to side, tension/release—was an inherently rhythmic wave, which she and others saw as the fundamental structure of nature. From Herbert Spencer to Wassily Kandinsky to Emile Jaques-Dalcroze, thinkers and artists had probed the mystic significance of rhythm. Spencer had explained rhythm as one of his "first principles" of the universe. Kandinsky was interested in translating musical rhythms into painting, and Dalcroze, a music professor who developed eurhythmics, was interested in transposing musical rhythm into movement.[78]

The rhythm and scale of Duncan's music—from delicate Chopin to monumental Beethoven—carried emotional, kinesthetic, and visual force. Generally, she followed the larger patterns of the music, keeping the rhythmic pulse with her legs while carrying the shape of the melody (rather than a note-by-note transposition) with her upper body.[79] But more than this, Duncan possessed an uncanny instinct for musicality—the expressiveness found in the way that music unexpectedly stretches out or rushes ahead. Instead of dancing squarely on the beat, she played with the elasticity of her accompaniment's rhythm, embedding hesitancy or fear or longing or a whole host of inner states in the way that she variously quickened or suspended her movement through time. Isadorable Maria-Theresa recalled:

> She was never concerned with the exact beat, but made her movements follow the broader line of rhythm with an unerring sense of musical flow, breathlessly holding back at times, enhancing the accent by a sharp turn or with vigorous movements of her legs, accentuating the principal modulation. In the more expressive slow largos and adagios of dramatic intensity, she followed the transitions of the musical themes with an uncanny suspense of motion, relying on the inner part of the composition.[80]

It was, arguably, through Chopin's trademark rubato that Duncan achieved her greatest musical effect.[81] And, in fact, concert pianist Harold Bauer (who learned from the very young Duncan about the gestural source of musical phrasing) discovered, many years after their collaboration in 1917, that her seemingly incorrect phrasing of Chopin's Etude in A Flat precisely matched the dynamic curve in the composer's own manuscript, which had been subsequently altered.[82]

Reviewers often articulated a distinction between what they perceived in Duncan's dancing and what they actually saw, because the stuff of her dancing was not physical. It was virtual. That is, there was something more happening on stage than a dancer simply moving her body parts. As back-to-nature reformer Bolton Hall described it:

> It is not dancing, tho' dancing is of it. It is vital motion, expressing emotion. Unlike the ordinary dancing, it has no set pattern or subordinate motif increasingly repeated.
> It has structure and design, but so closely allied to its beauty and grace that it can only be perceived, not seen.[83]

Forty years later, philosopher Susanne K. Langer explained the phenomenon quite eloquently, arguing that the essential sign of dance is "virtual gesture." That is, what we "see" in dance is not the bodily movement but the expressive volition—the force—that it suggests:

> The primary illusion of dance is a virtual realm of Power—not actual, physically exerted power, but appearances of influence and agency created by virtual gesture.
>
> In watching a collective dance—say, an artistically successful ballet—one does not see *people running around*; one sees the dance driving this way, drawn that way, gathering here, spreading there—fleeing, resting, rising, and so forth; and all the motion seems to spring from powers beyond the performers.[84]

Duncan's dancing embodied the virtual gesture par excellence. She gave the impression of dancing spontaneously, driven by some invisible necessity, even though her dances were choreographed. As Hall wrote, there was "structure and design," but spectators could not discern it while they were experiencing the dancing. They were not meant to discern it. The choreography was generally very simple, usually a gently repetitious, symmetrical scheme supporting the kinesthetic drama of the piece, primarily through the use of floor pattern (side to side, front to back, on the diagonal) and body level (low, medium, high). (George Balanchine—whose words for Duncan were generally unkind—did credit her with innovating the use of the stage floor for the whole reclining body.)[85] Again, as with her vocabulary, structure served only as a framework, meant to recede from view as the work was performed.[86] In the Chopin pieces, for example, Duncan used the relationship between the rhythm and dynamics of the body in order to choreograph the scale, shape, and dimension of the musical phrases.

Thus, for her American spectators between 1908 and 1911, Duncan's body effectively dissolved in the act of performance. H. T. Parker of the *Boston Evening Transcript* (a fine critic, who wrote on music, drama, and dance) described this phenomenon as "this idealized and disembodied quality in her dancing."[87] A perceptive anonymous critic from the *Philadelphia Telegraph* wrote similarly that Duncan was "an absolutely rare and lovely impersonation of the spirit of music, more like a sweet thought than a woman, more like a dream creation than an actual flesh and blood entity."[88] This was the paradox of her dancing: on the one hand, she revealed the physical body as it had never been revealed before on the concert stage, but on the other hand, her physical body disappeared, became force, or virtual gesture, on-stage. She "free[d] it from all that is material and of the flesh," as Chicago writer W. L. Hubbard described it.[89] For

Duncan, as well as her audiences, this was a transcendent practice. In dancing, she wrote, "the body becomes transparent and is a medium for the mind and spirit."[90]

What was so extraordinary, then, about Duncan for those early American audiences was that she appeared to make visible the inner impulses, stirrings, vibrations of the self, what she called the "soul." Ongoing movement became an allegory of the self. When Duncan initiated a motion from her solar plexus, then successively lifted her chest and raised her head heavenward or threw it backward Dionysically, it was a stunning embodiment of Will. The dancing body was no longer a product—of training, of narrative, of consumption—but rather a process. It was about *becoming* a self rather than *displaying* a body.

III

Behind the apparent artlessness of Duncan's dancing were years of conscious, laborious work, from a very young age. According to her best childhood friend, Florence Treadwell Boynton, there was a period when Duncan used her every action to practice gracefulness. "Everything that she did was studied (whether she sat down, rose, walked). It appeared to be stilted, overdone, affected, and looked cruder than a slow motion movie. She was never off guard in a single gesture or motion."[91]

Duncan was largely self-taught, but not entirely so. She took, of course, those infamous childhood ballet lessons, short-lived though they were. And there is evidence to suggest that she took lessons from a Delsarte instructor; at the Oakland Turnverein; and from ballerinas Marie Bonfanti and Katti Lanner. Apprenticeships in the theaters of Augustin Daly and F. R. Benson undoubtedly influenced her dancing as well. But at the root of it all was her older sister, Elizabeth, who taught her the social, or "fancy," dances of the day—the rhythmic stepping of the polka, waltz, and schottische, upon which she based her own movement vocabulary. "Even when a child," Elizabeth recalled after her sister's death, "Isadora grasped the slightest suggestion or remark about dancing with the comprehension of genius."[92]

Given the fact that Duncan's aesthetic was vehemently anti-ballet, it is no surprise that she would want to downplay any training she had received in the philistine form. Duncan managed to turn her youthful foray into ballet to her own advantage, for one of the cornerstones of the Duncan mythology is her youthful rejection of toe dancing. As she tells it in *My Life*, she was not pleased by her lessons with a "famous ballet teacher." "When the teacher told me to stand on my toes I asked him why, and when he replied 'Because it is beautiful,' I said that it was ugly and against nature and after the third lesson I left his class, never to return."[93]

Oakland music and dance critic Paul Hertelendy, however, has reported another reason for the dismissal of the ballet teacher, whom he identifies as Jay Mastbaum, a San Francisco dance instructor listed in the city directory from 1885 to 1890. According to Isadora's brother Raymond, Mastbaum commuted to Oakland for a short time to teach the children waltzes and social dancing. When he stalked out for good, it was after arguments with Mrs. Duncan "over her piano tempos."[94] Whatever the reason for the teacher's abrupt exit, the incident allowed Duncan a means of dramatizing her principled refusal of ballet.

Duncan received what was probably her most significant formal physical training from the Oakland Turnverein, one of the area's German-American clubs, which met at Germania Hall. Duncan took both dance and gymnastics there.[95] Most likely, her activities included dancelike exercises including skipping, follow-stepping, change stepping, and galloping.[96] In one of the many autobiographies she invented through the years (usually based loosely on the truth), Duncan claimed that her first public performance was for a "Great Charity festival before [a] public [of] 20000 people in Mechanics Pavilion," at age twelve.[97] This may be true, for in 1889 the Verein Eintracht (another local turnverein) held a Grand March at Mechanics Pavilion "representing 'Poets and Poetry' In 5 Divisions (350 Participants, 9 Floats), to conclude with a Menuet de la Cour de Louis XIV, at 9 o'clock precisely."[98] It is conceivable that they borrowed from fellow turnvereins to supply the pageant participants.

Duncan never admitted to taking any more ballet classes than those in the ill-fated childhood episode. Nevertheless, there is evidence enough to suggest that as a young adult she continued in ballet training, as a pupil of Marie Bonfanti and, perhaps, Katti Lanner.[99] Both had been famed ballerinas before settling down to teach, the La Scala–trained Bonfanti in New York and the Vienna Opera–trained Lanner in London, where she was ballet mistress of the Empire Theatre.

Bonfanti was an Italian prima ballerina who had come to America to star in the original 1866 New York production of *The Black Crook*, a spectacular production that initiated the immensely popular trend for extravaganzas across the country (figure 23).[100] (These spectacle-extravaganzas were loosely structured and designed to make the spectator marvel—at

Figure 23. Despite Duncan's claim to "Nature" as her only teacher, she likely took ballet classes from Marie Bonfanti, the Italian prima ballerina who had come to America to star in the spectacle-extravaganza The Black Crook. *Courtesy of the Theatre Arts Collection, Harry Ransom Humanities Research Center, the University of Texas at Austin.*

the scenery, the costumes, and the beautiful women. As the century wore on, the ballet dancing became less an expression of beauty and more a matter of technical virtuosity for the ballerina, and for the corps, little more than pretty posturing and display.) For the next thirty years after *Crook*, Bonfanti mostly toured the country, with several companies, including Augustin Daly's and the Kiralfy Brothers', and she spent several seasons in residence with companies such as the Metropolitan Opera.

In 1897 Bonfanti opened her own school, first in Union Square and then further uptown, on Broadway. According to a young California dancer named Lola Yberri, Duncan "used to take lessons of my teacher, Mme. Bonfanti, up to 5 o'clock in the afternoon, and then teach her own class."[101] Bonfanti taught the same principles she had learned from the master ballet teacher and theoretician Carlo Blasis in Milan: simplicity, logic, and clarity. "Slowness," she told her students, "is beauty." Duncan could have learned something of the beauty of the curve and the importance of artlessness from Bonfanti, who was renowned for her own "poetry of motion." Duncan may also have benefited by taking the ballerina's dramatic pantomime classes.[102]

Katti Lanner, daughter of the Viennese waltz composer Joseph Lanner, settled in London in 1875 after a distinguished career dancing and choreographing across Europe, Russia, and the U.S. She was known for her mime and her natural musicality—two traits she may have encouraged in Duncan. Lanner became an important force in improving ballet training, by serving as ballet master of Her Majesty's Theatre and directing the National Training School of Dancing. She also maintained a private school, where she taught and rehearsed her ballets for the Empire Theatre. A music hall where Lanner was ballet mistress for a decade, the Empire became one of the city's most active ballet platforms. Lanner choreographed thirty-six productions for the Empire alone, and her rarity as a female choreographer could have served as model for the aspiring Duncan.[103]

It may have been Augustin Daly who referred the young dancer to Lanner and Bonfanti, since he had worked with both ballerinas.[104] Daly, a significant theatrical producer who pioneered serious Shakespeare and other drama in his New York theater, probably deserves a bit more credit for Duncan's development than she gives him. Daly had broken from the vaudevillian structure that loosely strung together a range of novelties; instead he created a coherent, stylistically unified narrative in which everything contributed to the effect of the whole. In her autobiography,

Duncan tells the story of her first-night success as a fairy in *A Midsummer Night's Dream*, claiming that Daly dimmed the lights on her subsequent performances because he was jealous of the audience applause for her (figure 24). More likely, he was concerned that her number would be interpreted as a vaudevillian turn, disrupting the dramatic unity of the production as a whole. Indeed, the reviewer in the *San Francisco Chronicle* wrote: "In the dimness of the stage light the fairies dancing and singing might almost have been real fairies, for the effect was fascinatingly shadowy."[105]

From 1895 to 1897 Duncan performed in Daly's *Miss Pygmalion* (a musical pantomime starring Jane May); *A Midsummer Night's Dream*; *The Geisha* (a musical comedy, in which she played an attendant at the Tea House); *Much Ado about Nothing* (she performed the dance of the gypsies); *Meg Merrilies* (a musical, in which she was again a dancing gypsy); and *The Tempest* (as one of the chief spirits attending on Prospero).

Carl Marwig, Daly's master of dance, composed Duncan's dances for *Much Ado about Nothing*, *Meg Merrilies*, and *The Tempest*. A professor of dancing who came to New York City from Switzerland, he gave one of the earliest children's pageants in the country, in 1877. Later on he became a chief booking agent for New York showgirls and a ballet teacher of note. He was the dance master to whom Ruth St. Denis's mother had taken the young Ruthie, in order to have him determine her potential.[106] Marwig's classes began with a series of adagio movements and poses, the body swaying back and forth, with the arms outstretched or gracefully curved over the head as the feet moved forward and back, progressing into high kicks.[107] The classroom emphasis on grace through muscle control first, before the virtuosity of steps, could have helped Duncan to physicalize her ideas. So could have his insistence on the importance of the swaying of the body as a means of cultivating suppleness.

Duncan took another theatrical engagement in early 1900, in F. R. Benson's spring season at London's Lyceum Theatre. She again danced the fairy in *A Midsummer Night's Dream*, as well as a French camp follower in *Henry V*.[108] An actor-producer, Benson aspired to establish in London a revival of a stock company with a repertoire season; that spring, Benson produced seven Shakespeare plays and an Old English comedy. Duncan could have learned much from his *Midsummer Night's Dream* about the atmospheric production qualities that became so important to her own *mise-en-scène*. Benson's *Dream* was a poetic series of enchanting pictures, more like a masque than a drama. "The eye dwells with delight upon the woodland glade by moonlight," wrote the reviewer for the *Era*, "where

Figure 24. Before devoting herself to a solo career, Duncan danced roles in six plays and musicals produced by Augustin Daly, including that of a fairy in A Midsummer Night's Dream. *Courtesy of the Dance Collection of the New York Public Library for the Performing Arts, Astor, Lenox and Tilden Foundations.*

there is an admirable realisation of the beauties of an English sylvan scene."[109]

By the time that Duncan reached Paris later that year, she was still on the lookout for a teacher; she knew that she had not yet found a way to completely materialize her ideas about dancing. She wrote to Douglas Ainslie on 8 December:

> Also I was bitterly disappointed last night at the Opera—to see some "Greek Dancing" it was a sort of modified Ballet in white gowns—not in acme Greek—I thought I might find some teacher some help there—but it was all stupid, vanity and vexation—They do not dance for love—They do not dance for the Gods—There was not as far as I could see any Beauty or desire for Beauty—Not the slightest glimmering knowledge of Apollo—or the Graces—or even of the kindly Pan—There is no help for me there and so I [toddle] on in my own little way—at least *so*, life is joyous to me.[110]

Duncan was smart enough to *look* for teachers. After all, even though the training in her day would hardly be considered rigorous by today's standards, extended study under a master was still the paradigm of serious dance training.

Although Duncan found many teachers from whom to absorb some small thing toward her eventual aesthetic, she never found the "master" to whom to apprentice herself, for two reasons. First, no such person existed. A dance of "Nature" and "Beauty" as she conceived it at such an early age was, by definition, not to be found in any academy or institution. Second, the very concept of technical mastery was not consistent with Duncan's aesthetic. The dancing body Duncan eventually did construct was not an image of technical mastery, even though it did require technical mastery. The point of Duncan's practice was to reject an image of control and to replace it with one of release.

***

Duncan began to construct her dancing body by releasing it from literal physical confinement. The corset served only to squeeze off the upper body from the legs, and what Duncan was seeking was a holistic, single-unit body, in which movement could flow easily from one part to another. Toe shoes, to her, were merely a tool to defy gravity, which Duncan instead embraced as a choreographic partner. Gravity is, for example, used to initiate a run. Instead of starting with the feet, the Duncan dancer lifts up her body onto half-toe. She leads up and forward with her chest, "lengthening upward like a stretched bow,"[111] explains Duncan dancer Lori Belilove, until the weight of the entire body is pulled forward, and the feet must move ahead under the force of momentum. As the dancer continues running, she seems impelled by the space before her. In the same way, Duncan often choreographed diagonals into her dances; relative to the vertical stability of the human body, an arm or torso movement done on the diagonal forces the body off balance, and again, gravitational momentum thrusts it easily into a new course of energy.[112]

The basic body attitude of the lyrical Duncan dancer is one of suspension: the chest pulled high out of a low, grounded pelvis. She rises out of the legs and hips and into the solar plexus, and that energy continues through the head and arms. The torso (not the feet) propels the body through space, and the legs flow from an active, mobile pelvis. Control at the center is complemented by the grace of limbs (a direct borrowing from American Delsartism). The impetus of all movement originates in the torso, what she saw as the source of emotional life. This impulse travels outward, like a wave, into the extremities, which exhibit no obvious physical effort.

It was important that audiences imagine Duncan to be free from technical training, even from choreographic preparation, for she embodied a vision of spontaneity and complete freedom, born of "Nature." That was a large part of her appeal for a generation of Americans whose ambivalence toward modernism left them longing for things simpler, purer, more seemingly "authentic." But the claim to utter naiveté also worked against her wider reputation, both during her later lifetime and after her death, because as ballet and modern dance took a foothold in American culture, the display of "technique" became the generally accepted basis of theatrical dancing.

As early as 1910, when Duncan and famed Russian ballerina Anna Pavlova were touring simultaneously, they were constantly being compared in the press (figure 25). Pavlova's appearances, many said, were bringing ballet to America for the first time since Fanny Elssler's 1840–1842 tour, and the comparison of the two opposing aesthetics was inescapable. Pavlova, despite her admiration for Duncan, concluded to a *Musical America* reporter that "taken altogether, I think that my work is harder than that of Isadora Duncan. You see, she never has to get up and dance on her toes, and I do."[113] By the time that Sergei Diaghilev's Ballets Russes made its American tours in 1916 and 1917, the first one including the celebrated Vaslav Nijinsky, Duncan was not faring as well in the comparisons. Fervent balletomanes such as the Franco-Russian critic André Levinson

Figure 25. As early as 1910, when they toured the country simultaneously, Duncan's apparent "spontaneity" was compared with the technical prowess of the famed Russian ballerina Anna Pavlova. Photo: Mishkin. Courtesy of the Dance Collection of the New York Public Library for the Performing Arts, Astor, Lenox and Tilden Foundations.

considered her more a personality than a true artist, responsible for the encouragement of dilettantism. If Bonfanti did indeed teach Duncan, she either forgot or disdained to take credit for such heresy: "Isadora Duncan . . . Isadora Donkey! That is not dancing, whatever enthusiasts may call it. As if jumping around with bare legs were the first artistic principle of the dance. . . . Natural, spontaneous movements are always most awkward. To be sure, good dancing looks spontaneous and in a very definite sense it is, but it is the spontaneity that comes after training."[114]

As soon as Duncan died, the backlash against her antitechnical aesthetic swelled. Critic Valerien Svetloff, who had written admiringly of her early performances in Russia, wrote in the *Dancing Times* of December 1927 that, although something in Duncan's dancing may have been genuine and original, it attracted and encouraged only amateurs: " 'Duncanism,' in the long run, became the small change of the vainglorious, stage-struck tyro."[115] This debate between technically driven ballet and expressive modern dance continues with Duncan firmly at its center. Echoing the admiring yet damning argument of Svetloff, Lincoln Kirstein (cofounder of New York City Ballet) published his own indictment of Duncan, holding her responsible as recently as 1986 for the trail of untalented dancers who followed in her wake.[116]

***

In dance, "technique" is an academic term and concept, a mechanization and externalization of the body quite foreign to Duncan's essentially romantic impulse, which sought to penetrate the internal body by patterning movement after the harmonious workings of "Nature." "Technique" posits the body as an instrument of the self, and therefore distanced from the self, whereas Duncan conceived of the body as the self incarnate. If classicist Levinson metaphorized ballet as a machine,[117] Duncan metaphorized it as an organism—a plant, a wave, a bird. From the organism blossoms expression; the machine becomes a virtuoso. In ballet, technique is fused with style; it *becomes* style. In modern dance, beginning with Duncan, technique serves as a functional support beneath style. "Since I was a child I have spent twenty years of incessant labor in the service of my art, a large part of that time being devoted to technical training—which I am sometimes accused of lacking," explained Duncan. "That is because, I repeat, technique is not an end but only a means."[118]

Just because Duncan did not exhibit ballet technique does not mean that her dancing did not require technique, that is to say, according to Webster's, a consistent manner in which physical movements are made. Or, as Marcel Mauss defined it, in the plural, "the ways in which, from society to society, men [*sic*] know how to use their bodies."[119] Duncan's dancing body was indeed trained to move in a very particular way. Second-generation Duncan dancer Julia Levien recalls the exacting physical demands of her training: "Your knee must be turned out. Your hips must be thrust forward. Your breathing must be in a certain cadence. Nothing was left to chance."[120] This is only too evident when you look at a neophyte alongside a longtime Duncan dancer such as Lori Belilove, a third-generation dancer for more than twenty years (figure 26).[121] The differences in their identical gesturing and gamboling are immediately apparent in the resiliency of the ankles, the strength and flexibility of the back, the mobility of the pelvis, the articulation of the chest and neck, and the fluidity of the arms. The technique emphasizes contrast, an economy of means, and a supple connectedness between body parts. According to Irma Duncan, it requires "perfect nimbleness of limbs and body and genuine elevation."[122]

Anatomically, the movements originate from deep down in the abdominal muscles, which permit the deep backward extensions of the upper torso. The spine is strong and flexible enough to contract in both the lower and upper torso. The pelvis mobilizes the body's large actions forward, backward, up, and down from the ground. Although the dancer does not step on her tiptoes, she steps high on the balls of her feet, with an exquisitely developed arch; a pair of supple ankles facilitate the plush sinking and rising action. (Perhaps Duncan herself developed these ankles as a child, dancing on the beach. As an adult, dancing on a carpet probably helped to cushion the leaping and landing.) Arms held slightly forward keep the shoulders gracefully sloping downward. The lifting of the arm is precisely calculated: the elbow is rotated outward, and the lower arm hangs freely. The upper arm is tensed as it is raised until midpoint, when the full arm and chest are released upward together.

Duncan strategically choreographed such release spots into her dances, usually at the top of an extension. These were the moments of eternity when her body seemed to soar, when its reach exceeded its grasp and that "tremendous force of dynamic movement" that she saw in Duse penetrated the stillness. Anna Duncan talked about these moments as ones of "electrical energy," and Irma Duncan likened them to "dancing in water." The release has a sense of pressure, explains Levien. "It isn't a dead space. It's a sensual thing, because you must be so implicitly aware."[123]

These tension-and-release sequences are one of the fundamental ways in which the Duncan technique produces kinesthetic contrast, in order to suggest drama. The technique makes maximum use of the contrast

Figure 26. The rigors of the Duncan technique, exemplified by third-generation Duncan dancer Lori Belilove, result in the resiliency of the ankles, the strength and flexibility of the back, the mobility of the pelvis, the fluidity of the arms, and the articulation of the chest and neck. Photo: David Fullard. Courtesy of the Isadora Duncan Foundation for Contemporary Dance, Inc.

between the lightness of the upper body and chest and the strength of the pelvis; between the actions of rising and sinking; and between the contraction and release of the spine. There is the contrast inherent in spatial opposition, too.

It is essential that the flexion of the ankles, the mobilization of the pelvis, the extension of the torso, and the release of the head and arms be coordinated. This completely engaged body has the look of total involvement, which not only creates a sense of fullness but also gives the dancer's arm and hand gestures their monumental scale. The Duncan dancer is extended, but she never looks artificially stretched, because the extension of the limbs is mediated by constantly bending elbows and knees, and there are never any stabbing feet or locked joints. This kind of extension, which is spatial rather than muscular—aided by the dynamic pull of opposition, which often turns into a spiral—produces a body that is open and sculptural, rather than one that is closed and flat.

Irma Duncan, who wrote *The Technique of Isadora Duncan*, argued that Isadora had discovered a "Science of Movement," by which the body was taken through a logical succession of exercises.[124] Isadora outlined the system in a notebook:

> These exercizes shall begin with a simple gymnastic preparing the muscles for suppleness & strength only after these gymnastic will comes the first steps of the dance—the first to learn a simple rhythmical walk. Then to walk or pace slowly to simple rhythms Then to walk or pace quickly to more complex rhythms—Then to run—first slowly to simple rhythms then swiftly—to leap— [illegible] the ground to a certain part of a rhythm—These excercizes will acquaint their feet with the different rhythms
> The [Pexique] -u-/-u-/
> Iambique uu/-u-u/--uu/
> Sapphique ---u/-uu/-u--/
> and also some of the rhythms used in modern music In all movement, they will learn the values first of straight lines—then of angles & finally of curves— These movements they will learn consciously but they will also [possess] an unconsciousness in the execution of them as these movements will be so arranged as to be merely the expression of the unfolding of the Human Will in Bodily Movement. These exercizes will follow each other in natural sequence from the simple to the complex—they will be learning the notes as one might call them of the scale of movement from which later may be worked into Harmonies the most different & complex in structure.[125]

Using uncomplicated movements, Duncan emphasized rhythm, developed from the simple to the complex, whose variations, she seemed to suggest, can be used as a vocabulary in itself.

Unlike ballet, whose foundation is a series of still poses (the five basic positions), the basis of the Duncan technique is motion—namely, the walk. Out of the walk evolves skipping, running, leaping. (Even off-stage, Duncan was distinguished by her easy, swinging walk.)[126] But such a seemingly simple action is not so simple at all. First of all, the leg is not picked up off the floor by the foot; rather, it is lifted from the thigh muscles. The knee and relaxed lower leg follows, with a sense of weight and continued connection with the earth. It is the pelvis that propels the back leg forward, the hip disengaging in the process for a sense of earthy ease. The foot melts back into the earth, connecting on the ball first and rolling into the heel. There is a pause before the other leg moves forward, producing a distinct, stately rhythm.

***

Duncan, devoted as she was to establishing dance schools, was much less devoted to teaching. She herself admitted that she was not a teacher.[127] Isadora may have offered her students example and inspiration, but it was Elizabeth or Irma who had the daily task of giving class.

Elizabeth was the earliest codifier of the technique. In London, in 1900, when a woman approached Mrs. Duncan about dancing lessons for her daughter, she was told that Isadora did not teach, but that Elizabeth would take on the girl. Marie-Louise de Meeus recalls those classes in the Kensington Palace Hotel:

> The lessons were wonderful. She made me realise how movement must invade my whole being, from the poise of the head through the poise of the body, running like a current down the limbs, even to the tips of the fingers. All must be fluent, expressive. This being a nature-school, *tours de force* were rigorously excluded. The tip-toes of the ballet were condemned; the ball of the foot was alone created to carry the human body, so declared my mistress, adducing in support of her theory the classic frieze and the medieval painting. It was also a Duncan axiom never to stand squarely on both feet. One leg alone should bear the whole weight; the other leg, gracefully bent at the knee, should rest lightly on the side of the foot.[128]

Most of the young girl's training consisted of arm exercises, "though the whole frame had of course to participate in them to a certain extent, according to her inviolable rule." A rare glimpse into the early technique, de Meeus's account is worth quoting at length:

> I remember four of them, all founded on nature mimicry. The first and easiest was called the "Fern-frond." The pupil stood quite straight (for once!) with each arm curled closely upon the chest, the fingers rounded inwards on the palm, the outer edge of the wrists resting against each other. The head was bent down over the folded hands. Then the frond began to grow. To the sound of soft music the head was raised, slowly, steadily. Miss Elizabeth bade me feel how the muscles

tightened at the back of my neck during this action, as each section of my vertebrae played its part. Slowly, steadily, the chin was tilted, the eyes looked up. Meanwhile the arms began to move; they unfolded, always softly rounded; they rose above the head, stretched high; then, last of all, the fingers uncurled, straight to the very tips. Delicately must the movement flow, without a jerk, without an angle anywhere. The whole body remained thus a second or two, straining upwards, like a plant towards the sun.

Another exercise was named "Tree Branches in a Wind." As before, the feet remained still, while the body took on a swaying motion, accompanied by the rhythmic waving of the arms, and a peculiar dip and flutter of the wrists.

"The Waves" was perhaps the most difficult. Arms, wrists and fingers, stretched out at right angles to the body, had to assume a ribbon-like suppleness, and movement rippled along them, now deep and rolling like a stormy swell, now light and quick like a quiet sea.

"The Bird" brought the feet at last into play. The arms were extended in front, palm to palm, the hands faintly fluttering; then the action widened, the arms waving softly at first, then spreading out each side like wings, and beating ever stronger, till somehow, by the very force of suggestion, the dancer glided away in a floating measure, so airy, so free, that it really gave the performer the illusion of flight.[129]

In this country, the technique that has been handed down through at least three generations was codified largely by Irma Duncan. After Isadora's death, she stayed on at the school in Moscow and traveled to the U.S. in 1929/30 for a tour with some of her students. When they were prematurely recalled to Moscow, she chose to stay behind. Until her death in 1977, she remained committed to preserving the Duncan tradition by teaching several generations of students, staging the dances, donating her and Isadora's papers to the New York Public Library, and writing an account of her life with Isadora as well as one on the Duncan technique and one on Isadora's last days. Among Irma's students, Hortense Kooluris and Julia Levien continue to teach, reconstruct, and coach the Duncan repertory.[130]

***

It is ironic that what was called "natural" dance required technique, and the irony is further compounded by Duncan's gymnastic warm-up. But in the 1890s, the decade when Duncan was coming of age, gymnastics were an unprecedented means to greater physical mobility for women. With the renewal of the Olympic Games and the craze for bicycling during that decade, women were being encouraged to improve their health through exercise and fresh air. Public gymnasiums held classes for women in everything from swinging clubs to pulley weights, stationary bicycles to rowing machines, vaulting horses to tumbling. At the Olympic Amateur Athletic Club of San Francisco in 1893, where Duncan was then living, more than a hundred women attended gymnastic school twice a week.[131] Two years later, the "athletic craze [had] grown to such an extent that private gymnasiums [were] added to the nursery and boudoir," reported the *San Francisco Examiner*.[132]

Such concern with physical fitness was not new to America—it had just never caught on before. There had been enthusiasm for calisthenics, gymnastics, sports, and physical education[133] as early as 1830—by German idealist Charles Follen, who opened the first college gymnasium at Harvard University in 1826, and by Edward Hitchcock, the first American professor of physical education. The cause had been championed for the next three decades by reformers such as hydropathic physician Russell Trall and author/lecturer/advisor Catharine Beecher, by physical education instructor Dr. Dioclesian Lewis, and also by the German turnverein gymnastic clubs.[134]

The post–Civil War craze for fitness was in part a response to the increasingly urban, sedentary, bureaucratic nature of modern life. Neurasthenia, conceived of as the overwork of the brain at the expense of the body, was seen as a collective sympton of a deteriorating culture. So by the 1880s, with the pioneering work of educators such as Dr. Dudley A. Sargent, physical education became an established practice. An acrobat and weight lifter from the age of fourteen, Sargent directed the Bowdoin College gymnasium while he studied for his medical degree. He operated his own "Hygienic Institute and School of Physical Culture" in New York City, and then, in 1879, became the first assistant professor of physical training at Harvard. He used pulley and weight machines and what he called "mimetic exercises," which duplicated the activities of laborers and sportsmen.

At the same time that Sargent was developing his methods at Harvard, gymnastics was reaching its peak. The most accessible source of vigorous exercise came from the community turnvereins. A former "turner" herself, Duncan used gymnastics as a preliminary, in order to relax and limber both the legs and body and to develop elasticity in the ankles. At one point in her career, Duncan took Swedish gymnastics, and in 1908 she was reported to employ a trainer two hours a day to keep up her strength.[135] Irma Duncan outlines several of Isadora's exercises in her book on Duncan technique. For the legs, exercises such as high kicks and plies (without the turnout) were done at the barre, in a relaxed style; for the torso, there was a series of bends from the hips and hip circles and weight shifts.

Gymnastics, however, were meant only as a prelude to expressive composition. To think otherwise, as Duncan accused Emile Jaques-Dalcroze of doing, was a mistake. She criticized the Swiss composer's system of "rhythmic gymnastics," which was received with increasing seriousness in the United States during the early teens,[136] as "an illustration of the error that is born of imitation unsupported by original thought. They are good up to a certain point, but they are not creative"[137] (figure 27).

Despite her specifically expressive goals, classes in "aesthetic dancing" or "classic dancing" or "gymnasium dancing," inspired by Duncan's performances, became more and more popular as a new form of athletic exercise. For those authorities who objected to the fair sex turning to vigorous sports such as basketball or tennis, dancing was a graceful alternative. Sargent, for example, supported dancing as an effective means of exercise for women. This is how, in 1909, he evaluated the Duncan technique, in comparison to ballerina Adeline Genée's (figure 28):

> Miss Duncan is about sixty-six inches tall and 128 pounds in weight, and has seemingly a heavier trunk and heavier limbs than Miss Genee. The latter could easily duplicate the technical work of the former, though Miss Duncan could never duplicate the technical work of Miss Genee, because she lacks the local power in the feet and legs. Miss Duncan's dancing does not require extreme effort from any one group of muscles, but it does bring a great many groups into gentle activity.
>
> Miss Genee's best efforts are produced with straight legs and extended feet and flexed toes, while Miss Duncan's artistic attempts are made with bent knees or flexed thighs and extended toes. The repeated efforts made in drawing the knees upward in front and extending the legs and feet backward require a corresponding use of the arms and considerable extension and flexion of the trunk. For obvious reasons this style of dancing could not be done with a constricted waist or constricted limbs. So many groups of muscles are brought into action in Miss Duncan's dancing that we should expect her to have unusually good respiratory and circulatory power, and consequently great endurance.[138]

Although in her early years she lived simply and healthily, during one period waking early to run in a nearby park and then do some gymnastics,[139] Duncan became very inconsistent about her training. She told her pianist at the beginning of their 1916 South American tour that all she needed to keep fit was a few minutes of gymnastics and exercises, and yet there were times on the tour that she neglected even that, without any discernible deficit on stage.[140] In her last years, she would still attempt her

1   2   3

4   5

Figure 27. Duncan criticized the rhythmic gymnastics of Swiss composer Emile Jaques-Dalcroze, which were gaining popularity in the teens, as imitative rather than creative.

Figure 28. In 1909, physical education pioneer Dudley A. Sargent compared the overall "gentle activity" of Duncan's technique with the "local power in the feet and legs" of Danish-British ballerina Adeline Genée, whom Florenz Ziegfeld billed as "the world's greatest dancer" in his 1908 musical revue The Soul Kiss. Photo: Otto Sarony Co. Courtesy of the Dance Collection of the New York Public Library for the Performing Arts, Astor, Lenox and Tilden Foundations.

exercises, sometimes giving up the monotony. "An artist does not need muscles but should be porous," she explained to a companion. "I never was an acrobat, even in my youth, . . . and you will realize some day that I am the poorest of all professional dancers in the usual sense; when I was twenty-five, I used to throw spears at imaginary gods."[141]

3.

Just as Duncan had narrativized the origin of her dance practice by recounting her childhood rejection of toe dancing, so she narrativized the origin of her identification with "Nature." She claimed "Nature" as her first and only teacher, guiding her always toward a body unfettered, undivided, uncorrupted:

> When I was fifteen years old and I realized that there was no teacher in the world who could give me any help in my desire to be a dancer, because at that time the only school that existed was the ballet, I turned, as I had noticed all other artists except dancers do, to the study of nature. Is anything more marvellous or beautiful in nature than the study of the delicate love movements of plants? My imagination was first captured by Shelley's wonderful poem *The Sensitive Plant*, and for my dances I studied the movements of the opening of flowers, and the flight of bees and the charming graces of pigeons and other birds.[1]

THE *Natural* BODY

"The Sensitive Plant" notwithstanding, Duncan's idea of "Nature" was less transparent than she wanted her audiences to realize.

Far from being a tabula rasa, beyond the contingencies of culture and history, this "Natural" body was an artistic invention as well as a rhetorical strategy—a conceptual cipher for an ideal of harmony that embraced the Greeks and rejected "African savages." "Nature" was Duncan's metaphorical shorthand for a loose package of aesthetic and social ideals: nudity, childhood, the idyllic past, flowing lines, health, nobility, ease, freedom, simplicity, order, and harmony. Through a series of correspondences, she elided "Nature" with science, religion, the Greeks, and, finally, Culture. The "Natural" body was thus "civilized" (and white) as opposed to "primitive" (and black). Functioning as the foundational trope for her artistic practice, the grace and clarity of the "Natural" body thus served to purify and elevate the sullied image of the dancer in turn-of-the-century America. Functioning, too, as the foundational trope for her social agenda, it provided not just a blueprint for social order and harmony but also a template of social *control*, at a time of backlash against immigrants, whose numbers were growing, and blacks, whose ragtime music and dancing were penetrating urban American culture.

Much like the Arts and Crafts exponents, who looked back toward the medieval guilds for a model of handmade craftsmanship and design simplicity, Duncan bemoaned the losses incurred by modern life.[2] "With the first conception of a conscience," she argued, "man became self-conscious, lost the natural movements of the body; today in the light of intelligence gained through years of civilization, it is essential that he consciously seek what he has unconsciously lost."[3] Progressive advocates of a "simple life"—from naturalist John Muir and economist Thorstein Veblen to *Ladies' Home Journal* editor Edward Bok and craftsman Gustav Stickley—argued that the excessive nervous tension of the middle class could be cured by a cluster of practices outlined by historian David Shi as including "discriminating consumption, uncluttered living, personal contentment, aesthetic simplicity (including an emphasis on handicrafts), civic virtue, social service, and a renewed contact with nature in one form or another." The "simple life" was closely identified with the turn-of-the-century nature revival, which manifested itself in a back-to-the-land movement, a wilderness movement, and an outdoor fresh air movement.[4] "Nature" in its many guises—whether a country vacation or a stroll through Central Park, or a performance by Duncan—served as a rather nostalgic projection for the modern American, who sought some temporary respite from the anxiety of change and the complexity of the new. "In this present day of elaboration and artificiality," wrote an anonymous reviewer for the *Philadelphia Telegraph*,

> Miss Duncan's art comes as a pure breath from some pine-clad mountain height refreshing as its ozone, beautiful and true as the overarching blue sky. Entirely simple, natural and unaffected, she presents a picture of beauty, joy and abandon as one believes it must have been when the world was young and youth danced in the sunlight for the mere joy of life.[5]

For Duncan, as for many upper- and middle-class Americans dealing with the rapidly modernizing world at the turn of the century,[6] this idyllic vision of "Nature," whose origin was traced back nostalgically to the "glory of Greece," represented the romantic values that modernity threatened to destroy. Duncan's appeal to "Nature"—her interest in repose over efficiency—was an antimodern impulse, which refused to even recognize the modern body's inextricable dialectic with the modern machine, in whose grip, ironically, Duncan and her two children were to die.[7]

***

Duncan's trope of the "Natural" body was forged over a number of years, from a variety of sources. There were, of course, Percy Bysshe Shelley and John Keats. And there were also Walt Whitman, and Ernst Haeckel, and Sandro Botticelli, along with Johann Joachim Winckelmann, Friedrich Nietzsche, and Auguste Rodin. But before the dancer encountered any of them, there was California, whose natural beauty served as its animating identity. At the core of the "California dream," according to Kevin Starr, "was the hope for a special relationship to nature," which was "heroic, eternal, overwhelming," promising "a profusion of gifts: beauty, life, health, abundance, and, perhaps most important of all, a challenging correlative to inner aspiration."[8]

Duncan's deep affection for the Bay Area landscape was surpassed only by her love for dancing and for her children. In Budapest in 1902, when Duncan experienced her first public success and her first adult love affair, she drank in the spring, which flooded her with memories of her beloved California:

> In the world I am a pilgrim; a pilgrim and mendiante—from California I come—there as a child I played in the meadows—California is the land of gold—And [not] the gold which is carried in money but the free glad gold of the oranges and the California poppy—In Spring our fields dazzle the eyes—Dancing in the breeze laughing back its beams to the sun—a host of yellow flowers—Something of the Golden life of these flowers stole into my heart as a child—and I danced in the Meadows as Their sister—Could I dance as they swayed in the wind.—Could I dance their Golden messages—In the Summer the poppies vanish.—Back to the gold of the Earth they go—Back to the heart of the Sun—They disappear—but still their is gold in California in the long [illegible] beach strand by the blue Pacific—All during the hot summer the Gold burns As a child I danced on the sea beach by the waves—The hot sand burned my feet—The gold sand burned my eyes—The Sun danced on the waves—The movement of the waves rocked into my soul—Could I dance as they. Their eternal message of rhythm of Harmony?[9]

The gold of the orange groves and poppy fields may have been plentiful, but gold of the monetary sort Duncan never had as a child. The natural wealth of the California landscape provided the precocious young girl with a physical as well as a psychological respite from the less-than-idyllic reality of her fatherless, impoverished, itinerant childhood.

Sometimes, further down the road, when Duncan would tell her life story to the latest in a long line of interviewers, she imaginatively inserted her father into the tale, describing him as an authority on the ancient Greeks. To one reporter she even quoted a line of his poetry: "Greece is living Greece once more." To another she credited her "father's house" with the paintings that had inspired her "Natural" style of dancing:

> "I was brought up," she continued, "in San Francisco, where my father's house was plentifully supplied with reproductions of classic art in sculpture and engraving. In this artistic atmosphere I breathed the first years of my childhood. There I became inspired with high artistic ideals, and while a little girl my inborn taste for dancing was developed.
> "While playing in the garden of my father's house I tried by instinct to impart to my childish dance what I saw exhibited in the models of art. Thus, being deeply imbued with the perfect beauty of the copies of the great masterpieces, enhanced by the simplicity of the dress, from early childhood I have considered the freedom of my body essential to rhythm of movement. For this reason later on, with the development of my inborn disposition, a conscious study of the rhythm was at the same time promoted. Dressed in the beautiful ancient dresses I went on in the mode of dancing which I felt ambitious to render equal in beauty to the Greek dances of the days of old."[10]

One of those classic reproductions—which, at the time, were a popular means of circulating "Culture"—was Botticelli's *Primavera*, which Mrs. Duncan probably took along from her San Francisco home to hang prominently over the bookcase in their subsequent living quarters.[11] Here is the "free glad gold of the oranges," the soft, flowered earth underfoot, and the rhythmic steps of the dance. Duncan saw how the Three Graces' soft, round bodies—selectively revealed and enhanced by transparent drapery— became a part of the natural landscape. And she read the implied movement of the figures—the shifts of weight between their legs, the inflected necks, Venus's mysteriously beckoning gesture. Botticelli's painting made the connections among dance, "Nature," "Culture," and the Greeks. It suggested to Duncan ways of translating the private freedom she felt as a child frolicking au naturel on the beach into a public discourse: Greek gods and goddesses, she discovered, were forces of nature, and depicted as such in painting. Why not do the same in dance?

Flora, or Spring, from Botticelli's painting, was one of the first Greek figures whom Duncan impersonated. She composed several dances on the theme of spring while in New York in the late 1890s, and in London in 1898[12] and again in 1900, variously titled and accompanied. One such paean to the season of birth continued in her repertoire at least until 1909 as *La Primavera*, a painting that had been "done into dance." Duncan enacted a number of the figures in the painting, including Venus's compellingly enigmatic gesture, but it was Flora's costume that she chose to copy. A 1900 photograph shows Duncan in Flora's gauzy ankle-length dress, painted with flowers and ringed with blossoms at the neck and head (figures 29 and 30).[13] "And now with wreathing arms and undulating body and bare, twinkling feet," wrote a Munich correspondent in 1902, "she endeavors to present to us the vibrant atmosphere, the pulsing ecstatic quickening of all life, the langubrous [*sic*], delicious dolce far niente of this marvelous season as she reads it in Botticelli's masterpiece."[14]

At about the same time that Duncan was composing *La Primavera* in London, she was beginning her "studies" of Greek culture. A professor insisted upon teaching her Greek: she knew "Virtue is the cause of friendship" and "Friendship is the gift of the Gods."[15] A young poet, meanwhile, was entrancing her with the secrets of Apollo. "It was you," she later wrote to the young poet Douglas Ainslie, "who first put me on the way to seek Apollo, and since then how much I have longed for a wee bit [of] wisdom—strength to live that harmony of which you used to talk—beautiful form, color rhythm—."[16] Although Jane Ellen Harrison, the acknowledged leader of the Cambridge ritualists, who pioneered the use of anthropological theories in the study of ancient Greece, was listed as the reader on Duncan's 16 March 1900 program at the New Gallery, I have found no further evidence of a connection between the two women.[17] Duncan, who may or may not have been reading Harrison's *Introductory Studies in Greek Art* (1892), was indeed reading Winckelmann, the eighteenth-century German art historian and classical archeologist who, like her young poet Ainslie, emphasized the formal purity and passionless perfection of the Greeks—Platonic qualities echoed in the precise draftmanship and cool balance of Botticelli's *Primavera*. She danced out some Greek friezes with the same halcyon expression, which she described as "impersonal little friezes—of figures that have kept the same attitude for years and years—intent on their own meaning of grass and flowers and earth—with an exquisite aloofness from human things."[18]

But the Elgin marbles, which she undoubtedly encountered in her frequent visits to the British Museum, must have suggested something more to her about the Greeks, something that she later found articulated by

Figures 29–30. Botticelli's Primavera
*was "done into dance" by Duncan,
who must have read the implied
movement of the figures: the shifts of
weight, the inflected necks, and Venus's
mysteriously beckoning gesture. In*
La Primavera, *Duncan enacted a
number of figures in the painting,
including Venus's gesture, but it was
Flora's costume that she chose to copy.
Photo at top: the Uffizi Gallery. Photo
at bottom: Raymond Duncan.
Courtesy of the Dance Collection of the
New York Public Library for the
Performing Arts, Astor, Lenox and
Tilden Foundations.*

Nietzsche. The Phidian sculptures went beyond the delicate, neoclassical tastefulness of Botticelli. They were robust as well as refined, massive as well as buoyant; they were figures of force as well as repose. The reclining and the lunging of several figures on the East Pediment, as well as other Greek temples, soon made their way into Duncan's vocabulary (figures 31–34).

Nietzsche—whom Duncan discovered, through admirer Karl Federn, in Berlin in 1903—eventually converted Duncan from the Apollonian to the Dionysian. (Nietzsche could not have known the literal truth of what he wrote, that *The Birth of Tragedy*, which Duncan called her "Bible," "had a knack for seeking out fellow-rhapsodizers and for luring them on to new secret paths and dancing places.")[19] She no longer merely contemplated the spirit of the dance, as one who relates the story of something; she threw herself into the spirit of the dance, as one dancing the thing itself. Her pictorial "Done into Dance" aesthetic became less imagistic, less intellectual, less removed. With Dionysus, "Nature" took on a fiercer face, for the dithyramb united with a "Nature" that was sensual and even cruel. As Duncan developed as an artist, "Nature" was no longer just the lovely Flora, heralding the joy of spring; it was also the menacing Furies and the frenzied Bacchantes.

Duncan found early inspiration for this less idyllic side of "Nature" in Rodin's powerful, raw, un-"finished" sculptures, which she had admired since first seeing them in his retrospective exhibition, set up in conjunction with the Exposition Universelle in Paris in 1900. The young dancer, still in search of her aesthetic, must have thrilled to the importance he accorded the form of the body, to the figures' vivid sense of movement, to the pathos embodied in their gestures and postures. Sculptures such as the *Old Helmet Maker's Wife*, with her failing flesh, had helped to redefine the aesthetic concept of "ugly," turning it from a matter of appearance to a matter of Platonic essence. According to Rodin, "Whatever is false, whatever is artificial, whatever seeks to be pretty rather than expressive, whatever is capricious and affected, whatever smiles without motive, bends or struts without cause, is mannered without reason; all that is without soul and without truth; all that is only a *parade* of beauty and grace; all, in short, that lies is *ugliness* in art."[20] Rodin revealed the decrepit and the tortured as simply another side of "Nature." Much later in Duncan's career, when she advanced from her youthful idylls to the darker themes of grief and mortality, she echoed his words: there is nothing "Natural" that is ugly, for the inner "Truth" of "Nature" is always "Beautiful."

***

Figures 31–32. This reclining figure from the East Pediment of the Parthenon, kept by Duncan in her postcard collection, was adapted into her dance vocabulary. Photo at top: Courtesy of the Dance Collection of the New York Public Library for the Performing Arts, Astor, Lenox and Tilden Foundations. Photo at bottom: Arnold Genthe. Courtesy of the Museum of the City of New York and the Dance Collection of the New York Public Library for the Performing Arts, Astor, Lenox and Tilden Foundations.

972. Balustrade of Nike temple. Nikes and bull. A.M. Athens.

Figures 33–34. This lunging figure from the Nike Temple, kept by Duncan in her postcard collection, was adapted into Duncan's dance vocabulary. Photo at bottom: Elvira. Both courtesy of the Dance Collection of the New York Public Library for the Performing Arts, Astor, Lenox and Tilden Foundations.

As much as Duncan attributed the "Truth" and "Beauty" of the "Natural" body to the ancient Greeks, she founded its divinity in science. In the mid- and late nineteenth century, nature, evolutionary science, and theology went hand in hand.[21] Evolutionists such as Ernst Haeckel, a German, and Herbert Spencer, a Briton whose popularity in American outstripped that of Darwin, extended the paradigm from nature to culture, applying it to social life, art, and even religion.[22] Darwinism, as cultural historian Jacques Barzun has pointed out, "satisfied the first requirement of any religion by subsuming all phenomena under one cause."[23] Spencer generalized the basic premises of evolution, in a more accessible manner than Darwin's scientific rigor, into a totalizing cosmology, seemingly organizing all knowledge into an ultimate, unified reality. The novelist Jack London was awed by Spencer's *First Principles*, in which "all the hidden things were laying their secrets bare."[24]

Duncan's generation was enthralled by evolution theory, which they considered an intellectual revolution, either to absorb or to condemn it.[25] It is "hopeless to convey to a younger generation," wrote Edith Wharton about the significance of the theory of evolution, "the first overwhelming sense of cosmic vastnesses which such 'magic casements' let into our little geocentric universe."[26] At the same time that evolution theory opened up the small, geometric world of the nineteenth century into the potential vastness of the twentieth, it also explained the rampant progress of the day not just as a black void of the new but also as a development of the comfortable past. And, in a very important way, that is exactly what Duncan's dancing did—it brought along nineteenth-century transcendentalism into the modern age. In the tradition of Henry David Thoreau and Ralph Waldo Emerson, Duncan believed in an order of "Truth" that transcended the sphere of the external senses, a "Truth" communicated instead through the mediation of "Nature."[27]

Duncan was most influenced by Haeckel, the famous German naturalist and early Darwin supporter, whose *The Evolution of Man* (1874) was subtitled *A Popular Exposition of the Principal Points of Human Ontogeny and Phylogeny,* and whose *The Riddle of the Universe at the Close of the Nineteenth Century* (1899) attempted to tackle metaphysics by means of science.[28] His works, she wrote to him in a 1904 birthday greeting, brought her "religion and understanding, which count for more than life."[29]

Haeckel rejected the tradition of anthropism, which opposes the human organism to the rest of nature and places man at the center of a God-created universe. Merging the theory of evolution with the law of substance, which explained that the universe consists completely of matter and force, Haeckel replaced anthropist dogmas and the duality of orthodox religions with a comprehensive view of the universe. Monism, he asserted, "recognizes one sole substance in the universe, which is at once 'God and nature'; body and spirit (or matter and energy) it holds to be inseparable."[30] The monist position led to a religious pantheism, which replaced a creationist God with the natural forces of evolution. Thus man is not separated from God/"Nature"; rather, man is enmeshed in the divinity of "Nature," which *is* God.

The monist theology revered the trinity of "the True, the Good, and the Beautiful." "Truth" is to be found only in the rational study of "Nature"; "the Good" is found in charity and toleration, compassion and assistance; "the Beautiful" is found not in an afterlife but in this life, in the natural world. "The astonishment with which we gaze upon the starry heavens and the microscopic life in a drop of water," Haeckel wrote, "the awe with which we trace the marvellous working of energy in the motion of matter, the reverence with which we grasp the universal dominance of the law of substance throughout the universe—all these are part of our emotional life, falling under the heading of 'natural religion.' "[31]

This notion of essential unity and orderly design of the cosmos provided the fundamental template of *harmony* for mid- to late-nineteenth-century religion, art, and society.[32] "Nature" signified order. "Nature" served as a comforting, orderly matrix for all the fiercely multiplying, often contrary, elements in the universe—a universe whose microscopic and extraterrestrial boundaries were expanding daily, through the rapid-paced discoveries of science. In such an expanding yet enmeshed model of the world, the individual self, though just one link in this cosmic chain, was not diminished but rather ennobled by its connections with the rest of the universe. Thus "Nature" was no longer humbling, as it had been for artists earlier in the nineteenth century, but empowering. "Nature" provided a means for the individual to transcend the self and harness the cosmos.

After reading Haeckel, Duncan came to understand "Nature" not just as seasons or flowers or forces but as a comprehensive system whose inherent harmony she mapped onto her body. "I always put into my movements," she wrote, "a little of that divine continuity which gives to all of Nature its beauty and life."[33] The "Natural" body was one that moved harmoniously, as a single unit whose each minute part functioned interdependently. It embodied the basic wavelike force of movement in "Nature." For Duncan, "Nature" became more than just the worldly pleasure of an orange grove but also the transcendent joy of "the True, the Good, and the Beautiful."

As someone who proudly proclaimed to her young schoolmates that there was no Santa Claus, as someone who invented a father who had really departed in her early infancy, as someone who mastered the process of mythologizing herself, Duncan regarded the search for "Truth" as a complicated concern. And evolutionary science, premised as it was on the knowability of the universe, as revealed through the discoverable laws of nature, was a field of certitude and rationality.[34] This science, rather than myth or religion, was able to assure humankind that there was an ultimate order to existence. Duncan needed that reassurance. Darwin, she wrote to her lover, Gordon Craig, in April 1905, supplied her with

> "Divine Philosophy—
> & if read aright his observations teach the living truth of universal life and Love—
> And we must have Philosophy—Without that we would die of pain like dumb brutes. When they put on the torture then Philosophy is the thing—or call it what you will. Some people draw it from one source & some from another. A *Van Eyck* before me & a book of Darwin in my hands suits *me*—& Love in and over All—& now and then a Prayer to the Gods. Some people pray one way & some another—sometimes I *dance* mine & sometimes I think them."[35]

Duncan's faith in this "Divine Philosophy" did not endure, perhaps because the unity and order of her universe collapsed so tragically with the deaths of her children Patrick and Deirdre in 1913 and of her newborn in 1914. "What is the truth of a human life, and who can find it?" she wrote in her autobiography. "God Himself would be puzzled."[36] It is one of the few times that she ever wrote of God.

***

By the teens, Duncan's style of dancing became so popular that dance teachers were compelled to add it to their repertoires. They variously called the style "natural dancing," "classic dancing," or "aesthetic dancing," seeing no dichotomy, as we do today, between what is "natural" and what is "aesthetic." It was the middle term, "classic," that fused these two seemingly opposed ideals: the Greeks had rendered nature into art and, conversely, art into nature. By deploying the Greeks as a strategy to collapse art and "Nature," Duncan posited dance as a part of the cosmic unity and divinity of "Nature" and thus elevated dance into the realm of "high" art.

As a result, dance in America, or at least one major strain of dance in America, had become a band of barefoot nymphs in Greek tunics and head-bands, each with a knee lifted high and head thrown back, frolicking quite "artfully" 'round a tree or against the skyline (figures 35 and 36). How, in a matter of two decades, had Duncan appropriated the image and idea of the Greeks—as the connecting thread between "Nature" and "Culture"—to legitimize dance as an American "high" art?

By the time that Duncan reappeared in America in 1908, the newspapers had already reported her barefoot-scandal-turned-success, her unconventional costuming, her "reawakening of an art that has slumbered for two thousand years," and her pilgrimage to the heights of the Acropolis. The American press's amused depiction of her as a "Greek" dancer began in reports from Paris salon society in 1901: "Like an Ancient Greek Bas-Relief Come to Life She Astonishes Paris." The article, published with Duncan's byline, was a sensitive account of her ideals and theories. At its end, she made a subtle distinction between reconstruction and interpretation, which all the cable correspondents and metropolitan reporters, whose interest was more in eccentricity than in art, failed to recognize: "I drew my inspiration from Greek sources. Strictly speaking, I do not try to reconstruct Greek dances. This is practically impossible. The inspiration which I draw enables me to interpret what I believe to be not only the idyllic but the ideal dance."[37] Nevertheless, with her first trip to the land of Apollo and Dionysus in 1903, she encouraged the Hellenic link. For example, from an interview published in the *New York Sunday World*:

> My idea of dancing is to leave my body free to the sunshine, to feel my sandaled feet on the earth, to be near and love the olive trees of Greece. These are my present ideas of dancing. Two thousand years ago a people lived here who had perfect sympathy and comprehension of the beautiful in Nature, and this knowledge and sympathy were perfectly expressed in their own forms and movement.
>
> Of all the thousands of figures of Greek sculpture, bas-reliefs and vases there is not one but is in exquisite bodily proportion and harmony of movement.
>
> This could not be possible unless the artists of that time were accustomed to see always about them beautiful moving human forms. I came to Greece to study these forms of ancient art, but above all, I came to live in the land which produced these wonders, and when I say "to live" I mean to dance.[38]

Greece, she made clear, means "Nature" and "Art." And in connecting dance to Greece, she was also connecting dance to "Nature" and "Art."

Figures 35–36. By the teens, as a result of Duncan's success, dance in America meant a band of barefoot nymphs in Greek tunics and headbands, each with a knee lifted high and head thrown back, frolicking quite "artfully" around a tree or against the skyline. Photo at bottom: Underwood & Underwood. Courtesy of the Library of Congress.

Duncan's rhetorical dependence on classical precedents lasted from about 1901 to 1904, when she ended her experiment with a Greek boys' choir, singing "authentic" Greek music for her performances.[39] Although she would return to the Greeks later, in the 1910s, for different reasons, during this early period she was stressing the ancients' discovery of beauty in "Nature" and of "Nature" in the human form. The renewal of the Olympic Games in 1896 had sparked interest in the Greek ideal of the body, helping to reinforce Duncan's insistence on its beauty and nobility. Furthermore, the status of dance in Greek culture gave dancing a legitimacy it desperately needed for acceptance by her upper-class audiences. And, not inconsequently, Duncan's Greek rhetoric ended up functioning as a novelty in an era of novelty-driven theater and journalism. Just as Ruth St. Denis's gimmick was the "exotic" and Loie Fuller's was the "picturesque," so Duncan's was the "classical" (figures 37–39).

For America in the several decades before and after the turn of the century, "Greece" (conceived more from the likes of Keats's "Ode on a Grecian Urn" than anything archeological) was an idea about cultural legitimacy. An animating cultural fantasy since the Greek Revival in the early 1800s, Hellenist enthusiasm indicated the renewed aspirations of a burgeoning nation, without a pedigreed past equal to that of the great European states, to flourish in all its aspects—scientific, industrial, political, social, and cultural. Greek games flourished at colleges such as Barnard and Berkeley; outdoor Greek theaters, including the one at Berkeley, were built, too. In the wake of the 1893 World's Columbian Exposition, whose organizers purposefully chose a neoclassical architectural style over an incipient American modernism, civic and commercial buildings across the country—the courthouse, the state capitol, the university, the commemorative statue, even the firehouse—were being built in the image of the great Greek temple, its soaring columns and monumentality a visual declaration of collective ambition. In the flush of its imminent world-class status, America—as well as Britain and Germany and France—envisioned itself as the true heir of the great Greek civilization, in all its political, economic, and artistic glory.

So, in preparation for Duncan's August 1908 debut at the Criterion Theatre, producer Charles Frohman's press agents began spreading word of her "celebrated classical dances" before she even reached shore. This idea of translating Greek statuary into dance, however, was hardly new. Back in 1890, for example, at about the same time that "living statues" became a popular pastime for women, the *San Francisco Examiner*

Figure 37. Duncan's Greek rhetoric ended up functioning as a novelty in an era of novelty-driven theater and journalism. Just as Ruth St. Denis's gimmick was the "exotic" (figure 38) and Loie Fuller's was the "picturesque" (figure 39), so Duncan's was the "classical." Photo: Raymond Duncan. Courtesy of the Dance Collection of the New York Public Library for the Performing Arts, Astor, Lenox and Tilden Foundations.

*Figure 38. While Duncan attracted audiences with her allusions to Greek art and civiliza-
tion, Ruth St. Denis (pictured here in* Radha) *appropriated the costumes and imagery of the
"Orient" with equal success. Photo: Otto Sarony. Courtesy of the Dance Collection of the
New York Public Library for the Performing Arts, Astor, Lenox and Tilden Foundations.*

Figure 39. Before Duncan's fame as the "barefoot classical dancer," Loie Fuller was well known for the visual spectacles she created through the manipulation of light and fabric. Photo: Lafitte. Courtesy of the Dance Collection of the New York Public Library for the Performing Arts, Astor, Lenox and Tilden Foundations.

ran an article (could Duncan have seen it?) on two rather sophisticated Spanish skirt dancers named Carmencita and Otero, the latter of whom, "in her slow and sinuous movements, seems like a masterpiece of Phidias."[40]

Duncan seemed to make one last effort to qualify the "Greek dance" label before disembarking from London. "While my dancing owes inspiration to the Greeks," she told a reporter, "it is not Greek really, but very modern—my own idea. . . . Please don't say, by the way, that I dress in Greek style." Dutifully, the reporter set the record straight: "Miss Duncan really wears a Parisian Directoire lounging gown,"[41] which was then the most fashionable silhouette in Paris. Such subtleties, however, were the interest of neither press nor management. After several seasons of Indian incantations, Salome dances, and "La Loie" (Fuller) lookalikes, the "Greek" dance was a welcome distraction.

Despite Frohman's efforts to sell her as a Greek dancer, the Criterion audience was not totally responsive to such refined references. As a *Variety* reviewer, clearly more used to vaudeville (which had been showcasing the Brazilian Maxixe, burlesques of *The Merry Widow*, Princess Rajah's snake dance, and, of course, *Salome*),[42] explained:

> To one whose vision is perhaps somewhat warped by too frequent attendance upon vaudeville performances and whose culture in classic Art is rather less than inconsiderable, Isadora Duncan's attempt to monopolize a whole audience—and a $2 audience at that—for an entire evening, has very much the complexion of Paul McAllister's untoward experiment as a condensed "Hamlet" in vaudeville. . . .
>
> Now comes along Miss Duncan with an immense success in Europe as a recommendation and offers Broadway (as distinguished from East 125th Street) an entertainment the lofty pretension to Art of which is in about the same relation to the established standard of entertainment.
>
> . . . It is a fairly safe venture that a goodly percentage of the Criterion's audience who lent their applause to the none too plentiful gaiety of the evening did so because they thought that it was the proper thing to do and not because they found real delight in Miss Duncan's performance.[43]

This audience, which was accustomed to even lighter entertainments than usual during the summer season, was suspicious of anything pretending to "Art." (And yet the Variety review makes clear the very real pressure to recognize and acknowledge "Art.") Duncan had better luck with her northeastern out-of-town engagements, but when she returned to New York, she and Frohman canceled their contract. She began, instead, a series of immensely successful engagements with Walter Damrosch's prestigious New York Symphony Orchestra.

Her appearances with Damrosch were in concert halls and opera houses, such as the Metropolitan Opera, with a considerably different audience and set of critics. The audience was privileged, predominantly female,[44] and thirsty for "Art." Duncan performed excerpts from Gluck's *Iphigenia in Aulis* (1905–1915) portraying the Greek maidens as they played ball and knucklebones (figure 40) and spied the Greek fleet in the distance. Then she added *Iphigenia in Tauris* (1914–15) and *Orpheus* (1900–1915) to her American repertoire, strongly reinforcing her reputation as the "Greek" dancer. The critics flattered Duncan with grand comparisons, however undiscriminating: not only to Greek sculptures and vases, but also to Keats's "Ode on a Grecian Urn" and even to Wedgwood pottery. In order to describe Duncan, the *New York Daily Tribune*'s highly respected music critic, H. E. Krehbiel, invoked the British clergyman/botanist Charles Kingsley's fanciful description of Greek dancing, "in which every motion

Figure 40. When choreographing Iphigenia in Aulis, *Duncan may have been inspired by this image of a Greek knucklebone player from the British Museum, kept by Duncan in her postcard collection. Courtesy of the Dance Collection of the New York Public Library for the Performing Arts, Astor, Lenox and Tilden Foundations.*

was a word, and rest as eloquent as motion; in which every attitude was a fresh motion for a sculptor of the purest school, and the highest physical activity was manifested, not, as in coarse pantomime, in fantastic bounds and unnatural distortions, but in perpetual, delicate modulations of a stately and self-sustained grace."[45]

Although Duncan at times denied that she was imitating the ancient Greek dances per se, she did admit to copying Greek clothing, and her audiences immediately recognized the quotation. In the eyes of upper-echelon late Victorians, classical art had made the liberating connection between nudity and nobility that had been impossible within the Puritan tradition. As they saw it, the body, as depicted on the vases and in the statuary, was endowed with an ideal form both moral and beautiful. For women such as Mrs. William K. Kavanaugh of St. Louis, who defended Duncan against a minister who had characterized the dancer as a Midway come-on, Duncan was "an exquisite figure on an old vase that we are allowed to admire with all propriety."[46] As Americans constructed it, the unquestioned authority of Greek art *allowed* even a woman to contemplate the naked body with a good conscience and at the same time to congratulate herself on possessing an elevated taste (elevated socially as well as morally).[47]

Despite the identification of the "Natural" body with nudity, Duncan never actually performed nude, just as fifth-century Greek statues were never without some veil or drapery. Her Greek-style costume left her breasts unbound (early versions of the brassiere were not widely marketed as an alternative to the corset until the twenties)[48] but modestly covered her groin, hiding any pubic hair, as was done with the ancient statuary. Duncan's costumes were properly anchored to her body, "fastened on," she said, "with elastics over the shoulders and around the waist."[49] And, if we can extrapolate from what Irma's young American pupils wore to Isadora's own practice, the elastics were further anchored at the shoulders to a leotard-style undergarment made of silk jersey.[50] It is likely, too, that Duncan removed underarm hair, and possibly leg hair.[51] The warm glow of Duncan's stage lighting further softened the reality of bare flesh, as did pancake makeup later in her career.[52] Thus her audiences could accept her chiton as a transparent sign of nudity; moreover, they accepted it as a sign of *classical* nudity, whose claim to the "Natural" guaranteed the moral and the noble.

Besides Duncan's rhetoric, repertoire, and costuming, her movement vocabulary was also identified as classical. She seemed to broadly imitate the leaping, outstretched motions of the Greek vase figures. Sometimes she even appeared to bring a specific one to life: "One of the wildest of her dances she closed with arms outstretched and head thrown back almost out of sight until she resembled the headless Nike of Samthrace [*sic*]," observed a *New York Times* critic in 1909.[53] Dance critic/historian Deborah Jowitt has compared images of Duncan with photos of Greek sculpture, vase paintings, and bas-reliefs that the dancer likely saw, and demonstrated the close, sometimes exact, duplication of pose. Both sets of images, she found, shared "the resilient yielding to gravity displayed in reclining poses, the lift of the arms with which Duncan ended so many phrases, the head turned away from the direction of forward motion, the strong crossing of the lifted leg in a skip, the arch of the torso."[54]

The aura of Greece—as a symbolic suture between "Nature" and Culture—clung most fiercely to Duncan early in her American career, when her audiences needed to make sense of her unfamiliar style of dancing. After several rounds of tours, when she began dancing to symphonic music, the critics turned their attention to the appropriateness of dancing to concert music. By her next set of tours, in the teens, Duncan rekindled her celebrity through identification with heroic patriotism and maternalism. And by the 1920s, ironically, the same Greek source material that Duncan had appropriated for "Natural" dancing was being reappropriated as a precedent for its very antithesis, the ballet.[55]

***

By World War I, in large part because of Duncan,[56] dance had been transformed from entertainment into "Culture," at least in New York. Duncan not only reimagined the form and content of dance but also convinced an audience of its legitimacy as a "high" art. She created a "taste" for dance and, furthermore, made it a matter of "good taste." For working-class and immigrant girls and women, this style of dance literally added "class" to their lives, because it had become an emblem of "Cultural" refinement, in no small part as a result of its identification with classical Greece. Although Duncan claimed the idealized "Nature" of Greece as the source of her dance practice, her interest in Greece actually was sparked in London, after her formative experiences in California and New York. Greece was not the *origin* of her dancing body, as she claimed, but rather the *effect* of her desire to legitimize the dancing body as a "high" art.

What Duncan's identification with the Greeks served to accomplish was what historian Lawrence W. Levine has called the "sacralization of culture." By the end of the nineteenth century, opera and the production of Shakespeare—arts that had enjoyed a status both popular and elite in this country—underwent a process by which they were reconceived as unquestionably elite. Though symphonic music and the visual arts were never quite as popular, they, too, gained their cultural legitimacy through a newly institutionalized hierarchy that established standards and elevated taste. This ideal endowed an art "with unique aesthetic and spiritual properties that rendered it inviolate, exclusive, and eternal. This was not the mere ephemera of the world of entertainment but something lasting, something permanent."[57] Culture with a capital "C" became synonymous with the European products of the symphonic hall, the opera house, the museum, and the library, now seen as veritable temples, "all of which, the American people were taught, must be approached with a disciplined, knowledgeable seriousness of purpose, and—most important of all—with a feeling of reverence."[58]

Duncan gained this reverence for dance by deconstructing and reconstructing it as a practice of Western "Culture" for the privileged classes of northeastern cities. She used strategies of difference and exclusion, exploiting the conventional distinctions between high and low. Despite of—or because of—her family's poverty and fall from social grace, young Dora learned at an early age about the intimacy between class and taste, between social and artistic prestige. Denied the illusion of meritocracy that inheres in a comfortable middle-class upbringing, Duncan became a remarkable master of the signs and emblems of dominant taste, and she used that knowledge to gain distinction for her art.

With the nineteenth-century sacralization of culture, the arts had become implicated in class status. The Duncans, with Joseph at their head, established class status not just by virtue of his income but also by virtue of his publicly demonstrated aesthetic mastery. When the Duncans, sans Joseph, lost all their money and their social position, they endeavored to maintain, and later to increase, status through their refined "Cultural" sensibilities. Those evening salons functioned not merely as self-amusement but as the private performance of class. Duncan dealt with the considerable anxiety of her changing childhood fortunes by a flagrant lifelong disinterest in the management of money and thus a denial of its importance; she displaced the definition of class from money to art. If class brought "Culture" (as the nouveau riche took great pains to demonstrate), then could not "Culture" bring class? Duncan, and the girls and women who would later flock to Duncan-style dance classes, believed so.

Taste, according to French sociologist Pierre Bourdieu, is not disinterested; rather, it is rooted in social origin and in education. As an arbiter of taste, "Culture" is not just reflective but also productive. That is to say, it is not just "the state of that which is cultivated" but also "the process of cultivating."[59] This process of cultivating—which, similarly to Levine, Bourdieu calls "cultural consecration"—confers "on the objects, persons and situations it touches, a sort of ontological promotion akin to a transubstantiation."[60] By inscribing into perception and practice a "distinction" (difference that produces hierarchy) between the sacred sphere of legitimate, or high, "Culture" and the mere vulgarity of entertainment, "Cultural" practice thus fulfils a social function, whether conscious or not, of legitimating social—and specifically class—differences.

Duncan's construction of a "Natural" body did indeed imply a race and class hierarchy. It was not a willful flight from "Culture," off to some pre-civilized utopia. Neither was it a Whitmanesque celebration of the common folk, despite her genuine love for the poet's earthy vision. Duncan emphasized the noble over the savage; her model, after all, was the Victory of Samothrace, not Pocahontas. Duncan's "Natural" body was, rather, the artistic transformation of "Nature" into "Culture." It was artless artifice. Duncan espoused an ideal version of "Nature" as a newfound belief and joy in the worth of the human body, but she was careful not to let that joy slip into atavism, for "Nature" was "Nature" only when it was ennobled; otherwise it remained base primitivism: "People ask me, do you consider love making an art and I would answer that not only love but every part of life should be practiced as an art. For we are no longer in the state of the primitive savage, but the whole expression of our life must be created through culture and the transformation of intuition and instinct into art."[61] In other words, the "Natural" body is a "civilized" body.

Ever since her earliest society appearances in New York and Newport, Duncan had aligned herself with the elite—whether artists, celebrities, royalty, or the Four Hundred (figure 41). By invoking "Greece" in her dancing, her flowery prose, and her lifestyle, Duncan displayed signs of education and refinement. The Hellenistic practices also presupposed a certain class of spectator: not the likes of the *Variety* reviewer who mocked the artistic pretension of the "celebrated classical dances," but rather an educated viewer reared on classical literature and philosophy. Unsurprisingly, Duncan's noble Hellenic associations failed to make much initial connection

The Effect of the Revival of Classical Dancing on the "400"—as Seen by Punch. (Dedicated to Isidora Duncan, Loie Fuller et al.) 1909

Figure 41. Ever since her earliest society appearances in New York and Newport, Duncan had aligned herself with the elite—whether artists, celebrities, royalty, or the Four Hundred. Courtesy of the Dance Collection of the New York Public Library for the Performing Arts, Astor, Lenox and Tilden Foundations.

with vaudeville's working-class audience, but the link with Greece found believers among the wealthy, educated class of Americans who could afford tickets to see her at the opera house or concert hall and who could "read" her Hellenistic allusions as meaningful. When Duncan was denouncing African "primitivism," or invoking Nietzsche, or constructing herself as a Greek goddess, she was producing and reproducing social divisions along the lines of class and race. By operating strategically within the institutions and emblems of the privileged class, she was developing an audience and thus a "taste" for her art that drew upon and reinforced its distinction from all others—blacks, immigrants, the poor, the uneducated, the middle class.

In a way, Duncan, who believed that "education of the young is the only way to bring taste and understanding to the working class,"[62] was not so different from the self-described "merchants of culture, professional men and artists"[63] who started the Metropolitan Museum of Art. These robber barons–cum–culture brokers sought to establish "Culture" from the top down, so that eventually even the uneducated manual laborer could gain enlightenment through the love of the "Beautiful." For regardless of the country's industrial and commercial prosperity, explained one museum patron, it still needed to prove itself Culturally:

> The wealth of a nation lies not in its material pursuits alone. In a new country like ours they are the first to occupy its people, but when the forests are cleared, the roads built, the mines opened, the land tilled, manufactories in operation, and habitations are built, unless the higher part of man's nature is developed in the realm of art, whether useful, beautiful or romantic, like music and poetry, that nation relapses into barbarism.[64]

Duncan, too, was concerned that the masses not sink back into "primitivism," which, in the rhetoric of her later years, functioned as the paradigm of that precivilized state of being she endeavored to elevate. Duncan was interested specifically in going back to and appropriating the roots of *Western* (white) "Culture" in the Greeks; the Egyptians, she said, were origin of an-*Other* (black) race.[65] During her Argentinian tour of 1916, Duncan called her unfriendly audiences "niggers," assuming they were simply not advanced enough to appreciate her art.[66] As for ragtime and jazz, which rivaled her for the public's attention, she scornfully dismissed them on many an occasion as "this deplorable modern dancing, which has its roots in the ceremonies of African primitives."[67] Unlike some of her modernist European contemporaries, Duncan could find no inspiration in what she perceived as a vulgar aesthetic.

Duncan was not alone, however. "Officially and sincerely, most Americans," according to historian Henry F. May, "believed in the goodness of man. But the man they trusted was the educated and civilized man of the nineteenth century. Too much confidence in spontaneous emotion, too much dislike of rules might rouse passions which should not even be thought about."[68] Thus many social leaders agreed with Duncan that the "modern dances," as they were called, that saturated the country from 1911 to 1915 were unbecomingly violent and spastic. While many criticized what they saw as the seething sexuality of dances such as the black bottom, the fox trot, or the grizzly bear, Duncan objected to them as vulgar on different grounds. She railed against the uncontrolled character—the presumed *chaos*—of ragtime and jazz, because it threatened the moral *order* of civilization, which was precisely that moral order engendered by the harmonious ideal of "Nature" she gleaned from the Greece of Botticelli and the natural theology of Haeckel. Although a large part of Duncan's appeal was her seeming spontaneity (and she fed this illusion, that her dancing was improvised on stage), Duncan's dancing was far from wild. It was, according to *The Masses* editor Max Eastman, a perfect proportion of "art with nature, restraint with abandon."[69] Although "spontaneous," her movement style had a decided sense of flowing, unhurried gentility. Compared to what was described as the "spasms" or "paroxysms" of the African-inspired modern dances, she embodied a spontaneity tempered with the unspoken, unquestioned control that marked good breeding. In her mind, Duncan's body occupied the middle ground between the disciplined restraint of the ballerina and the grotesque excessiveness of the jazz dancer. Hers was an ease born of effortless control. This particular bodily hexis, to borrow Bourdieu's term for embodied dispositions of belief, was that of the privileged class.[70]

By constituting a "Natural" body as the basis for dance practice, Duncan effectively removed from it any vulgar requirement for labor, which would have smacked of the working class; instead, it could be imbued with an aura of the innate—of good taste, which is, by definition, effortless. Something that ballet, constituted as it was by its demanding technique, could not claim. Since the popular perception of the ballet dancer was collapsed into that of the untrained chorus girl, its social position was associated with lower-class women who turned to dancing as a means of making a living. Thus, even though ballet could claim the history of kings, it still required and connoted work.[71] On- or off-stage, Duncan always aligned herself with leisure, luxury, and ease—never with necessity. "When in doubt," she often said, "always go to the best hotel."[72]

Nevertheless, Duncan was not unsympathetic toward the American masses; in her late career, after encountering the Soviet experiment, she claimed them as her true audience. Inhering in Duncan's art, then, was this curious tension between the desire to legitimize dance as an art through a strategy of exclusion and the desire to spread dance as a cultural practice through a strategy of inclusion. Part of her desired to see the whole world liberate itself through dancing. But, really, she accepted the "masses" only on her own terms: as those who could be "uplifted" through the experience of "Culture" and, thus, affirming through their uplift the class difference that is ostensibly being erased. When she lauded the abilities of the tenement-dwellers on the Lower East Side to appreciate her art, for example, she did so primarily as a means of shaming unresponsive millionaires (who, it was implied, should know better) into contributing money for her to start a school.

In contrast to her experiences in Germany, France, and the Soviet Union, where she opened free schools for all kinds of children, she never was able to put her egalitarian educational ideas into practice in America. It was not Duncan herself but the Duncan-style dance schools that opened across the country in the wake of her appearances that forged contact between her ideas and the immigrant and working classes.[73] Despite whatever initial resistance they may have had to such high-falutin Hellenism, the pressure to revere "Art" soon brought them to the altar of dance as well, if not as consumers, then as students. For example, modern dancer Helen Tamiris's father, a Russian Jewish immigrant, sent her to Duncan-style classes at the Henry Street Settlement in order to get her off the streets of the Lower East Side. For decades, thousands of women and young girls like Tamiris (Duncan claimed 20,000 of them in 1922)[74] flocked to classes in "classic" or "natural" or "aesthetic" dancing, and in so doing, they acquired some longed-for "Culture."

4.

Since her premature death, Duncan has been both credited with and blamed for introducing the practice of "self-expression" into American stage dance. The detractions have been significant. The next generation of modern dancers constructed an aesthetic of objective form, in reaction to what they disapprovingly understood as Duncan's aesthetic of autobiographical emotion. Philosopher Susanne K. Langer called Duncan "sentimental" for her supposed belief that dance is generated by real emotional conditions—what dance aesthetician Katharine Everett Gilbert called "the floating dream and unavailable

THE *Expressive* BODY

ecstasy of Isadora Duncan."[1] Much more recently Lincoln Kirstein, apologist for classical ballet choreographer George Balanchine, curtly dismissed the very notion of self-expression in an article decrying "the curse of Isadora."[2]

If "expression" today is much maligned, having been relegated to the category of schlock and dilettantism after almost a century of aesthetic and ideological change, it was, nevertheless, a revolutionary ideal in Duncan's day. It meant the release from Victorian strictures and from European conventions; it meant the birth of modern art and the renewal of American society. It was a way of bridging life and art: expression, as it was preached in social realms ranging from home decoration to recreation to etiquette, was considered as much a way of life as it was a mode of artistic representation.

If the "Natural" body was a state of being, the expressive body was one of intense action, of seemingly authentic practice. "The world is always struggling to express itself," explained the young Robert Ames to the title character, a newly successful actress, in Theodore Dreiser's 1900 novel, *Sister Carrie*. "Most people are not capable of voicing their feelings. They depend upon others. That is what genius is for. One man expresses their desires for them in music; another one in poetry; another one in a play. Sometimes nature does it in a face—it makes the face representative of all desire."[3] Duncan expressed the world's desire not in her face but in her body. And in order to awaken the depths of that expressive body, she did away with the studio mirror, because it emphasized external image rather than inner impetus.

From the 1880s until World War I, from the stirrings of the Delsartean fad to the height of the craze for modern social dancing, the practice of "expression" animated the American imagination. In these years, Americans were vocal about the effete, overwrought, nervous condition of their age. According to cultural historian Jackson Lears: "For many, individual identities began to seem fragmented, diffuse, perhaps even unreal. A weightless culture of material comfort and spiritual blandness was breeding weightless persons who longed for intense experience to give some definition, some distinct outline and substance to their vaporous lives."[4] Expression, the bodily manifestation of inner impulses and feelings, was a way to give substance to the self, physicalizing it into a source of experience no less intense than manual labor or religious conversion.

The ideal of the expressive body was no longer as a container whose corset-armored skin and neatly circumscribed movements sealed off uncertain, and potentially dangerous, interior energies. Paralleling Freud's turn inward, the expressive body was conceived as depth, giving glimpse beneath the veneer of propriety to the depths of unspoken—and unacted—desire and emotion. It was here, in the space within the body, where the origin of the self was located—a pioneer-style self, independent and individual, unencumbered by external pressure but capable of outward projection.[5] The force of its depths streamed outward, unconstrained. It subverted the dividing line between the inner and the outer, between the private and the public, and in obliterating those boundaries, it held the promise of personal, political, and religious liberation.

Duncan's audiences found in her dancing a "release for [their] own impulses of expression," according to Augustin Duncan's second wife, Margherita. "In watching her we had a sense of satisfied longing."[6] From the beginning, Duncan sought to reveal not only her own inner stirrings but her spectators', too. "Come then and abide for an hour," she wrote in an 1898 program note. "Come for here is the mirror of your life to you, / Not a mirror of face, nor pink, nor white, / But the reflected soul of life."[7] From the mythic stage space to the familiarity of the music, from the accessibility of the vocabulary to the flow and ease of her movement style, Duncan constructed a literal and metaphorical theater environment that included the spectators. Duncan's early dances were essentially about the self in formation, whose fluid identity was metaphorized through constantly ongoing movement. Her audiences moved with this dancing "subject-in-process" (to borrow a term from Julia Kristeva),[8] whose unspecified longings they could fill in with their own. One writer recalled how he "shuddered with awe" the first time he saw her. "In this . . . free, simple, happy, expressive, rhythmic movement was focussed all I and a hundred others had been dreaming."[9]

For a time, her spectators reveled in this freely moving self, the metaphorical dissolution of social boundaries, for it offered them limitless possibilities. Artist Robert Henri saw Duncan as the prophetess of a world where full natural expression would be the aim of all people. She inspired poet William Carlos Williams toward the artistic life, and architectural critic Lewis Mumford admired her uninhibited vitality.[10] Artist John Sloan felt that "she dances a symbol of human animal happiness as it should be, free from the unnatural trammels. Not angelic, materialistic—not superhuman but the greatest human love of life."[11]

The avant-garde, in particular, was primed for Duncan's expressive body. In search of a new America, the artists, intellectuals, and radicals were galvanized by Duncan's enactment of release, what they saw as an icon of unbridled expression and, by extension, political and artistic freedom. The same year that Duncan returned to America, New York's "little Renaissance" was getting underway. Literary critic Van Wyck Brooks published *The Wine of the Puritans*, in which he set the basic framework for the period's social criticism, decrying both materialism and morality and embracing an ideal of "life." Journalist and social critic H. L. Mencken joined the staff at *Smart Set* magazine, in which he called for a new, broader-based American culture. An iconoclastic exhibition by the Eight, led by Henri, inaugurated the independent movement among artists unhappy with the tyrannical hold of the Academy over American art. Modern art was exhibited for the first time, at Alfred Stieglitz's 291 gallery, Auguste Rodin in January and Henri Matisse in April.[12] Charles

Caffin, in a review in Stieglitz's *Camera Work*, compared Matisse to Duncan, insofar as they both reached toward "an expression of primitive elemental feeling."[13]

For social critics, cultural nationalists, and the avant-garde alike, "expression" heralded the artistic enrichment of life and, conversely, the enlivening of art. For Constantin Stanislavsky, cofounder of the Moscow Art Theatre, Duncan provided the inspiration for a new method of acting, which eventually made its way back to America.[14] For the next generation of American modern dancers, "moving from the inside out," as Doris Humphrey described the expressive body, had, by the year of Duncan's death, become "the dominant expression of our generation, if not of the age."[15]

***

The middle- and upper-class preoccupation with "expression"— not just of body movement but of everything from colors to home design—was the fertile ground in which Duncan's art took root. They were playing out a self-consciousness about marks of identity that had been seeded not just by the social havoc wreaked by the country's swift industrial growth and by the muscle-flexing of the Spanish-American War, but also by the Civil War thirty years earlier. Torn asunder and patched back together, what, and who, was this United States of America, especially now, with its newfound wealth? It seems no coincidence that Walt Whitman, whose vision of American democracy (which paradoxically privileged *both* the individual and the masses) had been deeply affected by the divisive war, found belated acceptance among Americans in the 1890s. Whitman, argued literary and social critic Van Wyck Brooks later on, had "precipitated the American character. All those things that had been separate, self-sufficient, incoördinate—action, theory, idealism, business—he cast into a crucible; and they emerged, harmonious and molten, in a fresh democratic ideal, based upon the whole personality."[16]

Whitman's poetry was a celebration of the variegated folk of the great Union. One of the ways that he read expression was through the pseudoscience of pathognomy, formulated by the American phrenological theorist Dr. Joseph Rodes Buchanan and defined by the poet himself as "the expression of the passions—the science of the signs by which a state of a person is indicated by the soft or mobile parts of the body."[17] Pathognomy, or body expression, was an important element of Whitman's poetry, a part no doubt to which Duncan clung. From "I Sing the Body Electric": "But the expression of a well-made man appears not only in his face, / It is in his limbs and joints also, it is curiously in the joints of his hips and wrists, / It is in his walk, the carriage of his neck, the flex of his waist and knees, dress does not hide him."[18] Unlike David's biblical songs, Whitman's were not of God but of the individual—but, and this is important, the individual as connected to the unifying universal (not unlike Haeckel's monist universe). "One's-Self I sing, a simple separate person," the poet wrote, "Yet utter the word Democratic, the word En-Masse."[19] Whitman's artless, ample paeans to what he termed "personalism"[20] served as inspiration for several succeeding generations in search of themselves.

That search was conducted through a variety of "physical culture" practices, from elocution to gymnastics to statue-posing, all rooted in the Delsartean gospel imported to America by a young actor named Steele MacKaye. Shortly before Charles Darwin's *The Expression of Emotions in Man and Animals* was published, in 1872, MacKaye was introducing to America what would come to be called the "Delsarte System of Expression." The major New York dailies paid close attention to his speech "Science and Art of Dramatic Expression" at Steinway Hall on 24 April 1871. The lecture, reported one paper, "came rather as a revelation than a mere exposition."[21] MacKaye had returned from France only the year before, having apprenticed himself there to François Delsarte. A former actor and singer, Delsarte had devoted the better part of his life to observing and analyzing bodily expression. In his revolt against the stilted performance style of the Paris Conservatoire, he had, according to MacKaye, "lifted expression to the level of an exact science, for he found the fixed laws of art in nature."[22] Delsarte himself never wrote out his theories and methods, and neither did MacKaye; it was left up to others, such as MacKaye's student Genevieve Stebbins, to compile and disseminate them.[23]

Delsarte's work was dry and intellectually ambitious, invoking scientific method at the same time that it honored religious credo. In true nineteenth-century style, he devised a system that simultaneously embraced art, science, and religion. His "Principle of Trinity" established a harmonious theory of the human system: first, life, the sensitive state of the vital realm, expressed through the limbs and excentric (outward) motion; second, soul, the moral state of the moral realm, expressed through the torso and balanced motion; third, mind, the intellectual state, expressed through the head and concentric (inward) motion.

Besides dividing the body into zones and charting out the subtleties of meaning in the various configurations and inflections of each body part, Delsarte also generated a set of basic principles, including those of sequence, opposition, and correspondence—each of which was adapted by Duncan. The principle of sequence held that movements should travel through the parts of the body in fluid, wavelike succession. (MacKaye, finding that his students had great trouble with this, devised a training system of harmonic gymnastics, or "aesthetic gymnastics." Diluted Delsartism consisted primarily of these exercises, mistakenly attributed directly to Delsarte.) The principle of opposition held that a dynamic appearance is more powerfully achieved when two parts of the body move simultaneously in opposite directions. The principle of correspondence held that physical, mental, and spiritual states all are intimately interconnected and patterned.

Delsartism swiftly captured the attention of teachers, writers, and lecturers, who freely adapted—and often oversimplified to the point of distortion—the original system in order to suit their own purposes. By the 1880s, American Delsartism had developed into two often commingling streams. The first came out of the fields of elocution and acting, stressing the expressional vocabulary of gestures and postures (figure 42). The second incorporated Delsarte's ideas into the gymnastics and physical education movement, emphasizing exercise systems.

Whichever tradition they stemmed from, Delsarteans shared a concern with three basic concepts: repose, vitality, and poise. Repose, cultivated through "decomposing" exercises, was seen as a necessary balance for the constant high-energy business of modern life. It did not mean dead energy, however; repose was, rather, the luxuriant energy of inner calm. Vitality, encouraged through "energizing" exercises, was the name for life force, both in movement and in personality. One author analogized it to the "vibrancy" found in light and electricity—perhaps after Whitman's idea of the "body electric."[24] Poise referred not just to physical harmony and elegance but also to the assured balance among the psychic, physical, and moral realms.

What eventually became the pose-and-gesture school of American Delsartism was forged originally by elocution schools and actors. It gradually was adapted not just for professionals but also for laypeople, predominantly upper- and middle-class women, for both home entertainment and self-improvement. Schools and churches adapted the systems for creating pantomimes and theatricals, for which books such as Elsie M.

Wilbor's *Delsarte Recitation Book* (1890) and Mrs. J. W. Shoemaker's *Delsartean Pantomimes with Recital and Musical Accompaniment Designed for Home, School, and Church Entertainments* (1902) offered appropriate texts and songs.

The Delsartean pantomimes were extended into "living statues," which became a popular pastime for women in the 1890s. "I have seen a plain, uncouth girl fairly transformed by a month's daily drill," wrote one advocate of living statues. "It is so fascinating, this trying to reveal the inner or psychic through the medium of the outer, the material."[25] Stebbins, whose Delsarte matinees inspired Ruth St. Denis to an artistic career, distinguished her form as "artistic statue-posing," which, rather than conveying emotion, conveyed "the idea of absolute calm and repose of an immortal soul."[26]

Living statues, also called statue-posing, were much the same as tableaux vivants (whose tradition in New York City theater dates back to the 1830s),[27] only they moved, and their models were exclusively classical Greek sculptures, whose images were provided in manuals and magazines. Women with cornstarch-powdered hair, wearing gauzy Greek gowns and cheesecloth underskirts, melted seamlessly from one statue pose to the next. These "aesthetically educational entertainments"[28] had a group variation, too, called "expression groups," in which women formed tableaux such as "The Niobe Group" or "The Sacrifice of Irene" (figure 43). Interestingly enough, statue-posing caught on in vaudeville, too, in somewhat less elevated fashion. "Living Pictures," as they were billed, peaked in theaters from New York to San Francisco in the mid-1890s.[29] Duncan very well may have seen a performance of living pictures, and she could not possibly have been unaware of artistic statue-posings during her last several years in San Francisco. They were most likely another source of her Greek imagery.

Self-proclaimed Delsarte teachers of expression hung out their shingles all over the country. By the late 1880s it had become a popular craze distorted almost beyond recognition—a series of melodramatic gestures and postures pushed nearly to the brink of parody. "So much of the teaching known as Delsartism," lamented one teacher, "has resulted in posturing, posing, mechanical gesturing . . . that it is no wonder that there is considerable prejudice among educators and sensible people against anything labeled Delsarte."[30] Delsartism became an object of ridicule—the subject of farcical plays such as George M. Baker's *Forty Minutes with a Crank or The Seldarte Craze* (1889) and poetic ditties such as the following:

Figures 42–43. Duncan's expressive body was rooted in American Delsartism, whose expressional vocabulary of gestures and postures was extended into "expression groups" such as "The Sacrifice of Irene."

In former times my numerous rhymes excited general mirth,
And I was then of all good men the merriest man on earth;
[...]
But now how strange and harsh a change has come upon the scene,
And horrors appall the life where all was formerly so serene—
Yes, wasting care hath cast its snare about my honest heart,
Because, alas! it hath come to pass my daughter's learnt Delsarte.

[...]

   Where'er she goes,
   She loves to pose
     In classic attitudes,
And droop her eyes in languid wise and feign abstracted moods;
   And she—my child—
   (Who all so wild,
   So helpless and so sweet
That once knew not what to do with those great, big hands and feet)
Now comes and goes with such repose, so calmly sits or stands,
Is so discreet with both her feet, so deft with both her hands—
Why, when I see that satire on me, I give an angry start
And I utter one word (it is commonly heard) derogatory to Delsarte![31]

Meanwhile, those authors, lecturers, and teachers who concentrated more on exercises had conjoined Delsarte's ideas about the connection between inner self and outer behavior with the growing popularity of gymnastics, sports, and physical education. MacKaye's system of aesthetic, or harmonic, gymnastics provided a model, but authors also incorporated other physical training systems, such as military drills or Indian clubs. Emily Bishop, who frankly named her system and book *Americanized Delsarte Culture* (1892), began teaching at the Chautauqua School of Expression in 1887. Her lessons stressed six basic principles: correct use of the body; relaxation; gymnastics without apparatus; stretching; exercising when needed; and gymnastics accompanied by an "affirmative thought."[32]

These many systems became subsumed within a popular movement dubbed "physical culture," which, as the words imply, forged an essential tie (upon which Duncan seized) between body and soul. Moreover, the movement brought the two terms together in a balance that was missing from the gymnastics and physical education movement, which, though it sought to redress the physical effeteness of modern life, erred, many felt, in the other extreme. Physical culture advocates were constantly distinguishing their field from "mere" gymnastics, which, despite its growing popularity even among women, was still "associated in the public mind with prize-fighters and ruffian boxers."[33] Physical culture artfully engaged the physical, mental, and moral life, clearing the pathways among them for fuller expression in daily life. After all, it was physical *culture*, with the emphasis on "culture" as "self-improvement."

Despite this newfound emphasis on the body, the justification of physical culture on moral grounds bespeaks the period's lingering ambivalence toward the body. If the modern American had become effete, as author after author argued in justification for her/his physical culture treatise, then such brute physicality as was asserted by gymnastics would have been an ideal solution. But there was an enormous backlash—led by the physical culturalists—against such pure physicality. Bodily activity became respected in the highest sense only when it was rooted in the mind or spirit, or the emotions. Physical culture, thus, was not an unqualified embrace of the material body; it accepted the body only as a transparent representation, or "expression," of the soul. Body-building thus was another form of character-building.

Because of its claims to socially redeeming self-improvement, the increasingly eclectic field of physical culture was able to embrace the discourses of beauty and health, too. "Beauty" was redefined as the result of good health: not just physical health but moral health as well. As Mrs. H. R. Haweis assured her female readers as early as 1878 in *The Art of Beauty*, "It is possible to cultivate the inner and the outer grace together, and it is possible to actually open a way for the development of the moral good by smoothing the physical veil which encumbers and distorts it."[34] Physical culture became as important as etiquette in the development of social grace for the upper and middle classes. Its parameters expanded further and further, until it included even home decoration and clothing. Conjoined with aestheticism, whose life-as-art philosophy was being imported from England, physical culture was transformed into a lifestyle guide for the elite, whose reigning guru in the 1890s was Henrietta Russell Hovey.

Wife first of aesthetic proponent Edmund Russell, then of the American poet Richard Hovey, she brought Delsartism to the Four Hundred in Newport in summer 1891, the same year that she published a Delsartean treatise entitled *Yawning*, "a book intended to show the unity between the gymnastic methods of Delsarte and those of Nature, and to suggest the direction in which educational advance should be made."[35] Twice a week the likes of Mrs. W. C. Whitney, Mrs. William Astor, and Mrs. Stuyvesant Fish met "to writhe, wriggle, bend and sway; to relax and decompose [and to] form spiral curves and make corkscrews of themselves,"[36] an experience that, in effect, prepared them for the appearance of the young Duncan seven years later. Stressing grace, hygiene, and artistic poise,

Hovey added an emphasis on aesthetic dress to her Delsartean message. She lectured across the country with an extensive inventory of lecture categories, including the Personal Arts (featuring titles such as "Grace and How to Get It," "Gesture," "Ritual and Etiquette," "Bowing," "Poise"); Delsarte and Poetry; Architecture; and the Decorative Arts (featuring "The Making of a Home," "Dress as a Fine Art," "Line and Color in Costume," and "Jewels").[37]

Mary Perry King, based in New Canaan, Connecticut, carried the lifestyle gospel into the twentieth century with her 1900 book, entitled *Comfort and Exercise: An Essay toward Normal Conduct*. Starting with the Delsartean trinity of spirit, mind, and body, King's book conveyed an underlying message of balance and harmony in all things, what she called "this ideal of normal comfort: an ideal whose business it is to encourage impulse, to educate instinct, to inspire action,—to develop our humanity."[38] Such a "model ideal of comfort," she argued, pervaded all aspects of culture and conduct—education, occupation, home life, social life, and dress. As for expression, she deemed it

> one of the most elemental and undeniable demands of each solitary soul. . . . Our arts, our cities, our dress, our speech, our motion, our life from minute to minute, our civilization from age to age, are all varied forms in which human spirit is expressing itself. Our sole satisfaction in living is to find vent and scope for our aspirations and to embody them in expression.[39]

King's system of exercise was particularly sensitive and sensible, based on a sophisticated understanding of the body. Among her free gymnastic exercises were swaying, balancing, and turning; undulations of the full body and of the arms and legs; and bending, twisting, and deep breathing. All these were done in an orderly progression, with astute attention paid to successiveness and rhythm. In addition, she built in variations of force, shape, direction, and other subtle properties of movement that would be theatrically developed by Duncan. By 1910, King was lecturing on "poetic dancing and education."

The poet Bliss Carman, a student of Hovey and a friend of King, expanded the Delsartean principles into a handbook for modern living. *The Making of Personality*, published in 1908 (the year of Duncan's heralded reappearance in America), was lauded by novelist Gertrude Atherton and physical education pioneer Dudley Sargent alike.[40] With the Victory of Samothrace (a favorite image of Duncan's) as his frontispiece, Carman argued the need for his volume:

While general lack of taste in the art of living is only too prevalent, and prevents us from being sensitive enough to our physical defects, the over-strained and artificial conditions of modern life tend to aggravate those defects and to make it imperative that we should carefully reinforce and regulate our physical knowledge and procedure, correcting faults and supplying ourselves with legitimate standards of human excellence.[41]

Carman approached "personality" through the Delsartean triune of spirit, mind, and body. It is quite a remarkable book, embodying that turn-of-the-century romantic impulse that sought, with near-desperation, to unify the self through the guise of art, with the support of science. Progressing in the book from "The Beauty of the Foot" to "The Art of Walking," through dance and music to "The Leaven of Art," he insisted on the symmetrical cultivation of the body and the intellect as a prerequisite to happiness. In the face of advancing modern materialism, Carman's was a book about the meaning of life: the path to joy and happiness found in the art of living.

Was this fugitive "personality" that was sought through the practice of expression some deeply embedded, essential identity, which needed only to be located and liberated? Or was it something fluid that could be willfully reconstructed? The more practical of the Delsartean/physical culture manuals tended explicitly toward the latter premise, promising that if you carried yourself in a new way, you would be perceived in a new light. Perception was equated with reality, and persona with self. The individual was not *who* God made her; rather, she was *how* she acted. The self was not an essence to be improved, but the presentation of self was a behavior to be transformed. Thus life became drama: the *presentation* of self supplanted the self. Like an actor in rehearsal, the Delsartean sought to master the techniques of performance. And herein lies the rub. Paradoxically, in order to free the self for "spontaneous" expression, the techniques of expression had to be mastered, through repetition. In its most diluted form, physical culture became merely a series of rote exercises or a series of discrete poses: an updated substitution for Victorian strictures. For rather than freeing up individual expression, it dictated another set of conventions. The body was still something to be contained rather than a force to be released.

This milieu of expression, within which Duncan traveled from birth to international fame, was a transitional period in the American concept of self. It shifted from an image of self as container to an image of self as force, and from a mode of self-sacrifice to one of self-realization. It moved from the eighteenth- and nineteenth- century concern with "character" (identified with "manhood"), the enduring moral core judged by its relative strength, to a modern concern with "personality" (for both genders), an exchangeable exterior sheath judged by its likableness or "charm." Physical culture, which brought women into the discourse of the self, straddled both concepts: it emphasized the importance and changeability of exterior behavior while retaining the moral imperative. But, quite significantly, physical culture reversed traditional causality: the self no longer produced behavior; behavior now produced the self.[42]

***

Duncan no doubt took her share of Delsarte lessons as a child. There were plenty of teachers in the Oakland and San Francisco area, and one of her earliest dances, a gestural rendition of Longfellow's "I Shot an Arrow," sounds like something straight out of the manuals. In fact, the basic premise of her New York repertoire—her "Done into Dance" programs—was Delsartean, for each of three such programs had a piece of music or poetry literally transposed, or "done into" movement. She paid explicit homage to the Frenchman in an interview at just about that time. "Delsarte, the master of those principles of flexibility of muscles and lightness of body," she said, "should receive universal thanks for the bonds he has removed from our constrained members. His teachings faithfully given, combined with the usual instructions necessary to learning to dance, will give a result exceptionally graceful and charming."[43]

But Duncan never mentioned Delsarte again, maybe because, once she saw actresses Ellen Terry and Eleonora Duse in London in 1899, she realized the distinction between imitating emotion and summoning it. The Delsartean principles of succession and opposition, of repose and vitality, may have remained the underpinning of her movement style, but Duncan's understanding of correspondence developed far beyond any Delsarte pageant or statue-posing entertainment.[44] If Delsartism saw expression as overdetermined, with a "grammar of action"[45] laid out for all to replicate, Terry and Duse suggested that it was, instead, imprecise and resistant to formula, that is to say, sublime.

Duncan adored both Duse, who would be of great comfort to her after her children's deaths, and Terry, whose grandchild she would bear. Duse, the Italian, worked on an intimate scale, producing subdued, fluid, seemingly spontaneous nuances of feeling (figure 44). Terry, the

Briton, remained fresh, sweet, innocent, and girlish throughout her career (figure 45). She did not merely walk across the stage: she floated, danced, glided. Her emotions were fleeting rather than sustained. And she found her roles within her own personality, thus constructing herself, in the aesthetic tradition, as somehow natural and a work of art at the same time.[46]

At that time, female roles were changing from stylized mimetic performance to psychological realism. Instead of relying on conventional, broad gestures and stage business, actresses were aiming to suggest a particular character rather than an ideal type. Duse and Terry were able to manifest the very stirrings and trajectory of an intense emotion through the most subtle inflection of voice and body—and they did so with what appeared to be striking artlessness. This sense of reserved force became essential to Duncan's aesthetic: "Even violence is the greater when it is restrained," she wrote. "One gesture that has grown slowly out of that reserve is worth many thousands that struggle and cut each other off."[47] Such deep, spontaneous, authentic expression could not be so calculatedly created by technique alone, or so the great ladies claimed, in romantic fashion; Duncan explained to a reporter, "I do not dance every day, for the same reason that the Italian actress does not play every day. She told me that her physical strength was equal to it, . . . but she added that her emotions were not."[48] Duncan shared with Duse, in particular, an acute concentration, a sense of repose, a transparent, "natural" connection between the internal and the external, and an illusion of the improvised moment. Neither artist wanted her audiences to linger over her means of expression; Duse and Duncan wanted them to imbibe the emotion as it was stirred and made visible.

***

As the practice of expression was undergoing fundamental change in the theater, it was also being revolutionized in art. Since the rise of photography in the mid-1800s, the primacy of realism in the visual arts had waned. By the 1880s, mimesis was called into question, opening up the door to the major aesthetic issue of our own century, representation. "But whether psychological or idealist, semi-scientific or semi-philosophical," explains art historian Robert Goldwater, "the purpose [of art in the 1880s] is to establish the importance of the representation the artist has undertaken, and to establish it precisely by making it, in some

Figures 44–45. The sense of reserved emotional force which Duncan discovered in actresses Eleonora Duse (top) and Ellen Terry (bottom) became essential to the Dancer's own aesthetic. Photo at top: A. Dupont. Photo at bottom: Sarony. Both courtesy of the Library of Congress.

way, go beyond realism."[49] The symbolist preoccupation with expression and suggestion rather than mimesis placed more importance on the work of the artist than on the object being depicted, and yet the embrace of an inner, expressive reality did not immediately abolish a devotion to the outer, "objective" reality of the world. In fact, the diversity of styles during this period, according to Goldwater, was connected by the common "desire to make emotion meaningful, by connecting it with humanity at large and by seeing nature as its reflection."[50]

Artists such as Auguste Rodin were searching for art's own, primary existence (the modernist impulse) while still holding on to the last rhetorical vestiges of "Nature" (the romantic impulse). Rodin did not *copy* nature per se. He *re-created* it, having learned, according to poet and critic Arthur Symons, "to suggest more than it [the sculpture] says, to embody dreams in its flesh, to become at once a living thing and a symbol."[51] Yet Rodin always insisted that he did copy "Nature," despite the liberties he seemed to take with the surface and form of his sculptures. Remaining true to "Nature," he explained, was a matter of neither surface imitation nor aggrandizement. It was, rather, the artist's *in-sight* into what s/he saw. Rodin advised artists to "copy what you see" on the one hand, but to divine "the hidden truths beneath appearances" on the other. "The feeling which influenced my vision," he explained, "showed me Nature as I have copied her."[52] In effect, Rodin—and many of his fellow artists at the turn of the century—redefined "Nature." No longer was it the surface appearance of phenomena; it was the hidden essence, the noumena. Therefore, the artist's job was to "see" and "copy" that "*inner* truth," that "soul." Just as science had become religion, so "Nature" seemed to become metaphysics.

Like Rodin, whom she knew and greatly admired, Duncan did not separate objective perception from subjective interpretation. For her, dancing after "Nature" did not mean flapping her arms like a bird; it meant penetrating the inner essence of flight, as an anecdote by Irma Duncan illustrates:

> I still recall the initial lesson in dance composition she gave me privately and how miserably I erred in interpreting the Brahms song she had chosen. It began "If I were a bird," so I flew about the room as if I were a bird. When I stopped, I saw "that look" on Isadora's face. I was terrified. No, she explained, the song did not say "I am a bird," it said "If I *were* a bird." It meant, "I wish I could fly to you, but I am earthbound." From her couch, she demonstrated with beautiful gestures how the dance should have been done.[53]

Paradoxically, Duncan and Rodin demanded fidelity both to the object and to their own experience of that object. Furthermore, by attributing the artist's subjective experience to the object itself—its inner reality as opposed to a surface image—the artist's deviation from conventional mimesis could still be defined as being true to "Nature." Thus Duncan and Rodin transcended the traditional distinction between the outer reality of the phenomenal world and the inner experience of the noumenal world through the artistic process of "expression." Duncan did not admonish her pupils to *imitate* "Nature" as they *saw* it; she encouraged them to *express* "Nature" as they *felt* it.

***

From Duse, Duncan learned about the expressiveness of vibrating stillness. From Delsartism, she learned about the importance of the body's center (what she later identified as the solar plexus) as the source of physical expression. From the Greek vase paintings, she learned about "emotion taking entire possession of the body."[54] From Rodin, she learned that beauty is perfected in completeness of expression, not in surface imitation. Out of these sources she constructed an expressive body that was not just a means but an end in itself. Expression was nothing short of a virtue, and the central tenet of her very existence; it was her purpose in life, her religion.

It was no coincidence that her two greatest love affairs were with men similarly driven toward expression, Gordon Craig and Sergei Esenin. Both were revolutionaries, Craig in the theater and Esenin in poetry. Although Duncan could not read Esenin's poetry in its native Russian, she experienced the force, the passion, and the music of his recitations. Fellow poet N. G. Poletaev recalled that the young imagist "recited magnificently—somewhat theatrically, but magnificently, marvelously! I can imagine him now: tilting his luxurious yellow head forward . . . , all gesture, all mime and movement, he carefully shaded in his declamation the most subtle melody of his verse."[55] The writer Maxim Gorky admired his "enormous power of feeling, such perfect expressiveness."[56] Lola Kinel, Duncan and Esenin's interpreter, sat speechless before his "amazing gamut of expressions, from the very gentlest crooning, which was like a caress, to some utterly wild, hoarse shrieks."[57] Duncan, for her part, immediately fell in love with the "peasant" poet. They shared a disdain for anything prosaic, harnessing an appetite for heightened emotion that soon enough turned destructive.

Without any language barrier between them, Craig and Duncan were able to sustain a deeper level of idea and emotion. They met, in December 1904, at a fertile moment in their careers, each one rethinking the very premises of her/his respective art form. Both had apprenticed in the theater; both rejected its artificial conventions, seeking direction instead from poetry and painting. They matched each other in imagination, and it was mutually exhilarating; the passion was as much aesthetic as it was physical. They shared a primary belief in "Nature," in suggestion over realism, in the grandeur of simplicity, in the unity of *mise-en-scène*, in movement, proportion, and the Greek ideal. They believed in art as revelation. They envisioned a "theatre of symbols, a theatre of visions, a theatre of silence and movement."[58]

The idea that Duncan's practice was one of *self*-expression, however, is a mistaken one. Duncan's theory of expression—"the connection between passion and the storm, between the breeze and gentleness"[59]—was pointedly *not* a theory of *self*-expression. The trouble is, it lies scattered in bits and pieces across her writings and interviews, covered with the patina of romantic grandiloquence.

What, then, was Duncan's aesthetic theory of expression? To begin with, it was dynamic, not static. She suggested not only that emotion manifests itself in movement, but also that movement induces emotion: "That is only natural: the attitude we assume affects our soul; a simple turning backward of the head, made with passion, sends a Bacchic frenzy running through us, of joy or heroism or desire. All gestures thus give rise to an inner response, and similarly they have the power to express directly every possible state of the feelings or thought."[60] This idea she may have adapted from the American psychologist William James, who, despite the general belief that emotion precedes bodily expression, argued in his *Principles of Psychology* (1890) that emotion follows bodily expression.[61]

Duncan recognized three types of dancers: one who does gymnastic drills; one who conjures up a remembered feeling or experience; and one whose soul can express all humanity, "something greater than all selves."[62] The legitimate dancer is this last one, for dance is not about mere self-expression; it is about expression of the transcendent ("something out of another, a profounder world")[63] *through* the self, which she conceptualized as not just the individual but the individual as interconnected with the cosmos. Thus what is expressed by the dancer (whether it be an emotion, a mood, a thought, or an allegory) is not imposed by a single ego; it is acquired by merging the soul with the universe. This merging requires that the soul be "awakened" to the universal, by means of either music or "Nature." The soul, thus awakened, possesses the body, which becomes the manifestation of that soul. By reconstituting the body as an expression of the soul, Duncan thus transformed her dancing into a means of prayer and effectively consecrated the art form.

Duncan went even further, accounting for the production of meaning in her choreography. She followed Loie Fuller, the pioneer in movement and light who introduced Duncan to Vienna, in her belief that dance springs from music. But unlike Fuller, who believed that dance is the bodily expression of sensation,[64] Duncan saw dance as a matter of creating signs. (That is how several writers described her even before her first American tour, as being a "symbolic" dancer, because her pieces clearly meant something beyond their material existence.)[65] Duncan's aesthetic was an expression of effect, not form. She was at heart a symbolist long before she had ever read the poetry of Maurice Maeterlinck, or met with producer/director Lugné-Poë, or seen actress Suzanne Desprès. As she explained it to a reporter, Duncan had realized the advantage of the symbolic over the literal when she was just five years old:

> "I recited 'Ten Little Niggers' and made a great hit. I see, now,["] laughing merrily, "that it was a very inartistic performance. I had bought 10 little nigger dolls and had them sitting up in a box, and at the end of each couplet stuck one in my pocket. Now I see I shouldn't have had the dolls. One must have the symbols and not the real thing."[66]

Like the symbolists, Duncan looked for the suggestion of the thing rather than the thing itself.

In the following typescript of an interview by Redfern Mason, a San Francisco journalist with whom Duncan had an affair during her return there in 1917, she explained the chain of meaning in her dances. This transcript is an unusual Duncan document (whether it was ever published is unclear); nowhere else does she articulate in such specific terms the semiotics of her aesthetic:

> "Many people take my work too literally," says Miss Isadora Duncan, who is to give a Chopin recital with Harold Bauer at the Columbia Theatre this afternoon.
> " 'What is she doing now?' they seem to say, when I raise my arms or lower them, just as if I were doing a play in pantomime.
> "Now that is not the idea at all. The notion that every gesture has some precise meaning is all wrong. It is mood, not photography. Perhaps the music suggests to me the idea of the sea. In that case the undulating of my body will be inspired by the unrest of the billows. But the sea

is a symbol of passion or mental perturbation and to narrow my dancing down to the one meaning is to miss half its significance.

"First comes the music and it acts upon me in such a way as to produce a mind state of which the idyll I dance is a portrayal.

"The onlooker does not need to know just what it is I have in mind
in order to enjoy my art. Let him suffer the dancing to awaken in him
the vision to which his psychic constitution makes him prone. It may not
agree with the ideal formed by his neighbor. But for him it will be true
and, though the various interpretations of what I do may differ, I think
they will be found, on analysis, to have some factor which makes them
part of a common revelation.

"But the idea that a particular [music] should inevitably suggest this
or that gesture or movement of the body is an error. The music plays
upon my consciousness like light upon the dancing surface of the
water; I take my aesthetic color from it.

"When I am dancing, the movements succeed one another so rapidly,
so spontaneously, it would seem—though every effect is carefully
worked up beforehand, that I hardly know what I am doing and my state
of mind is akin to clairvoyance."[67]

Clearly, Duncan's dancing was not the spontaneous expression of her own
personal emotions. Neither was it the description of music, nor an imitation of "Nature." And she obviously rejected the reductivist Delsartean
notion that a catalog of discrete emotions are each ideally communicated
through one specific gesture or pose. Rather, music served as her starting
point, suggesting to Duncan visual/emotional imagery, such as the sea.
Duncan chose a kinetic aspect of that image—the unrest of the billowing
waves, for example—to be exemplified through movement—such as an
undulation. The shared quality of these movements—agitation, in this
case—further suggested an emotional state, such as passion or mental perturbation. Thus, emotion was provided not as the content of either the
music or dance, but rather as a sign into which both could be translated.
Duncan here is making a Nietzschean distinction: the music does not contain emotion, and neither is it the likeness or expression of emotion;
rather, the perceived emotion is a metaphor of (and after) the music and
dance.[68]

As far as Duncan was concerned, the fact that she was inspired in her
choreographic process by any specific image was unimportant to the
spectator's experience of the dance. For the spectator began from a different point in the chain of meaning, and s/he did not necessarily go
through each link. The spectator began with Duncan's dancing. Its
dynamic qualities (not any explicit imagery, necessarily)—which Duncan
had carefully abstracted from the expressive conventions of her day—suggested a mood, or emotion, or allegory. The spectator need not know that

Duncan abstracted her movement from the image of the sea, or why she connected the music to the sea in the first place. Duncan intended the interpretive process to be an open one.

Thus Duncan pioneered a new mode of representation in American dance at the turn of the century: the drama of the kinesthetic. Instead of sticking to routine denotation, she emphasized what aesthetician Nelson Goodman calls exemplification: the possession of a quality at the same time that it is referred to, just as a tailor's swatch at once possesses and refers to certain of a fabric's qualities, including color, texture, and pattern.[69] Duncan still used descriptive gestures, especially in narrative dances such as *Iphigenia* (1905–1915) and allegories such as the *Marseillaise* (1914), but she also mined the body's unique capacity for displaying in its form the subtlest shades of emotion or mood. Her body referred to states and emotions by actually possessing their various shapes, rhythms, and dynamics, as she found them coded in nature (the rhythmic force of waves, for example), in art (such as Botticelli's *Primavera*), and in everyday life (much as the Delsarte manuals must have taught her to do). As a choreographer, her talent was twofold: first, her ability to observe and absorb the conventional signs of emotions around her, and second, her ability to translate those signs into just the right combination of kinesthetic elements, in order to suggest a complex drama of states ranging from joy to oppression to grief.

***

An integral part of Duncan's kinesthetic drama was music: the emotional height of rhythm, the depth of melody, and the breadth of scale. It was fundamental to her expressive body, in terms theatrical, philosophical, and pragmatic. "It's this music question," she wrote in 1906 to her then-lover Gordon Craig. "I must settle *once* for all—antique? Early Italian? Gluck? Modern? or None?" A few days later, still struggling, she wrote again: "I would like someone to help me *learn* more about music, and study more *exactly* its different relations to dancing—It is a very interesting subject. . . . Tell me what you think: does the dance spring from the music, as I think it does, or should the music accompany the dance—or should they both be born together—or How?"[70] She settled "this music question" neither immediately nor definitively. Over the next twenty years, as her movement became increasingly minimal and dramatic and her music larger and less melodic, her compositions became less dependent upon musical structure.

In an early dance such as that to Beethoven's Sonata no. 8 in C Minor ("Pathétique") (c. 1904), for instance, the movement seemed to "spring from music." According to Paris critic Jean d'Udine, who described Duncan as translating melody into attitudes and movements, "All the curvings of the melodic line, all its events of structure: anacrusis, syncopations, groupings, even all its modulations find an echo in this body, inflections which are perfectly musical."[71] Duncan's *Blue Danube Waltz* (1902), to Johann Strauss's famous composition, was as transparent a dance as she ever composed. The breath, the wave, the musical phrase washed over and through each other. Duncan became the watery rhythm, rushing forward expectedly and back contentedly. In a later dance such as that to "Siegfried's Funeral March" from Wagner's *Götterdämmerung* (1918), however, movement and music seemed to be "born together," if not as twins, then from a larger dramatic idea about "deep grief transmuted into line, plane and mass," according to *Boston Evening Transcript* critic H. T. Parker. "She does not translate it as music into another medium, since her poses, gestures and facial play little heed its contours, inflections and rhythm."[72] Whatever the specific nature of their relationship, it is clear—starting with the fact that she did not title her dances but identified them solely by their musical accompaniment—that Duncan assumed the necessity of music to dance.[73] Her insistence on the suitability of dance to even the most revered symphonic compositions was one of her greatest legacies to twentieth-century dance.

Music had been a fundamental source of Duncan's expressive impulse ever since childhood, when in the evenings the piano became the center of the Duncan clan's attention. Mrs. Duncan played composers such as Schubert and Chopin, while little Isadora danced and danced, even after she was supposed to be in bed.[74] Duncan's musical tastes would never stray very far from the intensely melodic, rhythmic, and personal nature of romantic music: Schubert, Chopin, late Beethoven, Tchaikovsky, Wagner, Gluck, Brahms, Liszt. She advised the Isadorables to dance only to music that "goes from the soul in mounting circles," endorsing Bach, Beethoven, Schubert, and Mozart, but not the modernist Debussy. His music, she wrote, "is only the music of the *Senses* and has no message to the Spirit. And then the gesture of Debussy is all *inward*—and has no outward or upward."[75]

Duncan's youthful love of music later found intellectual justification both in Plato's *Republic*, which she invoked in support of Chopin and Beethoven and in contempt of ragtime, and in Nietzsche. Like Nietzsche, whose *Birth of Tragedy out of the Spirit of Music* she claimed as her "Bible," Duncan largely privileged music as the foundation of poetic expression. For music, along with "Nature," was capable of awakening the soul to its bodily expression. Nietzsche, following the lead of Schopenhauer rather than Wagner's *Opera and Drama*,[76] argued that music is the idea itself (the Dionysian), whereas drama or poetry only reproduces—in shadowy appearance—the idea (the Apollonian). Music is the essence that lies beyond mere appearance, that "allows the symbolic image to emerge *in its highest significance.*"[77] Just as Nietzsche believed that the creation of music comes from an "indecipherable" source beyond the self, so Duncan once explained to an interviewer that, although imitators seemed to think that her art consisted of certain stereotyped gestures, its virtue was actually to be found "in certain soul-states which are, in a sense, incommunicable."[78]

Duncan remained devoted to musical romanticism, whose early-nineteenth-century insistence on intimate—even mystical—subjective expression seemed, at the very least, inconsistent with late-nineteenth-century positivism. Compared to the radical realism of literature and painting, which more aptly embodied the massive cultural change of the late nineteenth century, neoromantic music might have seemed irrelevant. But instead, argues musicologist Carl Dahlhaus, neoromanticism's "untimeliness" enabled it "to fulfill a spiritual, cultural, and ideological function of a magnitude which can hardly be exaggerated: it stood for an alternative world."[79] Such "absolute" music (a term, in opposition to "program" music, coined by Wagner to mean music unmotivated— and uncontaminated—by linkage to poetry or drama) was privileged, as indicated in Nietzsche's aesthetics, as the one art that could express things inexpressible; it was essence, rather than mere representation, like literature and painting. It fit perfectly with the ideal world of free-playing expression that Duncan created on stage. Her dancing emphasized effect over form; suggestion over mimesis; internal experience over external appearance.

Duncan's early dancing was thus a paradigm of the symbolist aesthetic, captured in art historian Walter Pater's oft-quoted dictum "All art constantly aspires towards the condition of music."[80] Music was the symbolist art par excellence, because it was not tethered to the material world. To Pater and his followers, such as Duncan (one reporter spotted a volume of Pater's in Duncan's dressing room in 1908),[81] music was the purest art, without any representational ties to dilute its power to evoke the deepest of emotions. For art that merely imitates life, the English poet and critic Arthur Symons warned, "can have, at the best, but a secondary kind of imaginative existence, the appeal of the mere copy."[82] Unfetterred by character, plot, *mise-en-scène* or the conventions of the ballet girl, Duncan stirred the imagination with her "poetic" style. (She was billed as "The California Fawn, Poetic Dancing" in her first professional appearance in Chicago, on a "High Class Vaudeville" bill at the Masonic Temple Roof Garden on 21 July 1895.)[83] The term "poetic" was common then in critical parlance, referring to art whose symbolic significance traveled beyond the reach of ordinary prose. Her dancing, as the poet Shaemas O'Sheel wrote, was "no less than an interpretation of life in symbols."[84]

When Duncan choreographed, she began by listening to the music. According to Irma,

> Her creative procedure followed the natural sequence of closely studying the piece of music involved, which she usually did lying relaxed on a couch with eyes closed while it was being played repeatedly by her pianist, this in the quietude of her studio, with never a third person present even the musician had to sit with his back to her. She waited for inspiration to take over. Only after the idea for the dance creation and [illegible] the sequence of movements to illustrate it had formed themselves in her mind, did she venture to try them out on a physical level.[85]

While listening, Duncan entered into deep concentration. "No worries," wrote a friend, "and, in fact, nothing else in the world, existed for her at those moments."[86] In music, she said, she saw lines, to which she adapted her body, thus harmonizing the two art forms. "Music is sound, and sound is vibration; vibration is movement, and movement is the medium and root of dancing," she explained to a reporter in 1903. "Why, then, should it not be possible to directly transfer any musical sound into dance form?"[87]

The operative word there would turn out to be "any." Back in New York, Duncan had used an eclectic range of music, including one of Felix Mendelssohn's "Song without Words," Strauss waltzes, and several popular songs by Ethelbert Nevin. When she reached London's New Gallery, however, and the brief but formative tutelage of conservative music critic, editor, and scholar John Alexander Fuller-Maitland and preclassic music specialist Arnold Dolmetsch, she excised any popular material from her repertoire, focusing instead on more elevated fare. Fuller-Maitland claimed to have directed her away from recitations and toward Chopin, both significant turns in her artistic practice.[88] After a minor dalliance with seventeenth- and eighteenth-century dance music (an indication of Dolmetsch's influence) by masters such as Jean Baptiste Lully,

Claudio Monteverdi, François Couperin, and Jean-Philippe Rameau,[89] she set out on her lifelong course with romantic composers—not just the likes of Chopin and Schubert, but contemporaries such as Scriabin as well, who worked in a neoromantic mode. Most of the specific compositions she chose, moreover, were dance sections from familiar concert and opera standards, whose canonical acceptance among elite audiences brought a large measure of legitimacy to her own artistic practice.

When Duncan began appropriating nondance compositions, however, she was accused of committing sacrilege. It was justifiable for her to use Chopin's mazurkas and polonaises, or Gluck's ballet numbers, or even Wagner's dance music, but it was an indefensible breach of aesthetic convention to attempt any "interpretation" of the great, "absolute" concert and operatic works, which would be polluted by any association with the physical body.[90] Consequently, Duncan was severely chastised— really, only by a few highly placed critics—for dancing Beethoven's Symphony no. 7 in A Major in 1908 and then again in 1909, with Walter Damrosch and the New York Symphony Orchestra. "It is quite within the province of the recorder of musical affairs to protest against this perverted use of the Seventh Symphony, a purpose which Beethoven certainly never had in mind when he wrote it," commented music and dance critic Carl Van Vechten of the *New York Times*. "Because Wagner dubbed it the 'apotheosis of the dance' is not sufficient reason why it should be danced to."[91]

Despite the criticism, when she returned to the New York stage two years later, it was with an even more ambitious program, of Bach and Wagner. "If Bach did not intend that his music should be danced to," wrote Van Vechten a little more gently, "at least several of the numbers in this suite bear the names of dances, so Miss Duncan cannot be taken too much to task for employing them for her purposes."[92] Bach's "Suite in D" (1911) was one of Duncan's first experiments in tragic acting; unprepared for such a departure from her previously lyrical repertoire, the same music critics saw it as very uninteresting "pantomime." Wagner's "Liebestod," premiered the same year, also indicated the maturing Duncan's interest in the direction of tragic gesture and a corresponding shift in the relationship between music and movement. As a *New York Sun* critic described it:

> Mr. Damrosch played the prelude, and then the figure of Miss Duncan was dimly visible against the draperies at the back of the stage. When the finale began and the lights went up it was seen that she was lying

on her stomach. She arose in a few minutes to her knees. But it was some time before she got to her feet.

There were no long leaps upward and forward about this dance, if it could possibly be described as a dance, since it bore no more relation to that act than an occasional run backward and forward.[93]

The "Liebestod" had been placed last on the 15 February program, or so Damrosch dramatically forewarned the audience from the podium, so that anyone offended by the thought of rendering the dramatic finale into dance could take leave of the theater. Damrosch explained to the audience that, although the "Liebestod" originally was to be played only by the orchestra, he had seen only the day before Duncan's experiments with the music and thought them worthy of public viewing. Damrosch must have been the last to hear about the dancer's premiere, for press agents had been papering the critics for days with the news of the impending "Liebestod."[94]

***

Always music implied drama to Duncan: not in the Wagnerian sense of the word as spectacle, but in the Nietzschean sense of the word as transformation. Music, she told a reporter in 1915, is the inspiration of drama. "They should never be separated. On the other hand, they should never be confused. There is no such thing as music-drama. Wagner was a marvellous man. And when he made a mistake it was as great as his genius. He destroyed the actor. His operas are topheavy with music—all out of proportion."[95] Music provided the impetus for Duncan's expressive body in her early years, and along the way she experimented with music-drama-dancing, but in her later career she focused on the drama of gesture.

As a young artist in New York, Duncan spoke of her desire to produce an expressive fusion of dance, music, and poetry, but by the time she arrived at Bayreuth six years later, Duncan wrote, her "soul was like a battlefield where Apollo, Dionysus, Christ, Nietzsche and Richard Wagner disputed the ground."[96] Wagner clearly lost; Nietzsche and Dionysus emerged victorious. Like Nietzsche, Duncan recanted her unqualified admiration for Wagner. She retained her love for his music and admired him as the first to conceive of dance as born of music, but she rejected his notion that dance could not be an autonomous art. With sad surety she informed Cosima Wagner that her husband had been wrong: "The Master has made a mistake—as large as his genius. The music-drama, that's just nonsense."[97] Dance could indeed be independent of the music-drama, and her choice to choreograph Beethoven's Symphony no. 7 in A Major (1904) was perhaps one way of proving the point.[98]

After the New Gallery concerts in 1900, up until roughly 1913 (the year that her children Deirdre and Patrick were drowned), most of Duncan's choreography had been about dance as born of music. There were the Chopin evening and the Brahms waltzes, for example, Beethoven's Sonata no. 8 in C Minor ("Pathétique"), and, of course, the *Blue Danube Waltz*. This last dance, although hardly a complicated one (it was a public favorite that she tired of repeating), perhaps was the purest of her musical dances. It was a dance in which the rhythms of the body moving repeatedly forward and back melted into those of the music. "Her commencement of this dance is a marvellous expression of rhythm, balance, and intoxication," wrote one observer. "She stands poised on a step up at the back of the stage in her red [dress]. With a leap of joy like one arisen from some hiding place in the rocks, and shaking off the salt, fresh spray, she sways and sways till the big audience seems scarcely able to restrain itself from joining in the rhythmic motion."[99]

But Duncan paid increasing attention to drama, returning to her earliest interest in creating a kind of "total" theater, uniting music, drama, and dance. It was the chorus as Nietzsche defined it—the source and essence of Greek tragedy—that Duncan was thinking about. Her earliest public mention of the chorus seems to have been in 1908, when she told a reporter that her pupils at Grunewald, her first school, located outside Berlin, were "to be the nucleus of the great dancing chorus that will soon come into existence."[100] The next year, she told a Boston paper that she hoped "in time to revive the Greek drama and the Greek chorus. My dances, in fact, are a revival of the Greek chorus."[101]

By 1913, her idea of the chorus had fully formed. She told Russian dance critic Valerien Svetloff how her aesthetic had changed since she had last seen him, five years before. No longer was she devoted to the pure dance for dance's sake: "In the time of the ancient Greeks, dances did not exist separately, but at the beginning were tightly fused with music and poetry. And in just this united, indissoluble state was the dance recognized as a total artistic composition. To this fusion of three arts—according to my new outlook, indivisible—I do now call."[102] Already the chorus had inspired her earliest experiments with Gluck's operas, and it would continue to inform her drama-music-dancing productions in New York during the war as well as her later solos.

Duncan had spent years developing three full- or nearly full-length Greek tragedies: *Iphigenia in Tauris* (1914–1915), *Iphigenia in Aulis* (1905–1915; figure 46), and *Orpheus* (1900–1915). For all three, she chose Gluck's eighteenth-century opera scores, liberally excerpting and editing them, even borrowing from *Tauris* and *Orpheus* to add to *Aulis* at times.[103] In Gluck she felt she had found the spirit of the Greek chorus, "its rhythm, the grave beauty of its movements, the great impersonality of its soul, stirred, but never despairing."[104] In none of them did she ever portray any of the main characters per se.

Duncan premiered the evening-length *Iphigenia* program, assembled from the ballets, airs, and choruses of both *Aulis* and *Tauris*, in Amsterdam in 1905. She danced and mimed—with extraordinary effectiveness—such scenes as the young maidens of Chalkis playing ball and knuckle-bones; the robustly rhythmic spear-and-shield dance of the Scythians; and the passionate contortions of the maenads' bacchanal. Duncan toured the Netherlands that year with *Iphigenia* and the "Dance Idylls" suite (1900–c. 1903); in Haarlem, an off-stage choir accompanied the Greek tragedy.[105] It continued as a staple of the Duncan repertoire, and she danced the work in her premier American season with the New York Symphony Orchestra in 1908/09.

Very little description of *Iphigenia* was given in reviews,[106] so it is worth quoting at some length here from a description by Irma Duncan:

> Her Iphigenia program contained a medley of [illegible] operas. The lovely Overture to "I in Aulis" played by the orchestra before the closed curtain set the mood for the floor. When the curtain rose on the bare scene with a simple setting of a blue [illegible] originally but later with the tall blue-grey curtains she always used. Enclosing it on 3 sides she appeared dancing the Air Gai. Attired in a simple beige-[colored] chiffon tunic with a cross band on top and a band above the thighs to gather in the folds she gave as a first impression the effect of bringing a classic frieze to life crossing back and forth in the background across the stage from left to right. Young maidens playing the double flute and cymbals others strewing flowers in the path of a big procession for a wedding feast. So vividly portrayed one can almost hear the cymbals clash and see the flowers fall. Her feet marking time at the start of each sequence indicating the tempo the way a band leader would.
>
> In the andante that follows she changes tempo and walking with solemn hesitating steps, taking first a slow one then two quick steps in succession as the music indicates she lifts her hands close together before her as if carrying an offering to the Temple up the Temple steps and deposits the gift before Aphrodite, the goddess of Love. From there, slowly turning, she sees the Greek fleet approach in the distance and raises an arm in a gesture of greeting and a slow wave in that direction then returning once again to the "offerings" as the musical theme repeats itself.

Figure 46. Duncan in Iphigenia in Aulis, *by Gluck, whose music she considered the very spirit of the Greek chorus. Courtesy of the Dance Collection of the New York Public Library for the Performing Arts, Astor, Lenox and Tilden Foundations.*

[...]

In the second part of her program to the music of Gluck's Iphigenia in Taurus the mood changes from the lyric to the dramatic. In a short red tunic of heavy crepe de chine "a la greque," she presents a group of Warrior or Amazon dances. Here one can easily recognize the classic [illegible] of the Vase paintings she has absorbed and re-created. One warrior advances, attacking with a spear the other holding a shield, retreats and falls to [his] knees. He in turn rises slowly for the attack and turns back and forth. The various poses bring to life the frieze on the

Parthenon. A livelier war dance follows in which she engages in hand to hand combat raising and lowering the shield rapidly the feet moving in staccato fashion ending with a triumphant gesture kneeling over the adversary with shield raised. This dance she always had to repeat.

The illumination is more subdued for the solemn human sacrifices in the Temple in Taurus where Iphigenia was exiled after being saved from her own destruction by the goddess Pallas Athena. In a long gown a cadenced march with the sacrificial knife raised before her, she approaches the altar for the kill. First she engages in some sweeping movements back and forth dragging the victims to the altar. The chorus approaches slowly swinging censors (not real ones of course all imaginary). A cloud of incense pervades the dark mysteries of the temple.[107]

The Gluck tragedies were successful transitional works for Duncan, bridging her early, predominantly musical works with the later, primarily dramatic works. Gluck's scores had a purity of rhythm and melody that provided the musical backdrop for her familiar genre of pure dancing; at the same time, their embedded narrative provided the specificity of emotion for her wordless monologues. Duncan might have been responding, at least in part, to the popular misconception that she merely had been "interpreting" the works of master composers such as Beethoven and Bach. By taking on the role of the chorus, as opposed to that of Isadora Duncan, or of a character, she could invoke simultaneously its impersonality and its emotion. That the chorus was an *abstract* vehicle of emotion—"that wonderful impersonal sadness"[108]—was of prime importance to her.[109] Furthermore, Duncan identified the great Greek chorus—mother to all drama—as a glorious origin for an art form struggling for its legitimacy. Dancing, she wrote, "must become again the primitive Chorus, and the drama will be reborn from her inspiration. Then she will again take her place as the sister art of tragedy, she will spring from music—the great, impersonal, eternal and divine wellspring of art."[110]

With *Orpheus*, Duncan delved deeper into the dramatic mode. "In dancing the choruses and dances of 'Orphee,'" she wrote, "I do not try to represent Orpheus or Euridice but only the plastic movements of the Chorus."[111] The story of Orpheus's journey to rescue his wife in the underworld spanned almost the entirety of the dancer's career, from the New Gallery performances in 1900 to the 1920s. It expanded in scope and in fullness of production, culminating in a drama-music-dancing version complete with chorus and vocal soloist.

Her first *Orpheus* was modest—a minuet from Gluck's opera, part of her second New Gallery performance. For the next performance, she created a pictorialization of Sir William Richmond's painting *Orpheus Returning from the Shades* to the fourth act of Monteverdi's *Orfeo*. Between 1905 and 1908 she performed (on occasion with her students) a four-part version, to Gluck's opera: (1) "Lamento," (2) "Champs-Elysées," (3) "Recontre d'Orphée et Eurydice," (4) "Gavotte."

By 1911, she performed a greatly expanded version of the opera with Walter Damrosch and the New York Symphony Orchestra, a chorus, and a solo singer. The entire story was represented, episodically, with a happy ending: "In triumphal procession they are both brought to the temple of love."[112] Most of the main incidents of the libretto were represented, with the chief exception of the scene in which Eurydice persuades Orpheus to turn and gaze upon her face. A small chorus, seated among the orchestra, sang several of the choruses, and the soloist several of Orpheus's airs. According to critic Carl Van Vechten,

> In the first act, in a long robe of flowing gray, Miss Duncan represented one of the companions of Orpheus. Her poses and movements were intended to suggest the deepest grief. It was in the first scene of the second act, that of the scene in Hades, which was given in its entirety, that Miss Duncan, portraying one of the Furies, first aroused the enthusiasm of the audience. She indicated the gradual wavering of the Furies from the tremendous "No" in the beginning to the end when the Furies allow Orpheus to pass on to the Elysian Fields. The Dance of the Furies, with which this scene concludes, was a remarkable exhibition of dancing, evidence of high imagination.
> [. . .]
> Miss Duncan, as a Happy Spirit, was as much at home as she had been previously as a Fury. From here on a long excision was made in the score until the finale was reached; even the famous chaconne was omitted. In the final scene, in which the chorus again appeared, Miss Duncan indicated the triumph of Love.[113]

In New York, the critics admired certain passages, especially the Blessed Fields and the Furies, which, Duncan told a journalist several years later, she modeled after Botticelli's illustrations of the fiends in Tartarus in *The Divine Comedy*.[114] "The muscles harden in the face and limbs, the movements are abrupt, fierce, now bowed and now angular," described Caroline and Charles H. Caffin. "The carriage of the body is stiff and inflexible, and then quivers and vibrates like a bow-string, loosed from the hand."[115] But on the whole the critics were reserved, complaining about the lack of program notes and the overdependence on pantomime. Nevertheless,

Duncan performed a full-evening version the next year and in 1913 a production with the French tragedian Mounet-Sully, whose performance of Oedipus had inspired Duncan as a newcomer to Paris in 1900.

Orpheus, with lyric choruses written by Louis Anspacher and tenor airs sung by George Harris, Jr., was one of the dramas that Duncan mounted during her month-long Dionysion season at the Century Opera House in April 1915. Duncan's goal was not to reproduce Greek theater; rather, she aimed to adapt the spirit of the great Greek theater for the modern age: a unified vision of drama-music-dancing. With the Dionysion season, Duncan attempted nothing less than the fundamental re-creation of modern drama, which *New York Times* writer Hiram Kelly Moderwell—very sympathetic to Duncan's intentions—explained as merely seeking to duplicate everyday reality. Modern drama was, he continued, "largely a 'static' drama of dialogue; its movement is emotional rather than physical. And every now and then we find ourselves oppressed by its literalness and its prose. We find ourselves longing for movement and fresh air."[116]

To that end, Duncan choreographed the dancing, which included her students; Edward Falck directed the orchestra of sixty-five; and her brother Augustin coordinated the spoken drama. The very structure of the theater was reconfigured. A vast stage was extended out over the orchestra seats to create a kind of amphitheater, and the proscenium boxes and the sides and back of the stage were covered with long, neutrally colored draperies. The musicians were placed on the right side of the stage; the chorus sang from one of the boxes. Most of the light was projected from the top gallery.

Besides *Orpheus*, during the Century season, she created a new version of *Iphigenia*, a brand-new *Oedipus Rex*, as well as a Chopin evening and a Schubert-Brahms-Beethoven program. Even these musical evenings were laced with choral singing and readings (rather idiosyncratic choices that included the Bible and works by Edgar Allan Poe and Percy MacKaye)[117] by Augustin Duncan. For the *Iphigenia* program, the same episodes were chosen for representation, with the addition of spoken and sung choruses, written by Witter Bynner for *Tauris*[118] and by Louis Anspacher for *Aulis*. The speaking chorus consisted of dancers Irma Duncan and Helen Freeman as well as actresses Sarah Whiteford (Augustin Duncan's former wife) and Margherita Sargent (his current wife).

Prices for the Dionysion performances at the Century ranged from the popular (ten cents for the uppermost balconies) upward to two dollars, for the parquet circle. Fifty-three hundred people attended the first four performances, but interest eventually dwindled. With Otto Kahn contributing the use of the theater, Duncan spent $62,000, closing down the season with a debt of $12,000.[119] A good number of critics complained about poor singing, affected declamations, and indifferent orchestral performances, calling the production amateurish and inartistic. Others were kinder, suggesting that the great performer's reach was exceeding her grasp, and still others judged her art as potent as ever.

Duncan's most ambitious effort toward the Dionysion, and her first venture into the spoken drama, was her collaboration with her brother Augustin on *Oedipus Rex*. Their idea for such a collaboration went back to at least 1911, when Isadora wrote Cambridge ritualist Gilbert Murray, whose translations of the Greek classics she greatly admired, about Augustin's desire "to form a small Company of people about him, who will share our enthusiasm, and who for one year, will devote themselves solely under his guardianship to the study of three of your plays, with the object of producing them at the end of the year." In the meantime, Isadora would train twelve of her pupils for the choruses, and a composer, "whom we have still to find," would work on the music. "At the end of six months, we would then . . . all meet together and for the remaining six months, work together in some chosen place, so that, Music, Poetry, and Dance might grow in perfect sympathy and make a harmonious whole." Isadora telegraphed Murray a few months later, asking him to come hear Vaughn Williams "play Electra music," but the project, at that time, came to nothing.[120]

For *Oedipus Rex*, Augustin was in charge of words and management, and Isadora was in charge of the dances, the chorus, and the crowd scenes.[121] Augustin played Oedipus and Margaret Wycherly played Jocasta. Irma Duncan, Helen Freeman, Sarah Whiteford, and Margherita Sargent were the priestesses of Apollo. They contributed several dances and one particularly dramatic scene of mourning, but their main role was the graceful ascent and descent of the steps leading to Apollo. Duncan felt that the only music powerful enough to suit Oedipus was Beethoven's Symphony no. 5 in C Minor, the first two movements of which were played before the action, and the last two afterward. Duncan, leader of the chorus, danced the second, andante movement.

The critics reacted with mixed emotions to this "unaccustomed" version of Sophocles' masterpiece. The translated text, for one thing, apparently had taken on an unseemly colloquial tone. The *New York Times* described it as "commonplace and unfelicitous," abounding "in awkward verbal turns."[122] The lyric choruses, written by Percy MacKaye, drew criticism as well. Augustin's "liturgical" performance drew more displeasure than admiration: one critic pointed out the contradiction between the colloquial text and the overblown manner of delivery.[123] The *New York Telegraph* pointedly asked whether this Oedipus was "a Greek play in the Duncan manner or a Duncan play in the Greek manner."[124]

What drew nearly unanimous praise, however, was the *mise-en-scène*. "The suggestive lighting, the music, the costuming, and the groupings," wrote the *Times* reviewer, "were all devised so as to achieve the atmospheric effect which accompanies all Miss Duncan's productions."[125] Everything had been subordinated to the overall atmosphere of the stage picture. The Greek architecture was merely suggested by enormous steps at each side of the stage and two massive blocks at the rear, between which was a narrow entrance. According to Mary Fanton Roberts, the scenography consisted of these four sets of white, movable flights of steps and Duncan's trademark blue cheesecloth curtains, falling the full length of the stage space on all three sides. About a foot behind the curtains was a wall of boards, and in this space beween the curtains and the wall were placed lights. "The effect from the auditorium," Roberts wrote, "was as though one was looking into miles of azure air."[126]

The Dionysion season was the turning point for Duncan in America. She was no longer the youthful, innocent, gamboling dancer. She was older, thicker, and she realized the need to find and assert a mature aesthetic for herself. Drama, according to the precepts of the Greek tragedy, had held promise for such an aesthetic, but her execution was rather naive, and apparently more than a little clumsy. "With all these limitations," observed H. T. Parker of the *Boston Evening Transcript*,

> she still dances and poses with a beauty that she only among the dancers of our time may compass. It is a larger and more opulent beauty as of broad, full and expanding line. It is a more plastic beauty, that, were marble a fluid medium, might readily be transfused into it. Often, indeed, in arrested moments or in long-held poses, it is distinctly sculptural and it has become more and more suggestive of the figures upon Greek vases and reliefs. It is not a beauty that translates into itself the contours, the rhythms and the accents of music; but it is a beauty that is illusively symbolical of large and elementary moods and emotions and of their flow one into another. In these, her latter days, Isadora sculptures her dances and poses as she never did before. The impression and the illusion is of a static beauty, instant upon instant in quick succession. Dynamic force it has not, as it had in her young years. The old illusion of a lovely figure cleaving the air in as lovely motion has gone. In its stead, the spectator sees Isadora in a swift and plastic series of beautiful sculp-

tures, the medium of which is her own body. She now carves friezes upon the stage in plastic symbol.[127]

Duncan learned from this mistake; she never attempted the Dionysion-scale productions again. Instead, she developed her new, sculptural expressivity into solos—still tragic, but no longer literary. As early as 1911 she had been working with dramatic solos, with Wagner's "Liebestod" and the opening G-string air of Bach's "Suite in D."

In her later years, in dances such as Scriabin's Piano Etude op. 2, no. 1 (1924, commonly referred to today as *Mother*), Liszt's "Funérailles" (1918), "Siegfried's Funeral March" from Wagner's *Götterdämmerung*, sections of Tchaikovsky's Symphony no. 6 in B Minor ("Pathétique," 1916), and César Franck's "Rédemption" (1916), Duncan relied less on musical structure and more on the kind of emotional restraint that Duse had employed so effectively. Duncan performed fewer leaps and steps: her gestures became sparer and more monumental. She became less the dancer and more the tragic actress seeking "that tremendous force of dynamic movement" that she had observed in Duse's stillness. Sewell Stokes, a writer who befriended Duncan in her final year, recalled the last dance he ever saw her perform, a few months before she died:

> Isadora stood at one end of the studio, a motionless white figure clutching her draperies. Very slowly,—so slowly, in fact, that one scarcely saw her move—she made her way across the room, from time to time glancing fearfully behind her at the imagined shadow of death. Gradually the shadow, which one could almost believe one saw—so great was the power of her acting—advanced upon her, until at the end she remained standing perfectly upright, frozen in its grip.[128]

In plumbing the depths of mature emotion, Duncan relied more on an inner sense of space, out of which emerged extraordinarily compelling gesture—not isolated gesture, such as a hand waving, but a gesture created out of a full, postural movement of the body. In *Mother*, for example, as performed by second-generation Duncan dancer Julia Levien,[129] there is a moment in which the dancer, in a modified sitting position on the floor, forms her arms in a flat circle in front of herself. Her whole upper body begins to circle out horizontally from deep in her torso, but gradually the torso stills. Her arms keep making their rhythmic motion, however, still seeming to contain the space between them, gradually changing in rhythm, intensity, and spatial design until they become a pair of mother's arms rocking her baby. The movement is both a recognizable gesture and a formal abstraction integrated into the overall line of the choreography. And the sense of full-body support gives the gesture emotional gravity, both literally and metaphorically, for these later solos of Duncan's were a negotiation less between earth and heaven than between strength and dissolution. They were seen as the soul incarnate, made manifest through the expressive body, struggling between life and death, hope and despair.

5.

In late-nineteenth-century America, the popularity of the dancing girl
arose along with the development of theatrical syndicates, whose escapist
entertainments reflected the increasing commercialism of the theater. The
typical scenario:

> You enter. The audience, mostly male, eagerly eyes the stage. The
> air is heavy—the audience seems heavy. Smoke tickles the nostrils. All
> are prepared for a "good time." They know about exactly what's com-
> ing—the blaze of color, the stupendous efforts to amaze, pretty chorus
> girls and clever principals—legs, toes, arms, hips, breasts, eyes, hair, the
> whole mélange of stage femininity.[1]

The female body was a staple ingredient in the spectacle-extravaganzas
that dominated the stage (figure 47). The dancers' apparently nude legs
(actually covered in "fleshings," or flesh-colored tights) were just another

THE *Female* BODY

part of the *mise-en-scène*, to be marveled at along with the lavish costumes and incredible sets. Ironically, it was the legs that were objectified, and the scenery that was mobilized.

By the turn of the century, the "dancer" (implicitly female, but with little distinction between the trained ballerina, the entertaining skirt dancer, and the moonlighting factory worker–cum–chorus girl) was constructed as a highly paid, empty-headed, blonde soubrette of ill repute. In order to produce that fantasy, dancers were subject to the whims of the novelty-hungry audiences through the theater manager, who hired and fired them on the basis

Figure 47. In spectacle extravaganzas such as The Black Crook, *which dominated the stage in late-nineteenth-century America, the female body was another object in the* mise-en-scène, *meant to be marveled at along with the lavish costumes and elaborate sets. Courtesy of the Dance Collection of the New York Public Library for the Performing Arts, Astor, Lenox and Tilden Foundations.*

of their looks. An 1897 article in *Munsey's* described the dancer's working life:

> The salary of the dancing girl depends entirely on the proficiency she has attained in her art. The very best dancers are receiving as large sums for their services as any people on the stage. But while the *première danseuse* commands a high salary, the ordinary ballet girl receives very little pay—no more, in fact, than she could earn selling buttons in a dry goods store. The usual pay is six dollars a week. This is while her company is playing in the city. While traveling on the road, twelve dollars is generally paid. Even at this low figure three weeks' rehearsal must be given free. Some managers, however, when they require the girls to practise all day, allow them ten cents each for luncheon. In spite of the small wages paid, stages are not large enough, nor the demand for this sort of amusement strong enough, to give employment to half the girls who dream of becoming famous as skirt or ballet dancers. Those who succeed in reaching the top of the profession usually discourage beginners, though they may say that if they had all their hardships to go through again they would, nevertheless, be nothing else than dancers.
>
> Managers are very anxious to secure the prettiest girls possible. In first engaging the ballet they are obliged, of course, to take the comeliest that apply, but while the rehearsals are going on constant applications are made for positions, and a weeding out process begins whereby the plainer girls are dropped on some pretext or another, and more attractive faces take their places. It does not seem fair, but the managers say

it is business, and the rejected ones have to conquer their jealous rage and try again.[2]

As a product of commerce, then, the dancer was engaged according to her attractiveness, first as a *female* body, and only then, if at all, as a *dancing* body.

In her early auditions, Duncan was flatly rejected. Her dancing, the managers said, was more suitable for church than for the theater. Their audiences were interested not in the spiritual but in the physical. And regarding a woman, the physical meant the sexual. It meant shapely legs, unveiled silhouettes, smiles, availability. In mid- to late-nineteenth-century America, it meant Lola Montez, with her convulsing spider dance, and Little Egypt's shimmying hootchy-cootchy, and "the Naked Lady" herself, Ada Isaacs Mencken, so named for her apparently nude ride strapped atop a "wild stallion" in *Mazeppa*. It meant Lydia Thompson and her British Blondes, who transformed burlesque from its nineteenth-century emphasis on satire and parody into the twentieth-century striptease (figure 48).[3]

Duncan, and before her Olive Logan, endeavored to raise the status of the dancer in American culture. Beginning in the late 1860s, Logan, a former actress, campaigned nationally against the "leg business," which she defined as "the displaying, in public, by women, of their persons, clad in close-fitting, flesh-colored 'tights,' and as little else as the law will permit."[4] Initiated by *The Black Crook* (which opened in 1866 and ran through revivals for several decades), it had been fiercely popularized by the arrival of Lydia Thompson and her British Blondes. If *Crook* had offered scantily clad dancers portraying imps and demons, the British Blonde, Logan argued, "represents nothing but herself."[5] The reformer's attacks on the commercially driven stage nudity aimed to save the theater for legitimately gifted and intelligent actresses and dancers, who, she argued, could achieve some measure of equality and independence there.

Logan was an emblem of the late-nineteenth-century campaign for women's emancipation, called at that time the "woman movement." It was a celebratory movement, full of optimism for the empowerment of women—who were seen as distinctly different from men—in the cause of social reform. Shaped in midcentury by reformers such as Susan B. Anthony and Elizabeth Cady Stanton, the woman movement gained steam after the Civil War, when women such as Abba Woolson and Victoria Woodhull helped set forth new definitions and goals for womanhood.[6]

Figure 48. Lydia Thompson and her British Blondes helped to popularize the "leg business," which reformer Olive Logan decried as women "clad in close-fitting, flesh-colored 'tights,' and as little else as the law will permit." Courtesy of the Library of Congress.

Woolson, whose *Woman in American Society* was published in 1873, criticized the prevailing, male idea of female beauty as "petite and fragile, with lily fingers and taper waists."[7] Instead of the pale, languishing, and consumptive girls being bred into this notion of beauty, Woolson argued, they should develop their physical powers. Only then would women attain the higher level of intellect and morality needed in order to civilize and beautify the world.

Victoria Claflin Woodhull was an even more ambitious proponent of the woman movement. She and her sister, Tennessee C. Claflin, authors of books including *The Human Body the Temple of God; or, The Philosophy of Sociology* (1890), formed their own Wall Street stock brokerage company in 1870, and that same year started up a journal devoted to the equality of women. From 1869 to 1877 Woodhull traveled the national lecture circuit, speaking on female suffrage and women's political rights under the Constitution. It was, she said, a "question of raising society, through woman, to a higher standard of morals."[8] She believed that obscenity is in the mind and not the body, which is the temple of God; she argued that marriage, whose purpose should be love rather than comfort or status, is pure and holy; she asserted that women should own their own bodies, especially with respect to marital relations and childbearing; and she recommended sexual abstinence over birth control. "I would take away from marriage the idea that it legally conveys the control of the person of the wife to the husband," she proclaimed. "I would make enforced commerce as much a crime in marriage as it is now out of it, and unwilling childbearing a double-crime."[9]

As women's eagerness to expand their domestic sphere intensified, they began to form associations. Women's clubs, which gave women a forum for unity and fellowship and a way to fulfill their desire for knowledge and higher standards of social and intellectual life, were the first organizations to be controlled by women. In towns and cities across the country, they met weekly to discuss topics ranging from music to suffrage to the domestic arts, thus functioning as an informal college for thousands of middle-aged women and representing the interests of the home, as well as of philanthropy, reform, the arts, science, and philosophy.[10]

In their zeal to reform American life, women did not overlook the theater. At the World's Congress of Representative Women of 1893, held in conjunction with the Chicago World's Columbian Exposition, one of the most popular sessions was the one devoted to woman and drama. Actresses Helen Modjeska, Clara Morris, Georgia Cayvan, and Julia Marlowe each addressed a standing-room-only crowd, setting forth the claim for dramatic art "as a censor of social life, an inculcator of ethical principles, a critic of current standards, and an inspirer of devotion to the ideal."[11]

Duncan came of age in the midst of such woman-centered activity, and the sexual politics of the stage did not escape her. She understood that dance would never be accepted as a legimitate art as long as it was deemed a leg business, and that it would always be deemed a leg business as long as the female dancer was considered a fundamentally sexual body. So it was there that she began, with the female body.

Duncan did not have to start from scratch, because the nineteenth-century convergence of Darwinism with the woman movement had brought the female body smack into the center of "the Woman Question." A widespread discourse both popular and intellectual, "the Woman Question" sought to reexamine the biological nature and social place of woman in contemporary life. It was modern science, wrote Floyd Dell several decades later,

> which, by giving us a new view of the body, its function, its needs, its claim upon the world, has laid the basis for a successful feminist movement. When the true history of this movement is written it will contain more about Herbert Spencer and Walt Whitman, perhaps, than about Victoria Woodhull and Tennessee Claflin. In any case, it is to the body that one looks for the Magna Charta of feminism.[12]

Duncan worked with these preexisting lines of thought, bringing the female *dancing* body into feminist and radical discourses. It was because of her that Louis C. Fraina, a founding member of the American Communist Party and a literary critic who did a stint as an editor at the *Modern Dance Magazine* in the teens, could write:

> In this age of feminist aspirations, woman as beauty is subordinate to women as a New Being. Woman is seeking more than beauty—*individuality*; the beauty of a free personality. She shatters the shackles of sex-slavery. She wearies of the blight rampant masculinity imposes upon her. She shows disgust with the old-as-civilization traffic in sex— "legitimate" and "illegitimate." She would end the limiting demands imposed upon her—demands which deny her entity as an individual. And woman—the Modern Woman—is striving for all this with an energy, aye, a frenzy peculiarly adaptable to expression in the dance.[13]

***

Was Duncan a feminist? She certainly is painted as a rebellious, freedom-loving woman in popular culture and dance history, but whether she subscribed to what constituted feminism in her own time is another question.

In fact, the very word "Feminism" (capitalized in those early days) did not come into frequent usage in the United States until 1913. At that point, it represented a shift from the nineteenth-century "woman movement," which argued for female involvement in the public spheres of life on the basis that woman's unique moral superiority obliged her to improve society. Feminism, in demanding women's rights, was associated with a broader and more radical philosophy of equality between the sexes in all spheres of life, including sexual freedom and economic independence. Furthermore, Feminism was distinct from suffragism, which focused specifically on women's enfranchisement.[14]

Duncan combined, paradoxically, the Feminists' emphasis on radical individualism, on the one hand, with the woman movement's sense of social responsibility and the suffragists' social identification with women, on the other. She did not join in any organized efforts, choosing instead to be a force of one; however, she did, on occasion, engage in a rhetoric of the collective "Woman," most notably in the "Dance of the Future" manifesto. Duncan was not a suffragist: she saw the power for change as residing within the individual rather than in the state. The vote, she boldly told a room full of suffragists and Feminists alike, would not solve women's plight. She explained: "We women can get anything in the world we want without the vote. We doubtless wouldn't keep our own names even if we had the right of franchise. We start in life with a man's name—we marry and take another man's name. Now, Isadora belongs to me—Duncan is my father's."[15]

Duncan was talking amid the likes of writers Rose Young and Charlotte Perkins Gilman (whom Duncan greatly admired),[16] two of the suffrage luminaries who had been invited to Duncan's Fourth Avenue studio in February 1915 (the same year that New York defeated a suffrage referendum) for a "defense of motherhood" and a protest "against the useless torture now being inflicted on Ida Sniffen Walters in justice to her unborn child." Walters was a woman being tried for the murder of her two children, who had been born out of wedlock. She had been jilted by the children's father, a married man of some means (he was a lawyer) who had posed as her husband and promised to marry her, but then was about to desert her. In desperation, Walters poisoned herself and her childen; they died, and she survived. The case made sensational press for several months. In her salon, Duncan requested that her guests sign a petition urging that Walters "be set at liberty and cared for for the sake of her unborn child."[17]

Amid all the different concerns and ideologies that circulated in the realms of Feminism and suffragism during these years, Duncan's "doctrine of freedom"[18] focused on voluntary motherhood. "It is [to] the benefit of the State to support all children up to the age of 16," she wrote. "When people understand that love cannot be made 'legal' and that every woman has a right to children as a tree has to blossoms and fruit, perhaps some of these horrors of marriage, divorce and prostitution will cease."[19] The right of women to bear children out of wedlock, which linked the traditionally unacknowledged pleasure of female sexuality with the mainstream virtue of raising children, was more of a European concept than one that predominated in America. With the exception of the Village radicals or, earlier on, the rare writer such as Mona Caird, who wrote articles in the 1890s against marriage as the "dominant abuse of patriarchal life: the custom of woman-purchase,"[20] the call to replace marriage with "free love" never penetrated mainstream American Feminism.

Like Ellen Key, the radical Swedish reformer whose enormously influential books (including *Love and Marriage* and *Renaissance of Motherhood*) were being translated into English by 1909, Duncan made the radical move of yoking motherhood with sexuality, mother love with heterosexual desire. While American Feminists tended to focus on women's emerging roles and rights in the workplace, Key focused on woman's place in the home, where she should have legal and economic equality with her husband. Motherhood should be affirmed in its social importance, and women should exercise their individual freedom to engage in it as they please, whether inside or outside of marriage. She argued against the concept of "illegitimacy," instead championing the cause of unwed mothers, whose children, she argued, should be supported by the state. Key, along with figures such as Havelock Ellis, whose theories of female eroticism were circulated in books such as *Sex in Relation to Society* (1910), was a proponent of what was developed, in Germany, into "the New Morality."[21]

Although Duncan must have been aware of the American movements toward suffrage and dress reform, as well as the accompanying upsurge in women's clubs, and the demand for women's entry into higher education and the professions, she seems to have been most influenced by a Key-style approach to feminism. Key's *Love and Marriage* was published in Germany in early 1904—Duncan may well have read her, along with Nietzsche, or even met her, since Key's address was in Gordon Craig's address book at this time, during their affair.[22] And although the dancer claims in *My Life* to have decided her antimarriage stance at the age of twelve ("I decided, then and there, that I would live to fight against marriage and for the emancipation of women and for the right for every woman to have a child or children as it pleased her, and to uphold her right and her virtue"),[23] she probably first encountered it in a significant way through the radical German Mutterschutz movement.

By the time Duncan got to Germany in 1902, intoxicated by the German philosophers she was discovering, she was ready for the message of the German feminists. And their message, as opposed to the Anglo-American "Votes for Women," was one of "Mutterschutz" ("mother protection"), which aimed to reform the institution of marriage and to champion the victims of that institution, namely, unwed mothers and their children.[24] Surely Duncan's own early childhood, overshadowed by the shame of her parents' divorce and the void of an absent father, made the German feminists' ideas all the more resonant.

Key was on hand for the first convention of the Bund für Mutterschutz (the Union for the Protection of Mothers), which took place in Berlin in early 1905. Among the group's main goals were the legal equality of husbands and wives, state support of unmarried mothers, and the legalization of abortion. These German feminists, influenced by Nietzsche's exhortation that each individual live life to the fullest,[25] believed that women's emancipation was to be found not in the realm of politics, with suffrage, but with the social institutions regulating women's sexuality, namely, marriage and motherhood. The New Morality asserted that sexual love was the basis for marriage (whether it be legally sanctioned or not), which was defined as a free contract between equals. Not only would this liberate women from sexual subjection, but it would also grant the same legal rights to all children, whether born inside or outside of legal marriage. Mutterschutz called for the availability of contraceptives, the legalization of abortion, the recognition of free marriages, state support of unmarried mothers, as well as more general demands for equality between the sexes in regard to their personal lives.[26]

Duncan was headquartered in Berlin during the Bund für Mutterschutz conference. The conference, and the public controversy it provoked as chapters were established in many major German cities, were well covered in the press. Given Duncan's voracious appetite for German ideas at the time, it is likely that she read about the movement. And, at the same time, Duncan had begun her affair with Gordon Craig. When she became pregnant with his child in early 1906, she wrote to him about how, for her, the pleasure of sex had commingled with that of potential motherhood:

> I wish you would know that in all the hundreds of times you have kissed me there hasn't been *one* that every thing in me hasn't cried out—make me fruitful—give me a child—not once—I have always had that

constant longing impossible to control and I think if it hadn't come I would have gone crazy from the struggle—as it is I can't help feeling happy about it—I *can't help* it—I have the most exquisitely happy feelings at times—[27]

When the lady patrons of Duncan's school threatened to withdraw their support because of her pregnancy, the dancer retaliated by giving a speech on dance as an art of liberation, concluding with a talk on the right of women to love and bear children out of wedlock.

Duncan's iconoclastic views and practices, however, were not without their personal price. She and her mother, who had given extraordinary support to her daughter's youthful aspirations but disapproved of her out-of-wedlock pregnancy, became estranged not long after Deirdre's birth. At about the same time, Duncan—like many of her female contemporaries who struggled with their prescribed roles as women—suffered a bout of neurasthenia, or hysteria.

This extended postnatal period of neurasthenia—she was bedridden for six weeks—was her worst, but it was neither her first nor her last. She was racked with pain and fever, and she could not move. She was treated continuously and futilely with ice bags, milk with opium, powders, aspirin, and mustard plasters. The doctor laughed, telling her it was "neuralgia—just nerves—nothing." [28] She began to recover, only to relapse.

Historian Carroll Smith-Rosenberg has argued convincingly that hysteria was not just an individual psycho-physical condition but also, in part, a social role of hyperfemininity played by Victorian women who had no other way to resolve the double bind, dictated by social expectations, of being both a frail woman and a strong mother.[29] Duncan's condition fits the profile, with a slight twist. Her correspondence with Craig makes clear that her illness was a form of relief—whether conscious or not—from her stressful and increasingly untenable roles as both lover and breadwinner. "To live with him was to renounce my art, my personality, nay, perhaps, my life, my reason itself. To live without him was to be in a continual state of depression, and tortured by jealousy, for which, alas! it now seemed that I had good cause."[30] She recognized, only after much physical agony that failed to elicit any curative affection from Craig, that his demands were unreasonable. "You don't want a wife much or even a woman," she wrote to him, "but a sort of *Geni*."[31]

Duncan had spent nearly all her energies—already limited by a traumatic, debilitating childbirth—soothing Craig's volatile ego, keeping him romantically interested, and financing his artistic enterprise with a grueling touring schedule. Although he was supposed to be managing her tour, she was left to deal, quite ill-equipped, with unscrupulous promoters. And, at the same time, her baby's nurse unexpectedly quit, and her brother and sister both were wiring for funds. She was obviously looking for sympathy when she wrote to Craig that she felt "sad & distracted" but was trying to "be brave." Neither sympathy nor relief was forthcoming, and Duncan soon took to bed.[32] Not until she wrote him that it "looks as if I were turning into a Blooming Invalide!" and subsequently fell ill on stage did he come to visit her briefly, with rewarding devotion.[33] Nevertheless, her condition, which a doctor diagnosed first as internal neuralgia and then as a form of nervous prostration, persisted.

Duncan connected her malady with her gender. She wrote to Craig, "There is too much feminine in my composition—that's it—a silly mixture."[34] To her, the illness was a badge of womanhood: "Once I danced, yes then I was more like 'tree or wave,' but now I feel just the *beginnings* of being a woman—just the beginnings. The others at my age arrived at it long ago—& I begin to feel it's a d— pesky thing to be—Yes Infernal."[35]

This affair with Craig—an all-consuming one, a meeting of twin souls, she felt—from the beginning had provoked new and overpowering feelings in Duncan. She felt heady, complete desire for him. She wondered at the difference between being a man and being a woman. ("Woman's ought[n't] to swear—They ought to be meek & gentle & patient I aint— no no no," she wrote to Craig. "I wish I were a Man no no no no.")[36] She also worried about the effect of her sexual desire on her art:

> O you you you—I am slipping away from myself and becoming nothing but a longing and reflection, and I tried to tell you the other day my *work* was the principal thing. *Work*—I haven't a thought or feeling left for it—that's the truth—it's this Infernal feminine Coming out at all places.
> And yet—how far I am from wishing to be a Man!—but O how happy must the woman be who doesn't know what this tearing to pieces element means.[37]

Duncan felt a lifelong discontinuity between her roles as lover and as artist. Can a woman, she wondered, "ever really be an artist, since Art is a hard task-master who demands everything, whereas a woman who loves gives up everything to life[?]"[38]

But Duncan felt no tension between her roles as mother and artist. After all, art itself was an essentially generative act. "It is a question," she wrote in "The Dance of the Future," "of the development of perfect mothers and the birth of healthy and beautiful children."[39] Pregnancy, she tried to explain to an indignant American lady who pointed out that the dancer's second pregnancy was plainly visible from the first row, was a fundamental part of her dancing. "That's just what I mean my dancing to express—Love—Woman—Formation—Springtime. Botticelli's picture, you know—the fruitful Earth—the three dancing Graces *enceinte*—the Madonna—the Zephyrs *enceinte* also. Everything rustling, promising New Life. That is what my Dance means—."[40] That is why her school, where she functioned more as "mother" than as "teacher," was so important to her. It was a logical extension of her art.

Until they died, Deirdre (daughter of Gordon Craig) and Patrick (son of sewing machine heir Paris Singer) were never publicly acknowledged as Duncan's children. When she brought Deirdre on tour to the United States, Duncan told reporters that she was the school's youngest pupil: Ellen Terry's granddaughter, and Gordon Craig's daughter. Thus Duncan's maternal image in America, as it developed with her advanced age and the appearance of her students with her in performance, was that of a virgin: she was mother to *adopted* children, who were, not coincidentally, all girls (figure 49). Despite Duncan's private linkage of motherhood and desire, her public image was a traditional construction of maternity without sexuality.[41]

After Deirdre and Patrick died, in 1913, the dancer was enshrined by the press and the public as a great, grieving mother (figure 50). Her tragic loss must have been considered repentance enough for the sin of being an unwed mother, since her and her children's illegitimate status was never mentioned. Duncan became a maternal "expert" of mythic proportion, with articles on her school's system of child education abounding.

Except for one boy named Jean, who was enrolled for several years in the school at Bellevue, Duncan seems to have taught only girls.[42] But when she arrived in the Soviet Union in 1921, the situation changed.[43] She was teaching boys, although not as many as she had envisioned:

> I wanted very much to have five hundred boys and five hundred girls in my school. For my school is a school of life and not a school of dancing. It is a current opinion that dancing is feminine, and therefore only girls have joined my school. But I, personally, would have preferred boys, for they are better able to express the heroism of which we have so much need in this Age.[44]

In Duncan's day, the fact that women operated in a separate sphere from men was unquestioned; it was the size and boundaries of that

Figures 49–50. Duncan's maternal image in America was involved with the traditional construction of maternity without sexuality: she was "mother" only to adopted girls. She did not publicly claim her daughter as her own while on tour in America, and yet when Deirdre and Patrick died, in 1913, Duncan was enshrined by the press and the public as a great, grieving mother. Photo at top: Arnold Genthe. Courtesy of the Museum of the City of New York and the Dance Collection of the New York Public Library for the Performing Arts, Astor, Lenox and Tilden Foundations. Photo at bottom: Otto. Courtesy of the Dance Collection of the New York Public Library for the Performing Arts, Astor, Lenox and Tilden Foundations.

sphere that were being negotiated. Duncan, too, saw a distinct difference between male and female, in temperament and movement style. Judging from the scraps of quotes and writings that deal directly with the question, she seems to have considered her aesthetic as distinctly female, even if she did not code each of her roles as necessarily feminine: in some early dances, such as *Pan and Echo* (c. 1903) and *Orpheus* (c. 1905–1908), she "played" both the male and female parts; in many more dances, she took on the role of the Chorus, a universal being neither specifically "male" nor "female."

Nevertheless, the archetypal dancer of the future was Woman. Duncan tried to affirm this female body: to demystify—and therefore to defetishize—its sexuality. She wanted to make visible that which had been so repressed that it dominated the very idea of the dancer. She wanted to create a female dancing body in which sexuality circulated freely as a part of the *human* condition, without being objectified as a producer and product of specifically male desire. (It comes as no surprise, I think, that Duncan, who recalled all her male lovers as being "decidedly feminine," had at least one lesbian affair, with poet, playwright, and scriptwriter Mercedes de Acosta.)[45] The dancer wanted to reclaim the female body by redefining female beauty, moving it, literally and metaphorically, from the vaudeville house to the concert stage—from the realm of the commercial to that of the aesthetic. Then, perhaps, would women attend to their own "natural" bodily form, rather than to that of the corset.

Duncan's women spectators were particularly primed for the dancer's recasting of the female body, because beauty manuals had been invoking the Greeks as paradigms of the "natural" body for at least three decades. According to Mrs. H. R. Haweis's *The Art of Beauty* (1878), for example, the ancients' simple, unselfconscious attitude toward the body was an expression of inner grace and of the divine. This is what constituted "natural beauty." According to Haweis, "The Greeks were proud of their beautiful bodies, as we are of a beautiful face, and a bare leg was no more to them than a bare arm is to us. . . . But what was harmless in the early Greeks would be impossible in nations who have lost to a great extent the simple instinct of natural beauty, whilst they have grown abnormally self-conscious and reflective."[46] Similarly, Duncan wrote:

> As young girls grow up in our Countries they are taught not to think of their Body or its developing form [only] they are told that to show the form of their Breasts—their developing roundness is immodest—that the muscles which support the waist are unnecessary in the female form

although they are clearly named in the anatomy as muscles they are taught to think of them only as soft flesh to be compressed in a given measure usually—that the stomach is also immodest and should be compressed as flat as possible although the rump duly should be emphasized thereby. No, young girls they are not taught to think of the form of their Bodies they are rather taught to consider the forms of corsets and petticoats of the form of a fashionable dress makers models—and these [later] forms are not considered immodest nay they are even considered by most women to be Beautiful—47

Despite this emphasis on the experience of the material body, Duncan could not separate the physical from the metaphysical. Art must suture body and soul. Body knowledge, she suggested, was perhaps women's best means to understanding the "abstract idea of Beauty":48

Does the recognition of Beauty as the highest Idea belong wholly to the province of Man's Intellect? . . . Or do you think that a woman might also attain to a knowledge of the highest beauty? Considering women in our country as they are today, does it not seem that very few among them have a true feeling and love for beauty as an Idea? Does it not seem they have recognition of that which is trifling and pretty only, but are blind to true beauty?
[. . .]
One might well be led to believe that women are incapable of knowing beauty as an Idea, but I think this only seems so, not because they are incapable of perceiving but only because they are at present blind to the chief means in their power of understanding True Beauty. Through the eyes beauty most readily finds a way to the soul, but there is another way for women—perhaps an easier way—and that is through the knowledge of their own bodies.49

Duncan was not interested in privileging or denying either the physicality or the metaphysicality of the female body. She intended to simultaneously physicalize and abstract it. She wished to interfere with the conventional cultural and theatrical dichotomy between the sexual and the religious, between whore and virgin, between the physical and the metaphysical. By dismantling these sets of opposition that structured the image of the dancer in turn-of-the-century theater, Duncan hoped to free her of the leg business and elevate her into the category of "Art," which Duncan equated with the Platonic realm of "the True, the Good, and the Beautiful."

***

Did Duncan succeed in defusing the leg business? Was she able to deconstruct for her audiences the physical/metaphysical dichotomy that supported the conventional image of the dancing girl? How, exactly, did they interpret the sexuality of her lightly clad, bare-limbed female body?

Current feminist wisdom may suggest that by aligning herself with "Nature," Duncan immediately engaged in the very "Nature"/"Culture" dichotomy that relegates Woman to the lesser status of the primitive and the sexual. However, the discourses of "Nature" and "Culture" at the turn of the century were more complicated than this. "Culture" was not necessarily coded as masculine, and not necessarily the privileged of the two terms. And the two terms were not necessarily dichotomous. Duncan's alignment with "Nature" (a specifically Greek "Nature" that was collapsed into "Art") was, rather, a savvy rhetorical move that permitted the female body—if only for a brief while—to circulate in a space marked by something other than just sexuality.

If Woman was aligned with "Nature," she was seen as an antidote for corporate Man, who had fallen from "Nature's" grace. Typical of his day, Henry Adams believed that women were primarily wives and mothers, and that their special closeness to "Nature" would compensate for man's complicity in the industrial world.[50] Woman, then, represented the possibility of a return to Eden, after Man had been expelled into the modern world. In the context of encroaching modernism, the audience's identification of Duncan with "Nature" did not serve to sexualize her per se; rather, it served as a nostalgic link to a romanticized, preindustrial past. "The movements of Miss Duncan's graceful arms and feet and legs, her head and body, which accompanied that Allegretto, suggested to me an innovation," wrote one reviewer. "They were all chaste, because they implied that the dancer was unconscious of onlookers. To me she seemed some lovely woodland maid exuberant with the joy of life and youth, appealing to the skies and hills for sympathy."[51]

At the same time, however, Duncan served as a hopeful link to a liberated, post-Victorian future. For it was in the image of the female nude that modern artists, prominent among her spectators, were eliding "Culture" and "Nature," in order to justify the former within the discourse of the latter. The experimental artists associated with Alfred Stieglitz's *291* gallery recognized the difficulty of the nude as a genre: it had been rendered a merely physical appearance, and disgraceful. "Our morals, our climate, our mode of life have turned the nude into a phantom," explained a 1910 article in Stieglitz's *Camera Work*, "and it leads, alas! a phantom-like existence in the arts." In spite of this, or precisely because of this, they endeavored to reclaim the nude—specifically, a nude of "free and natural motion"—as a symbol of liberation. What marked the nude for these icon-oclastic artists was its *movement*, which symbolized a life beyond mere surface, beyond the visible and material:

> The nude body reveals its highest beauty only in fugitive visions and fragments. The exponent of the nude must follow a human body in all its actions, its slightest gestures, its almost insensible movements, and most delicate external signs. . . .
>   The expression, that immaterial quality which irradiates all matter, that changing force which invades the body and transfigures it, that vibrant power which superposes a symbolic beauty on the realities of line, form and color, will yield alone the highest beauty possible to the nude of today, as it offers a continual motive for emotions and dreams. . . .
>   . . . To assail the enigma of the human body and to discover all the uncreated movements that are hidden in its shrine—that is the goal that looms afar in the fantasies of the modern artist's soul.[52]

To that end, the Stieglitz circle constructed a soft-edged photographic image of the sinuous female nude set in the out-of-doors, usually echoing the line of a rock or tree or holding a glass ball.[53] These pantheistic photographs, many by women such as Frances Johnston (who photographed the Isadorables and other Duncan-esque dancers) and the Californian Anne Brigman, proliferated in the pages of Stieglitz's *Camera Work*. "In Mrs. Brigman's work," commented J. Nilsen Laurvik in that magazine, "the human is not an alien, has not yet become divorced by sophistication from the elemental grandeur of nature; rather it serves as a sort of climactic point, wherein all that nature holds of sheer beauty, of terror or mystery achieves its fitting crescendo."[54]

Why was the *female* body so important to this milieu? First, because it was the point of intersection between "Nature," which was already aligned with "Woman," and "Culture," which was newly aligned with women. For by the turn of the century, "Culture"—musical concerts, art museums, pageants, and the little theater movement—had been cultivated largely by women, as either artists or patrons.[55] This nude, a "Natural" body so much like Duncan's, functioned as a means of making the experimentalists' radical brand of "Culture" more acceptable, with its apparent association with "Nature." But, more important, the female body was marked and marginalized by its supposed tendency toward expression (e.g., the "hysteric"), and it was *expression* that the modern artists, as well as the political reformers and iconoclasts, saw as the radical means of exploding oppressive, outmoded traditions. In this manner, the female body functioned as a strategy of cultural subversion.[56] Duncan's female body, so full of movement, so full of expression, so full of kinesthetic drama, thus was read as the harbinger of a new America.

The vitality that was so appealing in Duncan's earlier dancing, then, was not read as sexual energy. To the reformers and radicals, both political and artistic, she enacted the overthrow of the old order. Her dancing was about transgression, but not primarily about sexual transgression. It was cultural transgression: a refusal to respect the boundaries between internal experience and external behavior, between the private and the public, between art and life. The spectator's pleasure lay in the play across the boundaries.

In their initial efforts to explain Duncan's larger significance, commentators tended to overcompensate by completely dismissing the fact of her female body. Critic Carl Van Vechten called Duncan "pure and sexless."[57] Conductor Martin Shaw wrote that "there was no sex appeal in Isadora's dancing. That in itself was new and strange."[58] Reviewer after reviewer stated unequivocally that there was nothing "sensational" about Duncan's dancing; it was, rather, quite "chaste." *Current Literature* reported:

> Miss Isadora Duncan has not given the Salome dance in her present tour through the United States. She refuses to sacrifice her art to the sensationalism and the vulgarity of the hour. In her dance the purely physical plays no part. She dances scantily clad, remarks a writer in the New York *Sun*. "The fact that her feet and legs are unclothed is forgotten. It is part of the picture. Miss Duncan therefore does not rely upon physical charms to add to her success, as do some of the so-called dancers who are at present doing various sorts of stunts on both sides of the water. Her success comes through her grace and ease of movement, not on account of her ability to kick or wiggle or do acrobatic tricks."[59]

And the *Chicago Daily Tribune* reported:

> To say that she appears with bared feet, legs, and arms, and so gauzily draped for many of the dances that the whole form is clearly defined, is to suggest to the reader something of the sensational and possibly the prurient.
> Nothing could be farther from the truth. Miss Duncan, when she is dancing, gives no hint to the onlooker of her being in anywise naked or unusually bared. The idea of sex seems wholly obliterated when watching her. The spirit of youth and of joyousness seems embodied for the moment before you, and there is nothing more of sex in her appearance than there is in boyhood or maidenhood.
> When the dancer comes forward to acknowledge applause she is unmistakably feminine—girlish, perhaps, but essentially of the woman conscious and confident. But when she is dancing, the fact of her being

a woman and of her feet and limbs being bare never makes itself realized. This is sincere commendation of her art and in fullest justification
of her manner of dressing for her dances.[60]

Duncan made it easy for the critics to write this way, since she never presented a sexually charged Woman-out-of-control. Compared to the
onslaught of Salome acts that dominated the season of Duncan's arrival,
she did seem sexless.[61] She presented to her audiences an oxymoron: *precise* abandonment. She was "Art" *and* "Nature," restraint *and* abandon—
her very movement style was based upon control at the center and
freedom of the limbs. Even the furies and the bacchantes, for all their passion, remained within a circumscribed vocabulary and floor plan. Duncan
bitterly denounced the excessiveness of jazz dancing, whose "primitive"
roots were anathema to her Nietzschean paradigm of art, in which the
Dionysian is always mediated by the Apollonian. Duncan's performances
always retained a modicum of white, male, upper-class restraint—constructed, in part, by her choice of exclusive venues, concert music, and (at
least initially) classical imagery.

Just because Duncan's limbs were bare does not mean that she was seen
necessarily as erotic, even in her 1898 appearances.[62] That is not to say,
however, that Duncan's reputation as a barefoot dancer was not in some
cases a titillating drawing card. Since the 1880s, images of ballet girls and
actresses ("stage beauties") had functioned as pinups in dubious publications such as the *National Police Gazette* and even in more respectable ones
such as *Munsey's*.[63]

But, as with striptease, as Roland Barthes has analyzed it, Duncan
desexualized herself; she covered her bare limbs with the cloak of the aesthetic (in this case, the Greeks), what he calls "the alibi of art."[64] Indeed,
her bare legs and feet were as potentially distasteful to some as they
were erotic to others, and considering that Duncan's earliest audiences were
women, it was probably the former rather than the latter reaction that initially predominated. Although Duncan rejected the tights that had previously functioned as the proper barrier between the spectator and the
dancer's legs and thus as a tool of aesthetic transformation, her smooth, hair-
less, pancaked body looked more like marble than flesh, further reinforcing
the classical reference to an inanimate sculptural object, an ideal of
abstract beauty removed from the taint of sexuality. Duncan's home-
made nip-and-tuck tunics, with their discreet, teddy-style undergarment,
were anything but glamorous. They offered a figure quite contrary to the

Edwardian era's erotic ideal of the small-waisted, S-curved silhouette. Fashion historian Valerie Steele has demonstrated that the corset, which produced this silhouette, was at least in part a potent symbol of female eroticism; when Duncan abandoned the corset in favor of the full waist of the classical nude (whose apparent chastity derived from its lack of that erotic waistline), the dancer was effectively shedding the most powerful sign of eroticism then available to her.[65] Furthermore, Duncan—from the very beginning—danced with her entire body, as an integrated whole; she did nothing to isolate and thereby heighten the sensuality of her breasts, legs, or pelvis.

The line between the chaste and the erotic is hardly a solid one, anyway. "The barriers between what is deemed licit and illicit, acceptably seductive or wantonly salacious, aesthetic or prurient," art historian Abigail Solomon-Godeau has pointed out, "are never solid because contingent, never steadfast because they traffic with each other—are indeed dependent upon each another."[66] Just as Solomon-Godeau has shown that, for photography in late-nineteenth-century Paris, the "chaste" had become "erotic," so for Duncan's audiences the "erotic" became "chaste."

Duncan, with her bare arms and legs, presented more of a material female body than had ever been seen before on the concert stage, and yet her kinesthetic drama, so unlike the stepping and kicking of the "dancer," drew the spectator so far into the physical that it became metaphysical. Shifting between these two interpenetrating realms, she was in the constant process of becoming. She never arrived, never could be "fixed" as "female."

If, after French theorist Julia Kristeva, we conceive of the "feminine" not as a definable essence to be fixed in representation but as a shifting position always relative to the dominant order,[67] then we can see that Duncan's extreme mobility, elusiveness, and fluidity were read as a metaphor of opposition to the nineteenth-century genteel tradition. It was not enough, exclaimed *The Masses* editor Floyd Dell, "to throw God from his pedestal, and dream of superman and the co-operative commonwealth: one must have seen Isadora Duncan to die happy."[68] She stood for everything her audience was clamoring for: "more Freedom, more Self-Expression, *more of Life* and its joy of expression."[69] She refused the static image of the dancer and reconstructed it as a female body seductive not in its sexual promise but in its subversive potential. "This solitary figure on the lonely stage suddenly confronts each of us with the secret of a primal desire invincibly inhering in the fibre of each," explained the poet Shaemas O'Sheel, "a secret we had securely hidden beneath our conventional behaviors, and we yearn for a new and liberated order in which we may indeed dance."[70]

Duncan denied the female body as it had been reified in the "dancer." But, paradoxically, she did draw upon the negativity—the Otherness—of that which was marked as feminine (or expressive) to subversive ends. And at that moment when her aesthetic was still new, and not yet completely readable, or fixed, in its codes, her spectators could move with her in a liberating space without definite boundaries. That is why so many different kinds of people—upper-class women, realist artists, abstract artists, communists, anarchists, progressivists—could all share such an intense pleasure in her dancing. It was the trajectory of the experience, rather than any definite destination, that was so pleasureable.

6.

*She rode the wave of the revolt against
puritanism; she rode it, and with her fame
and Dionysian raptures drove it on. She was
—perhaps it is simplest to say—the crest of the
wave, an event not only in art, but
in the history of life.*
—MAX EASTMAN[1]

By the teens, the Greeks no longer figured in Duncan's rhetoric. She did not even mention them during the war as a source of democracy. The Hellenic discourse and its corollary, that of "Nature," had been enormously useful to her as a way of establishing a universal, transhistorical cultural authority for dance in America at the turn of the century. With dance now accepted as a legitimate art, she no longer needed to justify the form of her practice, but could focus on its content—on social criticism.

Duncan's politics—constructed partly from a loose version of Plato's *Republic*, which she invoked more frequently as world war broke out and the Russian nation overthrew its tsar—came down to a series of contradictions. On the one hand, she called for a Whitmanesque liberation of every American body, from tenement dweller to millionaire; but on the other hand, she cultivated an idealized body marked by upper-class style

THE BODY *Politic*

and imagery, untinged by what was considered the excessive emotion of non-Western "primitives." Her ends may have been ostensibly democratic, but her means—wealthy patrons, high ticket prices at upper-class venues—were exclusionary. On the one hand, she espoused a radical American individualism that materially supported a wealthy elite; on the other hand, she professed a communist love for the masses. Although she regularly denounced the ability of the state to affirm a free life as she imagined it, she also suggested that the state support America's children. She may have denounced millionaires, but at the same time she felt a tremendous sense of entitlement to their money and their lifestyle. "When in doubt," Duncan was said to have quipped, "always go to the best hotel."[2]

Duncan may not have been a consistent social critic ("She was the apostle of action," recalled dance writer/publicist Merle Armitage, "untrammeled by plans or meditation"),[3] but she was, nevertheless, a persistent one, rooted in Progressive era reform and embraced by the later Village radicals. Ever since her first interview with the *New York Times* in 1898, she had underscored the social import of her dancing. It could not be divorced from life: it was about life, a part of life, a way of improving life. Nevertheless, like many anarchists of the period, she was not interested in the politics of the state. She denounced what she saw as the stupidity and inflexibility of the state's laws, "which make any real life impossible, and which would substitute for life a sterilized, machine-like existence founded on Duty."[4] She opposed the notion that social change could be effected through legal means: she saw no need, for example, for women's suffrage. The "law" was irrelevant to Duncan's politics, in which freedom was performed through the body, through expression. Freedom was agency erupting from within the individual, rather than being gifted en masse from without, by the state. She enacted—and "drove on," as radical writer and editor Max Eastman put it—the desire of the nation, that social and communal entity rising from below to challenge the tyranny of the state.

Expression, the hallmark of Duncan's aesthetic style and social criticism, was interpreted by a significant portion of her audience not just as a personal but also as a profoundly political issue. For during the period (1908–1917) dubbed the "New York Little Renaissance" by historian Arthur Frank Wertheim, the artists, intellectuals, and radicals of Greenwich Village saw expression as both the means and the end of their revolution.[5] These bohemians, the likes of whom gathered at Mabel Dodge's Fifth Avenue salon, read journals such as *The Masses* and the *Seven Arts*, paraded as nymphs and satyrs in "Pagan Routes," and frequented Alfred Stieglitz's 291 gallery, were, according to Adele Heller and Lois Palken Rudnick, "devoted as much to play and self-expression as . . . to labor unionization and the redistribution of wealth."[6] They privileged—as did Duncan—both the individual and the national community, refusing to see any tension between the two. Their politics may not have been intellectually rigorous, or supported by a specific plan of action, but their politics did visualize the possibility of a Whitmanesque future. It was, historian Edward Abrahams has written, "a libertarian and transcendental quest for boundlessness and self-expression."[7]

The Village supported a mélange of ideologies. Dodge described visitors to her salon, for example, as a mixture of "Socialists, Trade-Unionists, Anarchists, Suffragists, Poets, Relations, Lawyers, Murderers, 'Old Friends,' Psychoanalysts, I.W.W.'s, Single Taxers, Birth Controlists, Newspapermen, Artists, Modern-Artists, Clubwomen, Woman's place-is-in-the home Women, Clergymen, and just plain men."[8] This was a radicalism, wrote leftist political and literary critic Irving Howe, "in which native moral indignation and European political thought, a flare of cultural exuberance and some sharp-teethed criticism of our social arrangements all came together."[9] Waging a fight against the forces that were driving their country toward increasing standardization, mechanization, and materialism, they were a supremely optimistic and even innocent cadre, whose faith in the power of art and ideas to bring about social and political change would be destroyed by the end of the First World War.

The rebels were committed more to cultural transformation than to political reform per se. As with Duncan, theirs was not so much a politics of state power or policy; it was a politics of individual emancipation located in the realm of the nation, where art, feminism, and the masses all converged. It was a moment, exemplified by the Armory Show and the Paterson Strike Pageant, when cultural and political energies merged. Imagination overtook dogma. *The Masses* editor Floyd Dell described it as "that glorious intellectual playtime in which art and ideas, free self-expression and the passion of propaganda, were for one moment happily mated."[10] Echoing artist Robert Henri's call for "art that expresses the *spirit* of the people today,"[11] artists, radicals, and self-proclaimed Young Intellectuals called for a nationalism that focused not on militarization, but on culture. Art, they felt, should express American life, and furthermore should transform American life. To this audience, Duncan was the liberated American body writ large, the paradigm of a new national body that would release the force of freedom from within each individual.

In their quest to reconstruct the nation's culture, the "lyrical left" sought to fuse life and art, the personal and the political. Eastman recalled "a sense of universal revolt and regeneration, of the just-before-dawn of a new day in American art and literature and living-of-life as well as in politics."[12] It was this pervasive desire by the cultural and political intelligentsia for a "living life" that Duncan embodied so magnificently. "I went to see her dance whenever she appeared," wrote Dodge, "because she seemed to me, when she was on the stage, to be the most truly living being I had ever seen. There she made one live too, made one know more deeply and vividly the splendid and terrible potentialities one bore within oneself."[13]

Duncan's glorification of individual expression had an appeal that crossed ideological and aesthetic borders. Communist Louis C. Fraina, anarchist Emma Goldman, and socialist Leonard D. Abbott, for example, despite their disparate political orientations, all found respite in a dancing freedom. Goldman, an untiring social dancer, defended her own terpsichorean exploits as a fully appropriate symbol of the Cause, which she described as "freedom, the right to self-expression, everybody's right to beautiful, radiant things."[14] The list of nearly sixty Villagers who made up the "committee for the furtherance of Isadora Duncan's work in America" in 1915 spanned the spectrum: actor Jacob Adler, novelist Gertrude Atherton, activist John Collier, novelist Theodore Dreiser, politician Fola LaFollette, journalist Walter Lippmann, sculptor Paul Manship, music critic Hiram K. Moderwell, editor Mary Fanton Roberts, painter John Butler Yeats.[15]

The project of cultural nationalism was elaborated in journals such as the *Seven Arts*, the *New Republic*, the *Touchstone*, and *The Masses*, and in books such as *The Promise of American Life* and *America's Coming-of-Age*. With Walt Whitman as its patron saint, the *Seven Arts* was founded in 1916 by utopians who believed that America could be regenerated—or, rather, invented—through the expression of art.[16] "It is our faith and the faith of many," the magazine's credo began, "that we are living in the first days of a renascent period, a time which means for America the coming of that national self-consciousness which is the beginning of greatness. In all such epochs the arts cease to be private matters; they become not only the expression of the national life but a means to its enhancement."[17] Van Wyck Brooks, too, in *America's Coming-of-Age* (1915), called for a uniquely American literature. Herbert Croly, founding editor of the *New Republic* in 1914, wrote about the need for national cultural renewal as early as 1909, with *The Promise of American Life*. And so did Randolph Bourne, who wrote for publications such as the *New Republic*, the *Seven Arts*, and the *Dial*. Bourne's politics of liberation "stressed the cultural roots of social change, the necessity for diverse intellectual and ethnic communities, and, above all, the independence and integrity of the individual."[18]

"We shall not develop to the fullest as a nation," wrote Mary Fanton Roberts in 1912, "without the enjoyment of these emotional arts, because no people can achieve all that the sensitive among them desire without expressing the hunger for beauty that is deep in their hearts. A nation must sing, must dance, must make its own music to realize its portion of the world's power for beauty."[19] Roberts, editor of the *Touchstone*, the *Craftsman*, and *Arts and Decoration*, saw in both Duncan and the antiacademic group of artists known as The Eight a uniquely American expression of life—not a strident, patriotic Americanism but a quiet, organic one in which each artist, sensitive to the life of the time, devised her/his own means of expression.

Likewise, the artists and writers of *The Masses*—despite the varying shades of their aesthetic and political allegiances—saw in Duncan a mythic figure of liberation at every level—personal, cultural, national. For the guiding ideal of the magazine, Eastman explained later, "was that every individual should be made free to live and grow in his own chosen way."[20] Besides editors Eastman and Dell, artist John Sloan also admired her, and sketched her in the *Marche Militaire* (Schubert, 1909) for the May 1915 issue. All of the writers and artists of *The Masses* joined in a "rumpus of revolt," explained Howe, "tearing to shreds the genteel tradition that had been dominant in American culture, poking fun at moral prudishness and literary timidity, mocking the deceits of bourgeois individualism, and preaching a peculiarly uncomplicated version of the class struggle."[21] Here was the audience for Duncan—they were as innocent and vital and hopeful as she, as scornful of the Establishment, and just as faithful to the cause of Truth and Beauty. "Things move to Power and Beauty"; Alfred Stieglitz's *Camera Work* quoted H. G. Wells, "I say that much and I have said all that I can say."[22]

Artists as disparate in aesthetic as Stieglitz and Henri, Sloan and Abraham Walkowitz, all admired Duncan passionately. Whether Ashcan realist or emerging abstractionist, or something in between, the artists viewed Duncan in social rather than aesthetic terms. What mattered to them, as independents concerned with destroying the grip of the Academy over art in America, was that she broke with the genteel tradition and endeavored to construct a new kind of art—no matter what aesthetic choices she made in reconfiguring the broken conventions. Not until after the war, which dashed the radicals' utopian vision and their cultural nationalist reading of Duncan, would the dictum of modernism overtake such pluralism.

***

With the outbreak of the war, Duncan fled France for New York in November 1914.[23] At a time when polite society was going mad for Vernon and Irene Castle's sanitized Barbary Coast fox trot, Duncan's general welcome was less than overwhelming. Despite her embrace by the Village radicals, the reviews for her great Greek experiment, the Dionysion season at the Century Opera House in spring 1915, were mixed. And she ended up in well-publicized debt. Desperate for money to start up her dream of an American school, she asked for funds directly from the stage, but to no avail. As time wore on, she became more strident and bitter in her denunciations of the rich, pleasure-seeking philistine Americans.

Being back in New York, surrounded by so much conspicuous and yet inaccessible wealth, must have dredged up unpleasant memories for the dancer. As a child, her respected middle-class family had been ousted from the center of proper society by jail, divorce, and poverty, and she could only take glimpse of the Bay Area's finer families as their children's dance instructor. As an aspiring artist in New York, she entertained in the luxurious gardens and drawing rooms of the Four Hundred, while struggling to provide minimal support for her own family. These formative years in America had been spent grasping at the edges of the upper class, and even now, as an internationally famed artist, she was still grasping.

On the one hand, Duncan espoused a philosophy of liberation that depended upon the inner strength of the individual to overcome oppression—just as she had, ostensibly through sheer grit, risen from ignorance, poverty, and obscurity to a place of renown and respect. On the other hand, she remained wedded to an attitude of entitlement that was entrenched, no doubt, during her several well-heeled years as the lover of Paris Singer, heir to the sewing machine fortune. Because of her genius, she felt, she was *owed* a school, and it was the responsibility of the rich to provide the funding.[24] When they did not, Duncan retaliated. She implicitly criticized them by praising the Russian peasants and the tenement dwellers on the Lower East Side, lauding the emotional liveliness of "the masses" in contrast with the repressed "[upper] classes."[25] Furthermore, she called for a theater architecture that embodied democracy, without the distinction between first- and second-tier boxes and galleries.

Nevertheless, Duncan had chosen, as far back as San Francisco, to establish herself in the world of the elite. She chose to dance only in concert halls, and although this strategy aimed to legitimize dance as an art form, it also effectively narrowed her audiences. In America, her art was never really an art of the people, as she later cast it; rather, her art was a "high" art that required wealthy patronage.[26] When that was no longer forthcoming, Duncan turned her expectations toward governments— American, French, British, Greek, then Soviet.

In May 1915, after having already threatened to depart several months earlier, Duncan did indeed take her indignant leave of America, having shamed some of New York's moneyed art lovers into paying her $12,000 debt with outbursts such as this well-publicized one:

> I am going to an island in the Greek Archipelago to live on bread and onions and worship beauty.
> Because my own country doesn't want me I am renouncing America forever. It has shown me it doesn't want me by allowing me to lose my fortune here, because it does not know art. . . .
> It is the fault of the Government and the rich that you have no art here. It is not the fault of the masses.[27]

So she sailed for Athens, where politics, ironically, interfered with her plans for a school. She returned to war-shattered Paris for a while and then took on an ultimately unsatisfying tour in South America.[28] From there she traveled back to New York, in September 1916.

In New York, Singer arranged for Duncan to give a free, by-invitation-only performance at the Metropolitan Opera House on 21 November, in order to raise funds for the Oeuvre Fratérnelle des Artistes, an organization aiding the families of French theatrical and musical artists. France had been Duncan's artistic and spiritual homeland since her first success there in 1901, and she grieved for its losses. She even loaned out her magnificent school, Bellevue, as an army hospital only a few months after she had opened it.

The Metropolitan program had been given originally at the Trocadéro in Paris the previous April, as a charity benefit for the reconstruction of homes devastated in the war-torn Lorraine region. The first half began with the orchestra, conducted by Oscar Spirescu, playing from César Franck's Symphony in D. Duncan then danced Franck's "Rédemption" (1916) and Schubert's "Ave Maria" (1914). The second half featured Tchaikovsky's Symphony no. 6 ("Pathétique," 1916) and concluded with Claude-Joseph Rouget de Lisle's "La Marseillaise" (1914).

There, in the midst of artists, musicians, actors, intellectuals, and public figures including the Marquis de Polignac, Otto H. Kahn, Mayor Mitchell, Gertrude Atherton, Anna Pavlova, and Mrs. Dana Gibson, Duncan was given a standing ovation for her final number, a rendition of France's national anthem (figures 51 and 52). Duncan's body was enfolded in a blood-colored robe that bared her shoulders and, according to some reviewers, bared a breast at her moment of triumph.[29] Part of her effect was gained by gesture, part by the massing of her body, and the largest part by facial expression.[30] She was a heroic figure, towering aloft and spring-ing to action as the music sounded the call to arms. One reviewer, and prob-ably many more spectators, saw echoed in her poses François Rude's Arc de Triomphe sculpture of La Marseillaise, which was being reclaimed as a nationalist symbol in the work of the wartime Parisian avant-garde (fig-ure 53).[31] Duncan portrayed the departure of the troops to battle against the invaders, and as the dance went on, she was beaten to her knees, yet unconquered, and rose to triumph at the end. According to one account,

> In four stanzas Miss Duncan danced (or mimed) it, the first with mar-tial mien, the second in proud and triumphant fashion, the third as tho it were a prophecy of approaching glory amid the anguish of struggle, and the last with the hot intoxication of mob enthusiasm. There is no more potent music in the world than this song of the volunteer Marseillians. And Miss Duncan has never been more splendidly, more unapproachably, the artist.[32]

Duncan explained to one interviewer that the *Marseillaise* was more than just a call to arms: it was about the human determination never to yield, never to surrender.[33] In fact, this inner struggle against adversity became the overriding theme for the rest of Duncan's life and art: the liberation of individuals, of nations, and of all humanity from social constraints and political oppression. If Duncan's earlier dances followed the form of music and embodied a fluid self freely circulating, her middle and late dances, dating from this period, took the form of allegory, depicting a self triumphantly mastered, through adversity, oppression, and fate. In *Revolutionary* (Scriabin, c. 1924), for example, the soloist, representing the archetypal victim of oppression, unshackles her wrists and bangs at the door of the oppressor, finally freeing and empowering herself. Similarly, in *Marche Slav* (Tchaikovsky, 1917), a Russian muzhik rises from slavery to freedom. In some cases, however, fate won. Duncan saw Franz Liszt's "Funérailles" (1918), for example, as "a human being reaching for hap-piness and each time falling crushed to earth again."[34]

Duncan repeated her Metropolitan program—which had been widely reported in the press—for the public on 6 March 1917. On the eve of America's entrance into the war, she commanded one of the largest crowds of the season, the box office line rivaling that of a Caruso evening of grand opera.[35] The program notes framed the performance, in frankly political terms, as

> Miss Duncan's story of the present world struggle—from the opening number expressing the primitive struggle of man's spirit upward toward

self-mastery, to the finale, the most famous battle song and cry of man's right to freedom in the world—in which she pictures France, heroic, beaten to her knees, but unconquered and rising at last to triumph—typifying the cause of freedom everywhere.[36]

At the evening's end, after dancing the *Marseillaise*, Duncan made what was perhaps the grandest gesture of her American career. She peeled away her crimson robe, revealing the silken folds of the Stars and Stripes underneath.[37] The orchestra struck up the "Star-Spangled Banner," and the audience cut loose, some of them cheering "bravo" and others giving out a rebel yell. As Duncan repeated her gestures from the *Marseillaise*, the audience sang along with the orchestra. Still draped in the flag, she told the house that wartime is not a time for artists, who would rather be fighting in the trenches or nursing the wounded. After the war, Duncan promised, she would establish a school in America "to dance the songs of freedom."[38] She was greeted with thunderous applause, and the heavy golden curtains swung back many times for the dancer. It was a scene that one reviewer described as "the height of pandemonium."[39]

Duncan appealed to the American revival in patriotic idealism, which had begun even before the war. As early as 1912, the Progressives under Theodore Roosevelt proclaimed a "New Nationalism," and with the advent of war in Europe, the feeling intensified. According to historian Henry F. May, "The events of 1915–1917, with war alternately coming closer and receding, made the West impatient. The tendency that gained most from this impatience was neither isolationism nor interventionism but nationalism."[40] Hardly anyone remained unaffected by the war. Even Anatole France renounced his pacifism, and H. G. Wells was converted to patriotism.[41]

The Village radicals were a major exception, however, and Duncan's enthusiasm for the war, which allied her with the elite New Yorkers who were advocating intervention, cost her the support of some antiwar Villagers who had earlier idolized her. According to communist critic Joseph Freeman, the left-wing intellectuals, who opposed American intervention, were dismayed with her patriotic dances. Floyd Dell now "heaped . . . bitter scorn" on the woman he had once called a revelation.[42]

With the *Marseillaise*, and its "Stars and Stripes" variation, Duncan imbricated herself within the tradition of Woman-as-Nation, recalling France's mythical Marianne by way of the Statue of Liberty, which, modeled on Marianne, was gaining its belated status as an American patriotic icon through its prominence in the popular Liberty Loan posters.[43]

Echoing these and other war posters, many of which figured the nation as a towering and powerful woman wrapped in the flag (figure 54), Duncan played the benign Amazon, also recalling the immense central figure in Eugène Delacroix's *Liberty Leading the People*, which depicted a half-realistic, half-allegorical figure of Liberty emerging bare-breasted, with gun and flag in hand, from the barricades of the French revolutionaries during July 1830 (figure 55). Duncan was casting her American nationalism from a crucible of revived French patriotism, which was enthusiastically embraced by an upper class pushing to join the war on the side of the Allies.[44] No longer the gamboling nymph, Duncan was now the tragic heroine, à la Lady Liberty, whose maternal strength could, and would, lead the nation to a victory both political and moral.

Duncan's newfound role as symbol of wartime American nationalism was constructed partly from a recent change in her public persona. In 1913, her two children had drowned in the river Seine. Overnight, the American press made a mourning Niobe out of the dancer, never even alluding to the children's questionable paternity. She was now cast as the virtuous mother, a Madonna. When the papers narrated how she recovered from her tragic personal loss by tending selflessly to the needy in an Albanian refugee settlement, it was the first time that the American press treated her with unqualified respect rather than a mixture of admiration and bemusement. And when she landed back on American soil, with her students, in November 1914, the papers reported respectfully on the Duncan method of education. The dancer certainly produced and reproduced the Madonna image: she included her students in the New York performances; she spoke endlessly about her school, and she danced Schubert's "Ave Maria" along with patriotic allegories such as Tchaikovsky's "Pathétique."

The newspaper headlines described Duncan's *Pathétique* as a "war trilogy," whose patriotic fervor enthralled her audiences both in New York and in California, where she toured in December 1917. The first, adagio movement was played by the orchestra only. The second, scherzo, featured the dancer, in a springtime mood, ingenuously and inquiringly moving about the stage. Contrasted with that was the allegro vivace third movement, in which she made a repeated call to arms, a militant attempt to rouse an apparently unresponsive nation. The finale was an embodiment of utter grief and tragedy. One reviewer wrote:

> The gliding *scherzo* is a spring song of peace, say the fields of Picardy in July, 1914; the *Allegro Vivace* sets forth the approach of battle and the frenzy of physical heroism; the final *adagio* is an epic lamentation for the

Figure 51. Duncan's nationalistic rendition of the Marseillaise *during World War I (figures 51 and 52) recalled the French tradition embodied in François Rude's* La Marseillaise *(figure 53) and Eugène Delacroix's* Lady Liberty Leading the People *(figure 55) by way of the Statue of Liberty, which was transformed into a patriotic symbol by war posters (figure 54). Photo: Arnold Genthe. Courtesy of the Museum of the City of New York and the Dance Collection of the New York Public Library for the Performing Arts, Astor, Lenox and Tilden Foundations.*

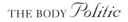

Figure 52. Duncan in the Marseillaise, *drawn by José Clará. Courtesy of the Dance Collection of the New York Public Library for the Performing Arts, Astor, Lenox and Tilden Foundations.*

Figure 53. François Rude's La Marseillaise.

Right is Might!

Figure 54. World War I poster featuring the Statue of Liberty. Courtesy of the Library of Congress.

Figure 55. Eugène Delacroix's Lady Liberty Leading the People. *Courtesy of the Louvre.*

slain. Let the spring song be what it will, Miss Duncan takes it as lightly as the young man's fancy his thoughts of love. She hippity-hops easily around the stage, gesturing pleasantly, and only at times making her dancing accord closely with the music. . . .

In the *Allegro Vivace* she seems to see herself as some goddess haranguing the people to battle. With curious gestures which we have not noticed before, she points to some distant field of conflict; at times she brings her hands near her breast and seems to plead; again she imperiously straightens up as tho to command. Her index finger becomes eloquent as it beckons or points the way.[45]

Again, Duncan invoked the nationalist/maternal Amazon, who encourages the good fight but also mourns her dead sons.

Duncan continued intermittently with her concerts at the Metropolitan through April, with the program only somewhat modified when accompanied by her students. The boxes were draped with the flags of the Allies for distinguished guests such as the mayor and the consul generals of France, Great Britain, Russia, Italy, Japan, Cuba, and Romania. Always, she concluded with her rousing renditon of the "Marseillaise." "At that time I believed, as did many others," she wrote in her autobiography, "that the whole world's hope of liberty, regeneration and civilisation depended on the Allies winning the war, so at the end of each performance I danced the 'Marseillaise.' "[46]

Duncan's patriotic dances were hailed as possessing a dramatic vigor and intensity rarely experienced in dance. Duncan finally had found content powerful enough to suit the tragic acting style she had first unveiled here in 1911, with the premiere of her *Liebestod*. The patriotic spectacles suited her titanic gesture, her imperious grandeur, her heroic build.[47] She was, after all, now forty years old. If critics and audiences had resisted the dancer's new works—clamoring always for her older, musical numbers in which she was the lithe, lyrical young goddess—now they cheered her new style, which critic Carl Van Vechten situated somewhere between dancing and pantomime. "Like any other new art," he wrote, "it is not to be understood at first and I confess in the beginning it said nothing to me, but eventually I began to take pleasure in watching it. Now Isadora's poetic and imaginative interpretation of the symphonic interlude from César Franck's *Rédemption* is full of beauty and meaning to me."[48]

Duncan had begun working on the basic gesture of *Rédemption*—one that began in black despair and ended in hope—in her studio before the deaths of her children.[49] After seeing her performance in Paris on 9 April 1915, the poet René Fauchois wrote a brief poem describing the dance as one in which a "damaged" soul in the black night struggles, like Michelangelo's slaves, to awaken to the dawn's first light, and then finally bursts forth, rising to stand triumphantly in the full light of day.[50] *Rédemption* was yet another allegory of struggle, but this time Duncan scarcely rose from her knees. Predating Martha Graham's formal experiments with minimal dances such as *Dance* (1929), Duncan used just her neck, throat, shoulders, head, and arms as her means of expression:

> Miss Duncan was discovered upon the deep shadowed stage, utterly prostrate, her white robes draped down upon her huddled figure as upon a thing grotesquely useless and inert. Then slowly, laboriously, the stir of life came, one could see it only in the trembling fingers at first, then along the uplifting arms. Then to knees, then to full height—and the figure could stride and assert itself in broad, deliberate motion. It was all a cycle of slow gestures, unalterably slow and stern, every inward impulse of it seeming to find fight and oppression from the unseen force without. And when, in the end, self mastery came, with head high and face gladdened with the pride of peace, it was as if a great battle of humanity unlimited had been enacted through one strong, transparent soul.[51]

Duncan's life had been spent freeing herself from any convention that stifled her artistic imperative, and within the context of the Village radicals her dancing had embodied a nationalism that focused on the Whitmanesque individual. Within the context of World War I, her dancing embodied a nationalism that focused on the allegorical, collective body. The *Marseillaise, Pathétique*, and *Rédemption* were some of her most praised and popular dances, at least in part because they yoked nationalism and motherhood into a sentimental American combination that exploited the country's residual Victorian moralism. For Duncan, who had been seeking a movement style appropriate for her maturing, thickening body, the heroic, martial image of a modern American Amazon was a successful way of insinuating herself into the nationalist discourse of the wartime elite, which emphasized the power, control, and moral righteousness of America. When she returned to America in 1922, however, after ten months in Soviet Russia, she would find herself branded as a traitor to that nationalist credo.

***

When the Russians overthrew their tsar in March 1917, Duncan paid tribute to the revolutionaries with a celebratory performance at the Metropolitan Opera House on Wednesday afternoon, 28 March.[52] Besides America and France, Russia (which she had toured at least six times since 1904) had been, and would continue to be, an important host to her art. She told a quite sincere—but nevertheless apocryphal—story in her autobiography about the shock of witnessing, on her first Russian tour, the mass funeral procession the morning after "Bloody Sunday," when the tsar's troops massacred crowds of peaceably protesting peasants: "There, before this seemingly endless procession, this tragedy, I vowed myself and my forces to the service of the people and the down-trodden."[53] She may have pitied the peasants, who could hardly afford tickets to see her perform, but she nevertheless enjoyed the luxury of the royal elite, who feted her grandly. Fifteen years later it was the young Soviet government, ironically enough, that offered her state sponsorship for a school.

With the Russian revolution, Duncan's philosophy of liberation found its ideal domain. The revolution gave substance to her vision of a communal dance school, where none of the students, who lived, learned, and played together, had to pay. It gave content to her utopian vision. It renewed her antipathy toward the rich, toward those who had the things she never had as a child, toward those who commercialized art. "In my red tunic," she wrote later on, "I have constantly danced the Revolution and the call to arms of the oppressed."[54] Duncan was enthralled by urgent human drama such as grief and oppression: that which is driven by inner necessity, which resists legislation. Thus the Russian revolution appealed to her as the upswelling of human suffering and injustice against its oppressor. "On the night of the Russian Revolution," she wrote, "I danced with a terrible fierce joy. My heart was bursting within me at the release of all those who had suffered, been tortured, died in the cause of Humanity."[55]

In April Duncan added to her patriotic repertoire another allegorical solo, this one to Tchaikovsky's "Marche Slav." It was similar in its dramatic trajectory to the *Marseillaise*, but this time representing the Russian muzhik rising from slavery to freedom. She did not aim to mirror the music, and she barely moved more than a foot from the spot where she began. This is how critic Van Vechten described the dance:

> With her hands bound behind her back, groping, stumbling, head bowed, knees bent, she struggles forward, clad only in a short red garment that barely covers her thighs. With furtive glances of extreme despair she peers above and ahead. When the strains of *God Save the Czar* are first heard in the orchestra she falls to her knees and you see the peasant shuddering under the blows of the knout. The picture is a tragic one, cumulative in its horrific details. Finally comes the moment of release and here Isadora makes one of her great effects. She does not spread her arms apart with a wide gesture. She brings them forward slowly and we observe with horror that they have practically forgotten how to move at all. They are crushed, these hands, crushed and bleeding after their long serfdom; they are not hands at all but claws, broken, twisted piteous claws! The expression of frightened, almost uncomprehending, joy with which Isadora concludes the march is another stroke of her vivid imaginative genius.[56]

The *Marche Slav* was greeted almost as enthusiastically as the *Marseillaise*.

At this point, before the Bolsheviks seized power, Duncan could intertwine the Russian revolution with Allied patriotism by appealing to her audience's sympathy for the politically oppressed and to their belief in the might of the right. But when Duncan returned to America in October 1922, after having established a school in Moscow, and with a "Red" husband, poet Sergei Esenin, in tow, the public's sympathies had shifted radically. The sort of innocent, nondoctrinaire "revolution" that Duncan represented was no longer possible. "Once the Soviet Union existed, a great deal of free speculation became difficult," intellectual historian Thomas Bender has explained. "Concrete positions on its policies seemed to be demanded. With the availability of such a litmus test, the tyranny of ideological correctness was encouraged."[57] Being a "revolutionary" was no longer a romantic badge of honor associated with the fight for democratic reforms; it now denoted a dangerous communist sympathizer out to destroy the American way of life. Where audiences once had seen freedom in the dancer's body, now they saw sedition.

***

Duncan was naive enough to believe in revolution without ideology. To her, communism was the renewal of democracy without the "greed" and "villainy" and "class injustice" of capitalism.[58] She saw no contradiction between her own American ideals and those of the Soviets. Thus she described the streets of Moscow as "the picture of the song of the 'Open Road' of Walt Whitman," whom she claimed as the first Bolshevik.[59] She could never understand why America, itself born of a revolution, did not support all revolutions, including the Russians' and including her own. "I am not an anarchist or a Bolshevik," she would later tell reporters as she left America for the last time. "My husband and I are revolutionists. All geniuses worthy of the name are. Every artist has to be one to make a mark in the world today."[60]

Duncan arrived in Moscow in July 1921.[61] She had accepted an invitation from People's Commissar of Education Anatoly Lunacharsky because, simply, she had no other. No doubt she would have agreed to a similar offer from any country, but the Soviet Union's anticapitalist ideology especially appealed to Duncan's disillusionment with the refusal of American millionaires to fund her school. "Perhaps I am becoming a Bolshevik," she said at one point, after having been accused of being one. "But all my life I have wanted to teach children, to have free schools and a free theater. America rejected this, but there they still have child labor, and only the rich can see the opera, and beauty is commercialized by theater managers and motion picture magnates. All they want is money, money, money."[62] The theater in America was no longer a temple, as she saw it, but a house of prostitution.

But Duncan herself had succumbed to a lifestyle of decadence in the West, admittedly as "a poor pagan sybarite, used to soft beds, good food."[63] Rhetorically, the austere postrevolutionary lifestyle offered her the opportunity to return to a purer place, with "Art" at its center: it promised to redeem her as an "Artiste." The dancer was no longer interested in the effete existence of an aesthete but in the vigorous life of a true artist, embedded within the sinews of revolutionary life. The young Soviet nation, Duncan claimed, offered her release from the oppressive laws of the state. "There is none of that restraint upon artistic effort that is found in all bourgeois lands," she explained to a reporter. "In the latter the conventions, the laws and the customs are such that no artist can attempt what is really in her soul. There is always the overhanging law, law, law, which may be one of law books, or one of mere social custom. But it is restraint, and there can be no art under restraint."[64]

Because Lunacharsky's project was to make art a thing of the people, Duncan could again indulge in the kind of unsullied idealism—the belief in universal love and harmony—that had originally fueled her. She arrived in Moscow full of what Lunacharsky described as her "militant communism."[65] She chided a group of Soviet leaders on their hypocritically bourgeois behavior at a party, and she volunteered to live in a peasant cottage. She lasted there only a week.

A month after Duncan's school finally opened, severe famine forced the hands of the Bolsheviks, who instituted the National Economic Policy, which allowed private enterprise and eased foreign trade. As Duncan explained it to a reporter from the *Daily Worker*, the American communist paper, "The brutal attacks from outside and the greed of many inside have forced a retreat to capitalism. We understand how necessary it has been, how unavoidable, yet the spectacle is a sad one."[66] As a result, Duncan's funding was cut, and she again was forced to raise school funds through her own performances. She toured the provinces, but without much financial gain, so she decided to return to the U.S., under the management of Sol Hurok. Whether America or the Soviet Union, nothing much had changed. She was still dancing for money. "My dream of a school devoted to the expression of life in terms of the dance came true in Russia," she lamented. "Unfortunately, the catastrophe of these last years, especially the famine, have ended the dream."[67]

Hurok recalled in his autobiography just how ignorant Duncan was of the America to which she had returned: "This, remember, was 1922. The wave of reaction to the war, to Wilson, to liberalism, was rolling up in a fearful tide. It was a year when red was the color of all evil, and to call a man a Bolshevik was to damn his eternal soul as well as to send his earthly body to jail."[68] Although the Red Scare had peaked in late 1919 and early 1920, when striking workers were automatically labeled "Reds," foreign language meetings were banned, union and socialist headquarters were raided by police, and alien dissidents were rounded up and deported en masse, by late 1922 America still was steeped in a postwar nativist mode that conflated immigrants, unions, radicals, and Bolsheviks. To the average American, who for several years had heard and read the propaganda manufactured by politicians, antiunion employers, veterans, racists, patriotic groups, and sensational journalists, Bolshevism meant anarchy and murder. Even more, it threatened to infect the rest of world—even our own shores—as communist revolution had already spread to Hungary and Germany. The Soviet famine elicited pity, and the National Economic Policy, an apparent turn toward capitalism, inspired optimism, but Americans still abided by the Wilsonian principle of "100 percent Americanism," which in the decade following the Red Scare translated into the continued drive toward an ideological conformity that left no space for organized labor, immigrants, and communists. Where the government's efforts left off, organizations such as the National Security League, the American Legion, and the Ku Klux Klan were picking up the slack: they endorsed immigration restrictions and opposed radicals, unions, and pacifists. The radical movement in general had been seriously curtailed by the Red Scare, and the two incipient communist parties in particular were driven underground. Their memberships dropped significantly. Not until 1923 did communists constitute themselves as a single, completely legal party, and not until the 1930s did the party gain its foothold in New York's artistic and intellectual communities.[69]

It is not surprising, then, that, Duncan and Esenin were denied immediate entry when they arrived in New York Harbor in early October 1922. They were detained aboard ship overnight; immigration officials questioned Duncan about her communist sympathies for two hours the next morning at Ellis Island. Reported on the front page of the *New York Times*, the situation gave Duncan an opportunity to insist publicly that her mission was artistic and humanitarian rather than political. As if to deflect any questions about her national loyalty, she pointed out that she was "the great-granddaughter of General William Duncan of the Revolutionary War."[70] When reporters asked her if she was a communist, she was reported to have replied, "Rot, rot, rot."[71]

Duncan was now forty-five, even though she told the press she was thirty-eight. She dressed quite fashionably, without a hint of the Greek.[72] Although her body was shorn of its lithe and supple youth, she appeared surprisingly slender and fit. Still, she was no longer a dancer of vivid motion. *Boston Evening Transcript* critic H. T. Parker explained:

> Instead, she is becoming sculptress, while the medium upon which she
> works is her own body, her own mantling raiment. For Miss Duncan no
> longer arrays herself in a few scarves of flying chiffon. Oftener than not
> last evening, she was clothed from head to foot in far-flung veils and man-
> tles that she might set them flowing in curves and lay plane against or
> upon plane. Becoming sculptural, she becomes also more indepen-
> dent of the music.[73]

For these late, sculptural dances, Duncan chose the large, flooding music
of Wagner and Tchaikovsky.[74] Wagner's, in particular, was more about scale
than rhythm, more about space than time—or, rather, a mythic space
unmarked by time. Ironically, it was through the work of the proponent
of "music-drama" that Duncan moved away from music or its story as the
architecture of her choreography. She did not "act out" the drama of
Wagner's scenes—the warrior maidens riding the skies, for instance.
Instead, she remained the chorus, abstracting and embodying distilled emotion through a minimum of means. With these solos she seemed to be coming ever closer to the "divine presence" that she had seen in Duse: that
tremendous force of dynamic movement communicated through stillness.[75]
A teenaged Helen Tamiris, who would develop into a leading modern
choreographer of the next generation, saw this quality in *Pathétique* when
Duncan performed it in Brooklyn:

> She started on the ground, lying close to the floor and—it took a long
> time—the only physical action was the very slow movement which
> carried her from prone to erect with arms outstretched. At the finish,
> everyone was crying and I was crying, too, although it took me many
> years to understand what she was doing—that she was living an action
> or inner motivation and I was living with her.[76]

In Louisville, John Martin, who later became the country's first major dance
critic, for the *New York Times*, and the chief apologist for modern dance, also
was moved to tears.[77]

By now, Duncan's audiences rather expected her to make curtain
speeches. The talks started out mildly, with the dancer invoking Whitman
and speaking of building a bridge between America and the Soviet Union.
Duncan told a Carnegie Hall audience that she did not preach Bolshevism
but only love—the love of mother for child, of lover for wife, and her own
for the top gallery.[78] But Duncan grew impatient as the papers became
more insistent on interpreting her as a communist sympathizer, ensconced
in the Soviet power structure. So she baited them. "There is a new idea

of living now," she told an audience in November 1922. "It is not home life. It isn't family life. It isn't patriotism, but the International."[79]

From New York Duncan went to Boston, where another brouhaha made the national headlines, setting the tone for the rest of the tour's coverage. After her opening night at Symphony Hall, many of the local papers ridiculed her performance, taking issue with the looseness of her tunics. She retaliated in her Saturday performance with a curtain speech, defending her theories. "If canned Greek art is permitted," she asked, pointing to the nude statues in the niches around the hall, "why object to the beauty of the living body?" As she waved her red scarf, the dancer explained it as "the color of life and vigor," while gray, the color of New Englanders, is "dull and gray." Only thirteen years before, Duncan had declared that Boston was Bacchic, but now it was "the hot-bed of Puritan prudery and vulgarity."[80]

When the mayor himself publicly accused Duncan's dancing of being indecent, she denied the charges, letting go her bluestocking indignation:

> "Every time I come to America they [the press] howl around me like a pack of wolves," she said plaintively. "They treat me as though I were a criminal. They say I am a Bolshevist propagandist. It is not true. These are the same dances that I danced before the Bolshevists were invented. In Boston the papers said I took off my dress and waved it crying, "I am red." That is an absolute lie. . . .
>
> [. . .]
>
> "Surely it [the red tunic] is not more indecent than the sight of forty girls in flesh colored drawers dancing the 'can can' on your vaudeville stages. They may be seen any day. But my daring, which has inspired artists over the world to a love of the beautiful, may not be seen because an Irish politician in Boston says it is not proper. There is American Puritanism for you."
>
> [. . .]
>
> "It appears my political sin is in asking America to help the starving Russian children. I have fifty gathered near Moscow now—children of exceptional talent. I do not know whether they have enough to eat or not. I wanted to bring them here to dance with me but there was not money enough. And so I must raise money to take back to them. As for politics, I am not interested except as every mother must be interested, for the sake of her children's future."[81]

Nevertheless, she was banned from the city, and three federal government departments ordered complete reports on her alleged Bolshevik declarations.[82]

The Boston scandal framed the rest of the tour. In Washington, the evangelist Billy Sunday demanded that the "Bolshevik hussy" be deported. In Indianapolis, the mayor ordered policemen to monitor her performance, lest the "nude dancer" sully his fair city. In Cleveland, Hart Crane—at the time a young poet still straining against his middle-class life—went to see Duncan in an all-Tchaikovsky program. He reported to a friend:

> It was glorious beyond words, and sad beyond words too, from the rude and careless reception she got here. It was like a wave of life, a flaming gale that passed over the heads of the nine thousand in the audience without evoking response other than silence and some maddening cat-calls. After the first movement of the "Pathétique" she came to the fore of the stage, her hands extended. Silence,—the most awful silence! I started clapping furiously until she disappeared behind the draperies. At least one tiny sound should follow her from all that audience. She continued through the performance with utter indifference for the audience and with such intensity of gesture and such plastique grace as I have never seen, although the music was sometimes almost drowned out by the noises from the hall. I felt like rushing to the stage, but I was stimulated almost beyond the power to walk straight. When it was all over she came to the fore-stage again in the little red dress that had so shocked Boston, as she stated, and among other things told the people to go home and take from the bookshelf the works of Walt Whitman, and turn to the section called "Calamus." Ninety-nine percent of them had never heard of Whitman, of course, but that was part of the beauty of her gesture. Glorious to see her there with her right breast and nipple quite exposed, telling the audience that the truth was not pretty, that it was really indecent and telling them (boobs!) about Beethoven, Tschaikowsky, and Scriabin. She is now on her way back to Moscow, so I understand, where someone will give her some roses for her pains.[83]

Back in New York, St. Marks-in-the-Bouwerie withdrew an invitation for Duncan to lecture on "the moralizing effect of dancing on the human soul." Esenin, in one of his drunken, violent spells, made anti-Semitic remarks at a gathering of Russian-Jewish poets in the Bronx, causing a scandal. At the Brooklyn Academy of Music, Duncan's pianist left the stage as she began an encore, which ended abruptly after she bumped into the piano. "The lurid headlines which trumpeted her march across the country caused mayoral apoplexy and occasional cancellations," Hurok recalled later on, "but they also assured long lines at the box offices where she did appear."[84]

Those lurid headlines were the product of a press still fanning the flames of nativism. The banner of the *New York American* (the flagship paper of William Randolph Hearst's national chain and news service), for example, included a bald eagle, on whose wings were emblazoned "Character," "Quality," "Accuracy," and "Enterprise." Above the eagle's head were printed the words "America First," and below, a banner read "An American

Paper for the American People." Headlines celebrated heroes such as Henry Ford and Charles A. Lindbergh and sensationalized sordid dramas. The Hearst chain, the most adroit at exploiting sex, crime, and scandal, seemed to dog Duncan around the country. Feeling badgered by questions about her personal life, she blamed the papers in general and Hearst in particular for the failure of her tour.

The reasons for its failure, however, lay deeper than that.

The moment that Duncan had accepted Lunacharsky's invitation to create a school for the fledgling communist country, she was labeled a "Soviet dancer" who had "joined the reddest ranks of Bolshevism."[85] Her comments and activities, her marriage, her performance to commemorate the fourth anniversary of the revolution, were all covered in the American press, so by the time she returned here, she had already been deemed a traitor. The former Lady Liberty, maternal and majestic, had transgressed a geographical/sexual/ideological border, and was thus branded a communist whore.

Even though she repeatedly disavowed any interest in preaching politics, and preferred to talk about her needy Moscow schoolchildren, Duncan was held responsible for the evils of communism, through her dancing, through her marriage to Esenin, and even through the color of her costumes. Red was the color that had signified life and passion to an entire generation of physical culturalists, and it had fueled the nationalist spectacles of the *Marseillaise* and the *Pathétique*. Now, after the display of red flags had actually been prohibited in twenty-eight states,[86] it was seen as brazen communist propaganda. Even her hennaed hair was described as "a Bolshevik shade of red."[87] Although her Carnegie Hall audiences—constituted, at least in part, by pro-Soviet liberals, leftists, and intellectuals—cheered her as ever, and even demonstrated Soviet sympathy, some of her old bourgeois friends and radical followers did abandon her. The population at large saw her as she was constructed in the newspapers: as the traitorous whore.

Duncan left America for good on 3 February 1923. Like many other artists and intellectuals after her, she spurned the country's growing materialism. Duncan was bitter about the scandal-mongering newspapers and about the petty parochial politicians. She abhorred Prohibition and despised the billboards cluttering the landscape. Among other things, she called America narrow-minded, hypocritical, loathsome, stupid, penurious, ignorant, smug, self-righteous, sanctimonious, and intolerant. She criticized the country's marriage laws, child-rearing practices, commercialism, and overall mental and spiritual slavishness. "Routine, weary routine, the same old table in the middle of the same old floor, the same old books on the same old table—that's America."[88] What more proof did the public need that Isadora Duncan was an undesirable? Even three of her own pupils, in anticipation of an American tour, felt the need to publicly repudiate their mentor's "political beliefs."[89] Soon after Duncan's fitful farewell, a Department of Labor hearing (arranged by an indignant secretary of labor) ruled that she was no longer an American citizen, because she had married a Russian.[90] The U.S. considered her a Soviet citizen, while the Soviet Union, ironically enough, considered her an American. The government effectively silenced Duncan by repositioning her as an "alien," literally and metaphorically sentenced to remain outside the country's borders until she could prove her loyalty.

7.

Isadora Duncan—both the woman and the legend—found herself out of step with her homeland by the time of her last tour. She was met with hostility, not only because her body politic was perceived as seditious by an anticommunist public, but also because her dancing body was considered old-fashioned by the postwar avant-garde and because her female body failed to resonate with the youth-oriented, pleasure-loving culture of flappers and Ziegfeld girls. Sol Hurok described her as "Hera, the queen goddess, ripened to the full curves of maturity, with the shadows of twilight already dark on her face."[1]

After she left America, the papers continued to carry news of Duncan's life in Europe, covering her financial woes, her marital exploits, her protest against the electrocutions of Sacco and Vanzetti, even her pitiable suicide attempt. She made good copy, a bizarre curiosity whose colorful

EPILOGUE: TWILIGHT OF AN AMERICAN *Goddess*

life could be rehashed for entertainment and shock value. In photographs she was no longer pictured full-length, as a dancer; instead she became a head shot, the disembodied journalistic shorthand for celebrity. Duncan was no longer an "Artist" but a mere "personality."

By the twenties, America was much more complex than Duncan's philosophy allowed. Walter Lippmann, who had helped promote the cult of experience before the war, described its naiveté from several decades' distance:

> We had vague notions that mankind, liberated from want and drudgery, would spend its energies writing poetry, painting pictures, exploring the

stellar spaces, singing folk songs, dancing with Isadora Duncan in the public square, and producing Ibsen in little theaters.

We seem completely to have overlooked the appetite of mankind for the automobile, the moving picture, the radio, bridge parties, tabloids and the stock market.[2]

Indeed, the twenties was an era of conspicuous consumption for the well-to-do, the dawn of the advertising industry, and, with the expansion of radio, movies, and print media, the start of a mass media culture. Trends were set by the young, "on the dance floor, in the beauty parlor, and the sports field."[3] The simple certainties of the late nineteenth century and the progressive movement had begun to disintegrate by the time the country entered the war, and by the twenties they had disappeared completely. Darwin was supplanted by Einstein, and Nietzsche by Freud. Instead of utopianism, intellectuals tended toward disillusion. Such were "the lost generation" of authors including Ernest Hemingway and F. Scott Fitzgerald, and the thirty writers who contributed to literary critic Harold Stearns's 1922 volume *Civilization in the United States*. They concluded that the country did not practice what it preached, deluded itself with an Anglo-Saxon self-image, and suffered from "emotional and aesthetic starvation."[4]

Avant-garde artists were less insistent on the unity of art and life, more interested in artistic experimentation for its own sake. They were no longer driven by a need for self-expression and spontaneity, but by a need for the discovery of the new. The kind of vague, utopian blend of arts and politics that characterized *The Masses* and the Dodge salon disappeared as cultural nationalism gave way to formalism. In the paintings of Max Weber, John Marin, Marsden Hartley, and Arthur Dove, nature moved from the ideal to the abstract. In poetry, William Carlos Williams symbolized that gradual shift from a love of the beautiful (he was an early admirer of Duncan's) to a more rigorous interest in creating new form.

As early as 1917, Margaret Anderson had accused Duncan of being a "pseudo-artist": "a woman of small intelligence, a monument of undirected adolescent vision, an ingrained sentimentalist."[5] Anderson was founder (in 1914) and editor of the *Little Review*, a prestigious literary magazine whose embrace of modernism was most profoundly exemplified by its serialized publication of James Joyce's *Ulysses*. Anderson had waited five years to see Duncan, and her report, in the April 1917 issue, of "Isadore [*sic*] Duncan's Misfortune" recorded her bitter disappointment. Self-consciously speaking for her entire generation, Anderson had no patience for Duncan's expressive body, which, "moving always *inside* the music, never dominating it, never even controlling it, never holding or pushing it to an authentic end,"[6] failed to foreground its own formal means. The dancer's privileging of effect over form was anathema to the modernist editor, for "the best—perhaps the only—test for Art is that your emotion is focused on the forms in the picture, not sidetracked to what those forms suggest to you or inform you of—as in descriptive painting or any other bad expression."[7] Anderson concluded that "the spectacle of her dancing draped in an American flag is bad enough; but her unconsciousness of how emotion must be transmuted through a significant medium is to me far more sad."[8] The manifesto completed, a passage from Joyce filled the rest of the page.

Duncan saw the formalist aesthetic advancing, and she attacked it directly: "I don't believe in the narrow bourgeois formula of art for art's sake," she told an interviewer. "Art must be based upon and flow from life."[9] As new as Duncan's dancing had been, it had been built upon romantic ideas about morality and spirituality that could not accommodate the more secular interests of modern art. She remained interested in effect over form, and, clinging to the monist ideal of continuity, she refused to celebrate the fragmentation of the modern, as epitomized by jazz dancing. Thus she participated in the "innovative nostalgia" that historian Robert M. Crunden has identified as the contradictory condition of progressive art, seen paradigmatically in the work of Charles Ives and Frank Lloyd Wright.[10] Duncan may have helped to negotiate the transition from late-nineteenth-century Victorianism to early-twentieth-century modernism, but she never did emerge fully into the new aesthetic order.

Similarly, Duncan remained devout to her Edwardian image of Woman. Ironically, as the American ideal of the female body became younger and more kinetic—from the wan, ethereal Steel-Engraving Lady to the younger, bicycle-riding Gibson Girl to the independent, boyish flapper—Duncan became older and less kinetic (figure 56). As a cultural icon, Duncan's aging body was eclipsed by a number of younger women: Irene Castle (figure 57), who popularized an innocent girlishness with her willowy silhouette and bobbed hair; the iconic flapper (figure 58), who worked as a secretary by day and danced the Charleston at night; champion swimmer Annette Kellermann (figure 59), who proved that the strength and endurance of the female body was part of its beauty; and Margaret Gorman (figure 60), the wholesome Mary Pickford lookalike who won the first Miss America Pageant in Atlantic City in 1921.

Figure 56. As the American ideal of the female body became younger and more kinetic, the dancer, here with husband Sergei Esenin in 1922, became older and less kinetic. Courtesy of the Dance Collection of the New York Public Library for the Performing Arts, Astor, Lenox and Tilden Foundations.

Figure 57. Ballroom dancer Irene Castle, here with husband/partner Vernon Castle, possessed the lean, girlish look required by the modern dances so popular in the teens. By that time, it was not Duncan but Castle, with her bobbed hair, who was setting the trends for American women. Courtesy of the Library of Congress.

Figure 58. In contrast to the streamlined clothing and motion of the youthful flapper, the aging and thickening Duncan appeared matronly. Courtesy of the Library of Congress.

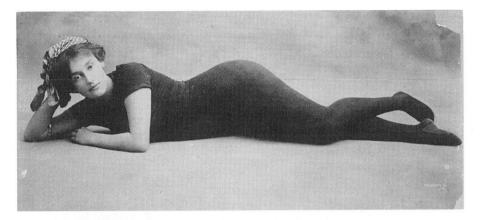

Figures 59–60. By the 1920s, Duncan's middle-aged body was eclipsed by a number of younger cultural icons such as swimmer/ beauty expert Annette Kellermann (top) and Margaret Gorman, the first Miss America (bottom). Courtesy of the Library of Congress.

Nevertheless, Duncan waxed nostalgic about her younger years when "thinness was not equivalent to spirituality."[11] Confronted by the narrow, streamlined, overtly sexual body image favored by the postwar generation, she argued for an older, voluptuous ideal of mature womanhood, embodied by actress Ellen Terry circa 1895:

> She was no longer the tall, slender girl who had captured the imagination of Watts, but deep-bosomed, with swelling hips, and a majestic presence, very different from the present-day ideal! If audiences of to-day could have seen Ellen Terry in her prime, she would have been besieged with advice on how to become thin by dieting, etc., and I venture to say that the greatness of her expression would have suffered had she spent her time, as our actresses do now, trying to appear young and thin. She did not look slight or thin, but she was certainly a very beautiful example of womanhood.[12]

By referring to diet advice as a threat "besieging" women, Duncan is critiquing the submerged violence she sensed in a bodily discipline of denial and internal regulation—the same discipline that she had opposed in the external form of the corset. Also, she is taking to task the diet and beauty industry itself, a booming twenties enterprise that ranked second, behind food companies, in money spent on advertising. New hair coloring and permanent wave processes attracted women to beauty parlors in unprecedented numbers, and an increasing number of cosmetics lines were available for the newly fashionable made-up look.[13] Female sexuality may have been transgressive in the teens (the flapper actually emerged before the war),[14] but it became a mainstream marketing strategy in the "dollar decade," when cosmetics companies, college sororities, and the Miss America Pageant were all used to sell sex.[15] If personality could be performed at the turn of the century, it could now be purchased. The flapper, a young, single working girl looking for fun and a husband, did not need intellect: she needed "It"—the name that romantic novelist Elinor Glyn gave to sex appeal and the quality that actress Clara Bow personified in the 1927 silent film simply titled *It*.

By that year, dancing had become a "path lead[ing] to cinema land" for Clara Bow want-to-bes,[16] and enthusiasts of popular culture, such as Gilbert Seldes, preferred the Ziegfeld Follies to civic pageants and Irene Castle to classical dancing. "We are an alert and lively people," Seldes wrote, "and our dance must actually express that spirit."[17] It is no wonder, then, that Duncan's "grand manner" was considered "absurdly out of place in our modern world." According to one newspaper eulogy, she was "not a modern woman at all; she was rather a creature out of Balzac."[18]

But the dancer would not surrender her high ground so easily. She launched her own counterattack, with her autobiography, written in the year before her death, in September 1927. At the end of the book, she reinvented herself once again, this time as the quintessential American, in the now-famous "I See America Dancing" essay, which embedded her Victorian ideals within the very terms of nativist nationalism that had positioned her as an outsider during her last American tour.

***

With the "I See America Dancing" essay, curiously wedged into *My Life* in between an account of Duncan's 1917 return to San Francisco and a meditation on truth in autobiography, Duncan restaged her origin for the last time. Years of Hellenic references notwithstanding, she insisted that her dancing was pure Americana. "It has often made me smile—but somewhat ironically—when people have called my dancing Greek," she wrote, "for I myself count its origin in the stories which my Irish grandmother often told us of crossing the plains with grandfather in '49 in a covered wagon."[19] This apparent shift in rhetoric prompted journalist H. L. Mencken, reviewing the autobiography, to dismiss Duncan as an uneducated, prancing woman: "With one breath she connects her dancing with the figures on Greek urns, and with the next she protests that it was completely American, and had Walt Whitman for its pa."[20] What Mencken failed to realize was that, although she shifted the terms of her discourse from "Greece" to "America," its underlying ideology remained consistent. With the same antimodernist impulse that had cast her as a Greek nymph at the turn of the century, she now appropriated the frontier rhetoric from the 1890s, and with the same nationalistic impulse that had wrapped her in the Stars and Stripes during the war, she now appropriated the nativist discourse of the 1920s. In so doing, Duncan made explicit what was there all along, underneath the veneer of idyllic Hellenism: the idea of a pure (white), premodern America and herself as the paradigmatic pioneer woman traversing the frontiers of self, art, and nation.

"I See America Dancing" was serialized posthumously in American newspapers, and since then it has become one of the most quoted passages in American dance history. Glossing a phrase of Walt Whitman's, "I hear America singing," the essay is an expanded version of a paragraph handwritten by Duncan in response to a press agent's copy during her American tours in the teens.[21] In its three and a half pages, the essay moves from Whitman to Duncan's grandparents, to an indictment of jazz, to the consideration of an appropriately American dance practice. "Why should our children bend the knee in that fastidious and servile dance, the Minuet, or twirl in the mazes of the false sentimentality of the Waltz?" she asks. "Rather let them come forth with great strides, leaps and bounds, with lifted forehead and far-spread arms, to dance the language of our Pioneers, the Fortitude of our heroes, the Justice, Kindness, Purity of our statesmen, and all the inspired love and tenderness of our Mothers."[22]

Duncan, her California childhood asserting itself again, romanticizes the lives of her westward-advancing grandparents, claiming that "the heroic spirit of the Pioneer," "the gestures of the Redskins," and "a bit of Yankee Doodle" were her true source material: "All this grandmother danced in the Irish jig, and I learnt it from her, putting into it my own aspiration of Young America, and, finally, my great spiritual realisation of life from the lines of Walt Whitman. And that is the origin of the so-called Greek Dance with which I have flooded the world."[23] Duncan further develops this pioneer narrative into an allegorical figure, a postwar version of "Liberty Leading the People," now a pacific Statue of Liberty literally embracing the expanse of the nation: "I see America dancing, standing with one foot poised on the highest point of the Rockies, her two hands stretched out from the Atlantic to the Pacific, her fine head tossed to the sky, her forehead shining with a Crown of a million stars."[24]

That figure, of course, is Duncan herself, with the land her stage and the heavens her *mise-en-scène*. Here she has imaginatively incorporated progressive historian Frederick Jackson Turner's popular notion, presented in a landmark 1893 paper, that the source of America's unique character—its rugged individualism, self-reliance, and resistance to direct control—lay in the space of its frontier.[25] Turner's theory was "obsessed with space and motion," historian Robert Crunden has observed. "To a country still discovering itself, Turner's vision produced a shock of recognition: the frontier, democracy, individualism, pioneering—surely these really were the essence of American experience."[26] Even though Turner had declared the American frontier extinct, the poetic metaphor endured: the frontier's actual disappearance seemed only to strengthen its imaginative reality. It was this "America" through which Duncan first had legitimized herself as an iconoclast, albeit beneath the more elevated discourse of "Greece," and it was this "America" to which she now explicitly returned, perhaps as a way of symbolically reclaiming her lost citizenship.

At this late date, Duncan shifted the negative term of her discourse: the enemy was no longer ballet but "the sensual lilt of the jazz rhythm," which only "expresses the primitive savage,"[27] because it was jazz, whose immense popularity, which began with ragtime in the teens, challenged the cultural authority of Duncan's practice. Her early, near-exclusive claim to the expressive body was displaced by ragtime, which, within the pages of the *Modern Dance Magazine* during the mid-teens, was discussed in the same language (self-expression, spontaneity, the living life, health, beauty, democracy) that had been used to describe classic dancing. By 1924, critic Carl Van Vechten, who was one of Duncan's most eloquent American interpreters, turned to championing the arts of Harlem.[28] Jazz, with its syncopated rhythms, overt sexuality, and vernacular sources, pointed the way to modernism, but Duncan would not follow. "Isadora was even more severe on Negro dancing and its imitations and derivations [than on the ballet]," recalled Harlem poet Claude McKay. "She had no real appreciation of primitive folk dancing, either from an esthetic or an ethnic point of view."[29]

To Duncan, the dance mania that had seized New York between 1911 and 1915[30] was a dance of spasms and angles, not of grace and curves. Whether ballet or jazz, her argument remained the same: the dancer was still aspiring to a "soul striving upward, through labour to harmonious life."[31] This she found neither in the "tottering, ape-like convulsions"[32] of the Charleston of the twenties, nor in the "animal dances" (fox trot, bunny hug, grizzly bear) of the teens, but in "the living leap of the child springing toward the heights, towards its future accomplishment, towards a new great vision of life that would express America."[33] She condemned the modern dances (as ragtime and jazz dancing were then called) as "the sensual convulsion of the Negro."[34] They were all Dionysian, without Apollonian reason (as opposed to ballet, which was all Apollonian, without any Dionysian abandon). They were "ignoble," "wriggling from the waist downwards,"[35] rather than soaring from the solar plexus. They were polluted, not "clean."[36] And, as she wrote elsewhere, they ignored the rhythm of the wave:

> Our modern dances know nothing of this first law of harmony. Their movements are choppy, end-stopped, abrupt. They lack the continuing beauty of the curve. They are satisfied with being the points of angles which spur on the nerves. The music of today, too, only makes the nerves dance. Deep emotion, spiritual gravity, are entirely lacking. We dance with the jerky gestures of puppets. We do not know how to get down to the depths, to lose ourselves in an inner self, how to develop our visions into the harmonies that attend our dreams.[37]

She dismissed the modern dances as "penny novels and bad poems" rather than true art.[38]

In a decade of intense nativism—when "Americanism," which had been promoted aggressively during the war, was enforced by immigration quotas and the Ku Klux Klan—Duncan's twinning of frontierist and racialist discourses is hardly coincidental. In fact, her argument closely follows that of conservatives such as Wilbur C. Abbott, who, in his case against the "lowering of our civilization"[39] caused by "the new barbarians," told the same story of national "boundaries [being] enlarged by those sturdy pioneers who pushed forward against the opposition of the savages and the wilderness."[40] At a time when the influx of immigrants from eastern Europe had sparked a national debate, reinscribing the "pioneer" into American nationalism effectively distinguished the "authentic" American from all Others: the immigrant, the African American, and the native American. "There is all the difference in the world between a pioneer and an immigrant," Abbott wrote, "between northern and western Europe, and southern and eastern Europe, to say nothing of Asia Minor."[41] As Andre Siegfried observed in his 1927 survey of the national landscape, Americans were preoccupied with cultural and moral standardization in the form of "assimilation," and the ideal of liberty had been replaced by that of prosperity. The formula operating here, he wrote, was "America for Regular Americans."[42]

The natural body, which Duncan cast originally as a product of the great Greek civilization (via her idyllic Californian fantasy, which, it is important to note, excised San Francisco's considerable Chinese population and Barbary Coast),[43] she now constructed as a product of the American pioneer's "Fortitude" and "Purity." The moral threat—the darkness—of the "uncivilized" body was left unspecified in Duncan's earlier, classical rhetoric. With "I See America Dancing," when an explicitly "American" identity is at stake, that darkness is named: the "Negro," the "African savage." Duncan's "America" is about a racially coded moral geography: a space vast and heroic and young, in which any "civilized"-enough individual can conquer the dark-skinned threat of "primitivism," whether it be the circling Redskins or the dancing Africans. (This Victorian distinction between the "civilized" and the "primitive" was embedded deeply even within the progressive movement: *The Masses* largely ignored race issues; the settlement movement failed to extend to African American migrants what it had offered to white immigrants; and the birth control movement embraced the eugenicist concern with "race purity.")[44] By reflexively defining her artistic practice in opposition to "primitive" modern dances, Duncan was effectively constructing the genre of American modern dance as whiteness. Duncan's dancing body was not only natural, expressive, female, and political, but white as well.

This defining American whiteness, as author Toni Morrison has persuasively argued, has been made possible only by an Africanist body. In her study of "American Africanism" ("an investigation into the ways in which a nonwhite, Africanlike [or Africanist] presence or persona was constructed in the United States, and the imaginative uses this fabricated presence served"),[45] Morrison demonstrates the ways in which Africanism—a trope, if not a reality—has produced "American" literary identity. In the realm of dance, Duncan's "I See America Dancing" is exemplary of "the self-evident ways that Americans choose to talk about themselves through and within a sometimes allegorical, sometimes metaphorical, but always choked representation of an Africanist presence."[46] For Duncan, who now found it wiser to describe herself as a puritan rather than a revolutionary,[47] the Africanist body did indeed provide "a way of contemplating chaos and civilization, desire and fear, and a mechanism for testing the problems and blessings of freedom."[48] More specifically, the Africanist body served to displace, away from Duncan, in her bid for legitimacy as an "Artist," the central cultural anxieties about the body as a respectable artistic medium: its hysteria (i.e., femininity), its distracting influence on the life of the mind, its sexuality, and its perennial potential for general social disruption. Projected onto the bodies of "Redskins" and "African savages," these threats were then symbolically conquered by the pioneer settlers, who, according to Duncan's fable, "tam[ed] the wild men . . . in a remarkable manner."[49]

Thus, in Duncan's final bid for the legitimacy of her dancing body, the very creation of that "American" self depended upon its distinction from the Africanism she projected to and from the modern dances. And she was not alone in this race-defined process of "Americanizing" dance. In his 1926 book, *The American Ballet*, Ted Shawn, husband and partner to Ruth St. Denis, constructed an even more aggressively dismissive and self-conscious Africanism in order to validate his own vision for an "American" dance practice. To claim jazz as an American expression is a "lie," he wrote. "Jazz is the scum of the great boiling that is now going on, and the scum will be cleared off and the clear fluid underneath will be revealed." That clear fluid is the country's Anglo-Saxon heritage, wherein "our most interesting [thematic] material lies, and our most American material, if we consider ourselves as more truly Americans than the two alien races of the red man and the black man."[50] Using a variation on the same strategy, Irene and Vernon Castle smoothed out the African American dances of the Barbary Coast for their exclusive cabaret clients, carefully emphasizing the civility of their own reconstructions and, at the same time, exploiting the illicit attraction of the originals.[51]

***

Today, Duncan's "I See America Dancing" essay reads as her nostalgic attempt, through the sinews of the country's rampant nativism, to reassert her idyllic idealism and to reclaim her discursive authority. She, like Whitman, came to realize in these later, dimmer years that her art would have to await its judgment by a future generation. "My Art was the flower of an Epoch," she wrote to Irma in 1924, referring to the students in her Moscow school, "but that Epoch is dead and Europe is the past. These red tunic kids are the future."[52] Depressed and sometimes even suicidal, she recognized that her day had come and gone. She died in a Bugatti on 14 October 1927, at age fifty.

Although Duncan has been written out of 1930s American dance history, in fact, the issue of an "American" dance that so dominated this decade was defined first by Duncan, as well as Shawn, and the Castles. Duncan projected an arc between late-nineteenth-century romanticism and the secular collectivism of the 1930s: she shifted between these two realms and facilitated the transition, although she never completed the leap. Nevertheless, I see more of a continuity than a discontinuity between the late Duncan—both in her rhetoric and in her movement style (compare Duncan's *Revolutionary* [1924] and Martha Graham's *Lamentation* [1930])—and the early phase of the next generation. For before Helen Tamiris's *Walt Whitman Suite* (1934) or Graham's *Frontier* (1935), or the Americana of Lincoln Kirstein's Ballet Caravan (which produced both Eugene Loring's *Billy the Kid* and Lew Christensen's *Filling Station*), Duncan already had considered what it meant to be an "American" artist.[53] And before the social and political agendas of the Workers Dance League and the New Dance Group, Duncan already had established the dancing body as a site of cultural debate. She showed that the deepest, most highly contested discourses of American life could indeed be "done into dance."

NOTES

PREFACE

1. There have been a number of films depicting Duncan's life, including *The Loves of Isadora* (1968), Ken Russell's *Isadora Duncan, the Biggest Dancer in the World* (1966), and *Isadora* (1969), with Vanessa Redgrave. This last one garnered substantial publicity when it opened; today, it is still replayed on television and was featured prominently in cable network A&E's program guide, whose blurb for the movie describes Duncan as "the tempestuous dancer who jolted turn-of-the-century America and Europe with her torrid lifestyle and sensual modernistic dance" (*A&E Program Guide* 6, no. 3 [March 1991]: 36). I thank Bud Coleman for alerting me to this program guide material.

2. Ruth Kozodoy, *Isadora Duncan* (New York: Chelsea House, 1988). Part of a series devoted to "American Women of Achievement," this book uses information, such as Duncan's birth date, that had been revised by scholars twelve years earlier. The play *When She Danced*, by Martin Sherman, produced in New York in 1990, was about Duncan in her later years, a fat, drunken woman with an abusive young husband. An article on Duncan's last choreography (Ann Daly, "The Continuing Beauty of the Curve," *Ballett International* 13, no. 8 [August 1990]: 10–15) prompted an indignant letter to the editor vehemently clinging to notions about Duncan's dancing being produced by trance.

    A trio of articles devoted to Duncan in the Spring 1994 issue of *American Studies* indicates, perhaps, a reversal in this trend, at least in academia.

3. To refer to the dancer by her given or family name was an issue for me. On the one hand, "Isadora," as she is commonly called, is a kind of shorthand for the sensational haze that has hidden from view her artistry; on the other hand, she herself claimed "Isadora" as her true name, as distinct from the name of her father, Duncan (Janet Vale, "Interviewing Isadora," *New York Morning Telegraph*, 14 February 1915, 5). Because calling women by their first names today is a way of inscribing their inferior social status (the implication is that they are not important enough to be addressed formally, as a sign of respect), I have chosen to refer to her as Duncan, as part of my project to reestablish the seriousness of her artistic practice.

4. Duncan persuaded photographer Edward Steichen to go along with her to Greece in 1921 by promising that she would let him make motion pictures of her dancing on the Acropolis. "When we got to Athens, she changed her mind. She said she didn't want her dancing recorded in motion pictures but would rather have it remembered as a legend" (Edward Steichen, *A Life in Photography* [Garden City, N.Y.: Doubleday, 1963]).

5. I borrow from Marcel Mauss the term "body techniques," by which he means "the ways in which, from society to society, men [sic] know how to use their bodies" (Marcel Mauss, "Techniques of the Body," in *Incorporations*, ed. Jonathan Crary and Sanford Kwinter [1934; reprint, New York: Zone, 1992], 455).

6. Fredrika Blair, *Isadora: Portrait of the Artist as a Woman* (New York: William Morrow, 1986); Deborah Jowitt, "The Search for Motion," in *Time and the Dancing Image* (New York: William Morrow and Co., Inc., 1988); Elizabeth Kendall, *Where She Danced: The Birth of American Art-Dance* (New York: Alfred A. Knopf, 1979); Allan Ross Macdougall, *Isadora: A Revolutionary in Art and Love* (New York: Thomas Nelson, 1960); Nancy Chalfa Ruyter, *Reformers and Visionaries: The Americanization of the Art of Dance* (New York: Dance Horizons, 1979); Francis Steegmuller, ed., *"Your Isadora": The Love Story of Isadora Duncan and Gordon Craig* (New York: Random House and the New York Public Library, 1974).

7. Clifford Geertz, "Thick Description: Toward an Interpretive Theory of Culture," in *The Interpretation of Cultures* (New York: Basic Books, 1973), 20.

1. PROLOGUE

1. Refuting Marcel Mauss's argument that there is no such thing as "natural" behavior, Douglas suggests that the body is *both* natural and culturally defined. (For a structuralist who relies on the defining properties of oppositions, there can be no nature without culture, and vice versa). "Here I seek to identify a natural tendency to express situations of a certain kind in an appropriate bodily style. In so far as it is unconscious, in so far as it is obeyed universally in all cultures, the tendency is natural. It is generated in response to a perceived social situation, but the latter must always come clothed in its local history and culture. Therefore the natural expression is culturally determined" (Mary Douglas, *Natural Symbols: Explorations in Cosmology* [1970; reprint, New York: Pantheon Books, 1982], 69). Douglas seems to identify the "natural" (universal) dimensions of bodily symbolism as structural rather than substantive. Her delicate negotiation between the natural/cultural, physical/social seems to presage Bourdieu's mutually informing dialectic, in his case between individual will and social structure. Like Douglas, Bourdieu posits the general, if not exact, consonance of bodily style (*hexis*) with social structure.

2. Pierre Bourdieu, *The Logic of Practice*, trans. Richard Nice (Stanford: Stanford University Press, 1990), 68.

3. Shaemas O'Sheel, "Isadora Duncan, Priestess," *Poet Lore* 21, no. 6 (1910): 480.

4. Biology was the most important science in the years after the Civil War. When I use the term "science," it is largely referring to the realm of biology.

5. Mark Johnson, *The Body in the Mind: The Bodily Basis of Meaning, Imagination, and Reason* (Chicago: University of Chicago Press, 1987), xiv.

6. Ibid., xv.

7. Ibid., 13–14.

8. Specific force structures include compulsion (being moved by external forces), blockage (encountering obstacles in the environment that block or resist our force), counterforce (head-on meetings of forces), enablement (awareness of our sense of power or lack of power to perform an action), and attraction (gravitation toward an object). Ibid., 45–47.

9. Isadora Duncan, *The Art of the Dance*, ed. Sheldon Cheney (New York: Theatre Arts, 1928), 96.

10. Isadora Duncan to Douglas Ainslie, [1899], Douglas Ainslie Papers, Harry Ransom Humanities Research Center, University of Texas at Austin.

11. Julia Levien, "Sources of Style in the Dances of Isadora Duncan," *Ballet Review* 6, no. 4 (1977–78): 45–46.

12. Kristeva uses the term "subject-in-process" to emphasize the constant change and movement of the self (Julia Kristeva, *Revolution in Poetic Language*, trans. Margaret Waller [New York: Columbia University Press, 1984]).

13. Mary Douglas has explicated the consonance between social boundaries and bodily boundaries. See Douglas, *Natural Symbols*; Mary Douglas, *Purity and Danger: An Analysis of the Concepts of Pollution and Taboo* (1966; reprint, London and New York: Routledge, 1992).

14. Pierre Bourdieu, *Distinction: A Social Critique of the Judgement of Taste*, trans. Richard Nice (Cambridge, Mass.: Harvard University Press, 1984).

15. See Toni Morrison, *Playing in the Dark: Whiteness and the Literary Imagination* (Cambridge, Mass.: Harvard University Press, 1992).

16. Floyd Dell, "Who Said That Beauty Passes Like a Dream?" *The Masses* 8, no. 12 (October 1916): 27.

17. Cultural historian Hillel Schwartz has convincingly argued that the kinesthetic force of "torque" was pervasive throughout early twentieth-century America in bodily practices such as Duncan's modern dance, powered flight, penmanship, drawing, sports, and motion picture acting (Hillel Schwartz, "Torque: The New Kinaesthetic of the Twentieth Century," in *Incorporations*, ed. Jonathan Crary and Sanford Kwinter [New York: Zone Books, 1992], 71–126).

18. W. R. T., "Classical Dancing in England," *T. P.'s Magazine*, May 1911, 119, Isadora Duncan Dance Reserve Clipping File, Dance Collection, New York Public Library for the Performing Arts (hereafter cited as DC).

19. Karl Federn, "Nach fünfundzwanzig Jahren," in Duncan, *Der Tanz der Zukunft* (Jena, 1929). Translated and quoted in Irma Duncan, "Isadora Duncan: Pioneer in the Art of Dance," *Bulletin of the New York Public Library*, May 1958, 9.

20. He wrote to his friend and collaborator Martin Shaw on 3 March 1905: "I am drinking in 'American *push*'—Walt in a book is alive—but Walt walking, dancing, is LIFE." Quoted in Francis Steegmuller, *"Your Isadora": The Love Story of Isadora Duncan and Gordon Craig* (New York: Random House and the New York Public Library, 1974), 72, n. 1.

21. André Levinson, "In Memoriam," reprinted in *Ballet Review* 6, no. 4 (1977–78): 16.

22. Howard Mumford Jones, *The Age of Energy: Varieties of American Experience, 1865–1915* (New York: Viking Press, 1971).

23. Hillel Schwartz, "The Zipper and the Child," in *Notebooks in Cultural Analysis*, vol. 2, ed. Norman F. Cantor and Nathalia King (Durham, N.C.: Duke University Press, 1985).

24. Schwartz, "Torque."

25. Thomas J. Schlereth, *Victorian America: Transformations in Everyday Life, 1876–1915* (New York: Harper Collins, 1991).

26. Gertrude Stein, "The Gradual Making of the Making of Americans," in *Gertrude Stein: Lectures in America* (1935; reprint, London: Virago Press, 1985), 161.

27. Historian Robert M. Crunden describes progressivism as a "climate of creativity," rooted and defined by Protestantism but secularized into the "civil religion of American mission" (Robert M. Crunden, *Ministers of Reform: The Progressives' Achievement in American Civilization, 1889–1920* [1982; reprint, Urbana and Chicago: University of Illinois Press, 1984], ix, x).

28. Lewis Mumford, *My Work and Days: A Personal Chronicle* (New York: Harcourt Brace Jovanovich, 1979), 21.

29. Carl N. Degler, *Out of Our Past: The Forces That Shaped Modern America*, rev. ed. (New York: Harper Colophon Books, 1970), 369. See also Henry F. May, *The End of American Innocence: A Study of the First Years of Our Own Time, 1912–1917* (London: Jonathan Cape, 1960).

30. Isadora Duncan, letter to the editor, *New York Evening Sun*, January 1915, quoted in "Isadora Duncan and the Libertarian Spirit," *Modern School* 2 (April 1915): 38.

31. Eric Howard, "Famous Californians: Isadora Duncan," *San Francisco Call and Post*, 26 January 1923, 23.

32. Duncan routinely capitalized these words, as an expression of their timeless and universal significance. On the one hand, I want to retain her sense of the words, but on the other hand, I do not mean to suggest their transparency. Therefore, I will retain the capitalization as a reminder of their meaning to Duncan and also place the words in quotation marks, to indicate a critical questioning of that meaning. Also, for the purpose of distinguishing between "culture" in the anthropological sense of the word and "Culture" in the aesthetic sense of the word as Duncan intended it to mean "high art," I will capitalize the latter. Again, I will place the word within quotation marks.

33. From the start, the British theater designer and theorist Gordon Craig, Duncan's lover from 1904 to 1907 and the father of her first child, Deirdre, identified "Americanness"—and Duncan—with Whitman. Both Duncan and Craig were enthralled by Whitman's work. According to Francis Steegmuller, editor of the Duncan-Craig correspondence, Duncan apparently traveled with Whitman's complete works during 1905 (Steegmuller, *"Your Isadora,"* 73). In the lovers' letters, Whitman often is invoked, much as one would mention an intimate friend in passing. At one point, Craig shared with Duncan one of the Whitman manuscripts that his mother, the famed actress Ellen Terry, had brought back from America, much to the dancer's delight.

34. Walt Whitman, *Leaves of Grass* (1892; reprint, New York: Bantam Books, 1983), 10.

35. See also Ellen Graff, "Walt Whitman and Isadora Duncan: The Construction of a Personal Mythology," in *Proceedings Society of Dance History Scholars*, comp.

Christena L. Schlundt (Riverside, Calif.: Society of Dance History Scholars, 1987), 177–184.

36. See Kevin Starr, *Americans and the California Dream, 1850–1915* (New York: Oxford University Press, 1973).

37. Because of the San Francisco earthquake and fire in 1906, in which city records were destroyed, there is no birth record available for Duncan. Her baptismal record at Old Saint Mary's Church, however, indicates that she was born Angela I. Duncan on 26 May 1877. The middle initial "I" is presumably for Isadora, shortened to "Dora" when she was a child. Although Fredrika Blair (*Isadora: Portrait of the Artist as a Woman* [New York: William Morrow, 1986]) identifies Mrs. Duncan as Mary *Isadora*, all other records (including Isadora's birth certificate) and biographies from primary sources refer to her as Mary *Dora*; however, as with her daughter, "Dora" may have been short for "Isadora." Indeed, the dancer refers to her mother as "Isadora" in her autobiography (Isadora Duncan, *My Life* [New York: Boni and Liveright, 1927], 126).

38. Joan M. Jensen and Gloria Ricci Lothrop, *California Women: A History* (San Francisco: Boyd and Fraser Publishing Co., 1987), 20.

39. Florence Treadwell Boynton, quoted in Millicent Dillon, *After Egypt: Isadora Duncan and Mary Cassatt* (New York: A William Abrahams Book, Dutton, 1990), 162.

40. Jensen and Lothrop, *California Women*, 42.

41. Duncan, *My Life*, 22. Josephine DeWitt Rhodehamel and Raymond Francis Wood, *Ina Coolbrith: Librarian and Laureate of California* (Provo: Brigham Young University Press, 1973), 133.

42. William Halley, *The Centennial Year Book of Alameda County* (Oakland: William Halley, 1876), 457, 454–455; J. P. Munro-Fraser, *History of Alameda County, California* (Oakland: M. W. Wood, 1883); James Miller Guinn, *History of the State of California and Biographical Record of Oakland and Environs*, vol. 1 (Los Angeles: Historic Record Co., 1907).

43. It has been suggested that Coolbrith and Joseph Duncan were lovers, but I have found no evidence for this assertion.

44. Later, in court, Duncan claimed to have "sacrificed everything" for the benefit of the depositors (*San Francisco Bulletin*, 25 February 1878).

45. See Harry Mulford, "Notes and Items Relating to Joseph Charles Duncan (ca. 1823–1898) Father of Isadora Duncan," Isadora Duncan Collection, Performing Arts Library and Museum, San Francisco, California.

46. Starr, *California Dream*, 240.

47. As Raymond Duncan recalled, "One key was my maternal grandmother. She was Irish. And she was a remarkable woman. It was she who gave me the lesson of my life when I was about six years old. She said, 'Raymond, you must never do what everybody does'" (Interview with Raymond Duncan by Marian Horosko, "World of Dance," 28 November 1964, DC).

48. Gelett Burgess, *Behind the Scenes: Glimpses of Fin de Siècle San Francisco* (San Francisco: Book Club of California, 1968), 15.

49. Douglas Tilden, "Art, and What California Should Do about Her," *Overland Monthly* 19, no. 113 (May 1892): 509.

50. See Marvin R. Nathan, "San Francisco's *Fin de Siècle* Bohemian Renaissance," *California History* 61, no. 3 (Fall 1982): 196–207; Starr, *California Dream*; Jensen and Lothrop, *California Women*.

51. Gertrude Atherton, *Ancestors* (New York and London: Harper and Brothers, 1907), 369. Quoted in Starr, *California Dream*, 261.

52. Max Eastman, "Isadora Duncan Is Dead," *Nation* 125 (September 1927): 310.

53. *Dionysion*, pamphlet published for performances at the Metropolitan Opera House, October 1914, DC.

54. Duncan, *Art of the Dance*; Duncan, *My Life*; Steegmuller, *"Your Isadora"*; Franklin Rosemont, ed., *Isadora Speaks* (San Francisco: City Lights Books, 1981).

55. Ivan Nikolenko accompanied Duncan, Mary Desti, and Alice Spicer on their 1927 motor trip from Paris to Nice, where she died. In anticipation of a film of Duncan dancing the *Ave Maria* and the *Internationale*, Nikolenko took a test print of Duncan holding a cigarette and smiling and sitting in the automobile (Alice Spicer to Juliet Rublee, folder 2, Isadora Duncan Miscellaneous Manuscripts, DC). Irma rented the film from Spicer in January 1929 (folder 14, Irma Duncan Papers, DC) and lost it when she lent it to a friend for showing on his projector (folder 117, Irma Duncan Papers).

    Anna Duncan, too, left moving picture films (possibly including the Nikolenko) and equipment in a vault of the old Fry estate in Greenwich, Connecticut, in 1945. By the time that Irma went to reclaim them years later, the estate had been sold and the films were unlocatable (folder 65, Irma Duncan Papers).

    There is a very brief film fragment of Duncan performing at a garden party included in the "Dance in America" documentary *Trailblazers of Modern Dance* (1977) that tells us little.

    A short movie, titled "Animated Picture Show," was thought by dance critic Walter Terry to feature Isadora Duncan as the dancer (Walter Terry, "World of Dance: Fabulous Find in the Files," *Saturday Review* 52 [8 March 1969]: 113–115). Elias Savada of the National Center for Film and Video Preservation, however, has identified the film as a British production shot circa September 1903 (Elias Savada, letter to author, 10 October 1990). Since Duncan was in Greece at this time, she could not have filmed "Animated Picture Show."

56. Marie Theresa Duncan, "Isadora, the Artist: Daughter of Prometheus," in Abraham Walkowitz, *Isadora Duncan in Her Dances* (Girard, Kans.: Haldeman-Julius Publications, 1945), 5. (Later in her professional life, this Isadorable was known as Maria-Theresa.)

57. Irma Duncan, *Duncan Dancer* (Middletown, Conn.: Wesleyan University Press, 1966), 122–123.

2. THE DANCING BODY

1. Edith Wharton, *A Backward Glance* (New York and London: D. Appleton-Century Co., 1934), 321.

2. Ibid.

3. George Seldes, "What Love Meant to Isadora Duncan," *The Mentor*, February 1930, 64.

4. Folder 64, Irma Duncan Collection of Isadora Duncan Materials, Dance Collection, New York Public Library for the Performing Arts (hereafter cited as DC).

5. According to her biographer Allan Ross Macdougall, she was heard to say this at various times during her later years when asked about the origins of her dance (Allan Ross Macdougall, "Isadora Duncan and the Artists," *Dance Index* 5, no. 3 [March 1946]: 61).

6. James Oliphant, "Plain Words about Dancing," *Westminster Review* 136, no. 1 (July 1891): 59.

7. Skirt dancing, a hybrid form of classical ballet and theatrical step dancing, developed in London throughout the 1870s and 1880s. It became hugely popular in music halls and vaudeville theaters in the United States in the 1890s. See "Skirt-dancing," *Saturday Review*, 25 June 1892, 741–742; Martie Fellom, "The Skirt Dance: A Dance Fad of the 1890s" (Ph.D. diss., New York University, 1985); "The Poetry of Skirts," *Cosmopolitan* 28, no. 6 (April 1900): 617–618; "The Skirt Dance," *Scientific American* 74 (20 June 1896): 392.

8. Elizabeth Beland, "The Eldest of the Arts," *Cosmopolitan* 10, no. 6 (April 1891): 644.

9. "Dancing as It Is Taught, How Muscular Instruction Is Given Classes on the East and West Sides. Popular Songs Enliven the Steps. Vigorous Methods Needed for Awkward Lads, but the Girls Learn Readily," *New York Herald*, 7 October 1894.

10. Lady Battersea, "Ethics of Amusement," in *World's Congress of Representative Women*, vol. 7, ed. May Wright Sewall (Chicago and New York: Rand, McNally and Co., 1894), 135.

11. "Dancing Literature and Dogma," *Saturday Review* 60 (1 August 1885): 151.

12. Herbert Spencer, "Professional Institutions. III—Dancer and Musician," *Popular Science Monthly* 47 (July 1895): 364–374; Herbert Spencer, "Professional Institutions. III—Dancer and Musician," *Contemporary Review* 68 (July 1895): 114–124.

13. Mrs. Lilly Grove, *Dancing: A Handbook of the Terpsichorean Arts in Diverse Places and Times, Savage and Civilized* (London: Longmans, Green and Co., 1895). Also see Susan Leann Foote, "Lilly Grove Frazer and Her Book *Dancing* " (M.A. thesis, York University, 1986).

14. Lee J. Vance, "The Evolution of Dancing," *Popular Science Monthly* 41 (October 1892): 739–756; J. F. Rowbotham, "Dancing as a Fine Art," *Eclectic Magazine* 52, no. 1 (July 1890): 16–23; Amelia E. Barr, "Characteristic Dances of the World," *Lippincott's* 27 (April 1881): 330–341.

15. Allen Dodworth, *Dancing and Its Relations to Education and Social Life, with a New Method of Instruction* (New York: Harper and Brothers, 1885), 3.

16. On the ideology of the body produced by dance technique, see Susan Foster, "Dancing Bodies," in *Incorporations*, ed. Jonathan Crary and Sanford Kwinter (New York: Zone Books, 1992), 480–495.

17. Judson Sause, *The Art of Dancing* (Chicago, New York, San Francisco: Belford, Clarke and Co., 1889), 128.

18. See Robert C. Allen, *Horrible Prettiness: Burlesque and American Culture* (Chapel Hill: University of North Carolina Press, 1991).

19. Philip Hayman, " 'The Magic of Dancing Is Sorcery Sweet,' " *Theatre* 36 (1 May 1891): 238.

20. Isadora Duncan, *Der Tanz der Zukunft* (Leipzig: Eugen Diederichs, 1903), 23.

21. "Emotional Expression," *New York Herald*, 20 February 1898. Duncan may have picked up her ideas about the character formation of children while in Oakland or San Francisco, where Emma Marwedel, a pioneer of Friedrich Froebel's kindergarten plan as a method of education reform, was laying down its American foundations. Marwedel and other education progressives believed that free kindergartens, as a means of "character training," began the path leading to the emancipation of childhood, the perfection of motherhood, and the regeneration of the human race—Duncan's own concerns, too. Wealthy women

such as Mrs. S. B. Crocker and Mrs. Stanwood were underwriting the establishment and maintenance of free kindergartens there (Fletcher Harper Swift, "Emma Jacobina Christiana Marwedel: Pioneer of the Kindergarten in California," *University of California Publications in Education* 6, no. 3 [1931]: 139–216). Also see Jane (J. C.) Croly, *The History of the Women's Club Movement in America* (New York: Henry G. Allen and Co., 1898), 258.

22. Quoted in Michael Steven Shapiro, "Froebel in America: A Social and Intellectual History of the Kindergarten Movement, 1848–1918" (Ph.D. diss., Brown University, 1980), 44. Although I have found no evidence directly linking Duncan and Froebel, her ideas seem to echo his. He believed in the correspondence between the evolution of natural forms and the stages of a child's growth and stressed an ethics of unity as an expression of God's plan for order. The purpose of children's education, then, was to lead them toward the "inner law of Divine Unity." Froebel's techniques included singing, marching, and dancing. Shapiro's dissertation establishes the high profile of kindergarten in San Francisco and around the country during the 1880s and 1890s, which further suggests Duncan's likely exposure to these ideas.

23. Stephen Kern, *Anatomy and Destiny: A Cultural History of the Human Body* (Indianapolis and New York: Bobbs-Merrill Co., 1975), 64–65.

24. "Emotional Expression."

25. "The Dance and Philosophy: Music and Poetry Illustrated by the Misses Duncan at the Home of Mrs. Dodge," *New York Times*, 16 February 1898, 2.

26. Dorothea Andrews, " 'Dance of Life' Instructor Urges New-Fashioned Selves," *Washington Post*, 28 March 1948, Mary Fanton Roberts Papers, Archives of American Art, Detroit, Michigan. Also see John Martin, "The Dance: Memorial; Elizabeth Duncan—A Great Figure Passes," *New York Times*, 19 December 1948, Mary Fanton Roberts Collection, Theatre Collection, Museum of the City of New York.

27. In an advertisement for "Miss May [Elizabeth] Duncan, teacher of Physical Culture and Dancing," references are given for "Miss Lake's School, Miss West's Seminary, Peralta Hall, etc." (*Our Society Blue Book, 1891–92* [San Francisco: Hoag and Irving, c. 1891], lxxviii, San Francisco Room, San Francisco Public Library.

28. Walt Whitman, *Leaves of Grass* (1892; reprint, New York: Bantam Books, 1983), 124.

29. Paul Hertelendy reports this finding from the memoirs of Florence Treadwell Boynton (Paul Hertelendy, "New Light, Old Legend: Isadora's Early Years," *Oakland Tribune*, 18 December 1977, Isadora Duncan Collection, Performing Arts Library).

30. See Croly, *Women's Club Movement*; Patricia Albjerg Graham, "Expansion and Exclusion: A History of Women in American Higher Education," *Signs* 3, no. 4 (Summer 1978): 759–773; Theodora Penny Martin, *The Sound of Our Own Voices: Women's Study Clubs, 1860–1910* (Boston: Beacon Press, 1987).

31. Isadora Duncan, *The Art of the Dance*, ed. Sheldon Cheney (New York: Theatre Arts, 1928), 99.

32. Isadora Duncan to Douglas Ainslie, Berlin to London, Douglas Ainslie Papers, Harry Ransom Humanities Research Center, University of Texas at Austin.

33. Duncan, *Der Tanz*, 12.

34. Never mind that Nietzsche rejected Darwin's fatalistic, mechanistic principle of natural selection and supplanted it with the power of the individual free will to create change. This basic incompatibility (among others) between her sources

was not important to Duncan's purpose. Rather, she drew upon Nietzsche's poetic vision of the future and the power of the will.

35. In 1908, the year of Duncan's first American tour, H. L. Mencken's *The Philosophy of Friedrich Nietzsche* (Boston: Luce and Co., 1908) was an immediate success. By 1925 no European thinker of the nineteenth century, except for Darwin, Spencer, and possibly Thomas Henry Huxley, had been so widely reprinted. There had been 200,000 copies of his works printed in the U.S. since the first, in 1899 (Melville Drimmer, "Nietzsche in American Thought, 1895–1925" [Ph.D. diss., University of Rochester, 1965]).

36. Duncan, *Der Tanz*, 26.

37. See John E. Atwell, "The Significance of Dance in Nietzsche's Thought," in *Illuminating Dance: Philosophical Explorations*, ed. Maxine Sheets-Johnstone (Lewisburg and London: Bucknell University Press and Associated University Presses, 1984), 19–34; Friedrich Nietzsche, *Thus Spoke Zarathustra*, trans. Walter Kaufmann (New York: Viking Press, 1966).

38. Duncan, *Art*, 101.

39. Isadora Duncan, blue notebook, 1904, 83–84, folder 141, Irma Duncan Collection of Isadora Duncan Materials, DC. I have retained Duncan's original spelling and punctuation in my citations from her unpublished writings.

40. Ibid., 87–89.

41. Whitman, *Leaves*, 315.

42. Nietzsche, *Zarathustra*, 34.

43. Duncan, *Der Tanz*, 24.

44. Duncan, *Art*, 122.

45. In this sense, Duncan's practice was a conservative one, preserving boundaries which she would extend racially. I will deal with this issue in the Epilogue.

46. Nietzsche, *Zarathustra*, 75.

47. Neal Jahren, "Using Schopenhauer and Nietzsche as a Foundation for Modern Dance: A Study of Isadora Duncan's Philosophical Sources," unpublished manuscript, 8–9. Duncan articulates a connection between individual and cosmic will in "The Dance of the Future" (Duncan, *Der Tanz*, 13).

48. Isadora Duncan, "Form and Movement," *The Theatre Dionysus* notebook, Mary Fanton Roberts Collection, Collection of Isadora Duncan Materials, Museum of the City of New York.

49. Ibid.

50. Ibid.

51. Duncan, blue notebook, 96–97.

52. Duncan told a reporter: "One works for years to perfect some one artistic thing like that of merging one motion into another, but what difference does it make? Who sees it? Nobody understands" (Arthur Ruhl, "Some Ladies Who Dance," *Colliers Weekly*, 5 February 1910, Isadora Duncan Clippings, DC).

53. Duncan, *Art*, 69.

54. Ibid., 99.

55. Isadora Duncan, "The Dance," *Theatre Arts* 2, no. 1 (December 1917): 21; see also Duncan, *Art*, 99.

56. Duncan, *Art*, 101.

57. Irma Duncan, *Duncan Dancer: An Autobiography* (Middletown, Conn.: Wesleyan University Press, 1966), 54.

58. Lucile Marsh, "The Shadow of Wigman in the Light of Duncan," *Dance Magazine* 16, no. 1 (May 1931): 62.

59. Sewell Stokes, *Isadora Duncan: An Intimate Portrait* (London and New York: Brentano's, 1928), 74.

60. Ibid., 82.

61. Duncan, *Art*, 121.

62. For an overview of the Duncan iconography, see Allan Ross Macdougall, "Isadora Duncan and the Artists," *Dance Index* 5, no. 3 (March 1946): 61–82.

63. Robert Henri, "Isadora Duncan," *Playboy* 1 (January 1919): 12.

64. Genthe, one of the most popular and versatile American photographers in the early twentieth century, was one of the first to experiment with filming dance. He made films of Duncan's older pupils. Besides *Isadora Duncan: Twenty-Four Studies*, the earlier *Book of the Dance* chronicles the dancers of his day, including the Isadora Duncan School, Maud Allan, Ruth St. Denis and her school, Anna Pavlova, and the Duncan-style Noyes School and Morgan Dancers. Genthe's photographs of Duncan are housed at the Library of Congress and at the Museum of the City of New York. (Arnold Genthe, *The Book of the Dance* [Boston: International Publishers, 1920]; Arnold Genthe, "The Revival of the Classic Greek Dance in America," *Dance Magazine* 11, no. 4 [February 1929]: 22–23, 61; Arnold Genthe, *Isadora Duncan: Twenty-Four Studies* [New York: Mitchell Kennerley, 1929]; Arnold Genthe, *As I Remember* [New York: Reynal and Hitchcock, 1936]; Toby Gersten Quitslund, "Arnold Genthe: A Pictorial Photographer in San Francisco, 1895–1911" [Ph.D. diss., George Washington University, 1988].)

65. Isadora Duncan, *My Life* (New York: Boni and Liveright, 1927), 327.

66. See Kent Smith, *Abraham Walkowitz Figuration, 1895–1945* (Long Beach, Calif.: Long Beach Museum of Art, 1982), 17.

67. Quoted in ibid., 18.

68. Quoted in "Charles H. Caffin in the 'N. Y. American,'" *Camera Work* 41 (January 1913): 29.

69. Smith, *Abraham Walkowitz*, 15–17.

70. See Ivor Guest, *Adeline Genée: A Lifetime of Ballet under Six Reigns* (London: Adam and Charles Black, 1958); Camille Hardy, "The American Debut of Adeline Genée," in *New Directions in Dance*, ed. Diana Theodores Taplin (Toronto: Pergamon Press, 1979), 121–133.

71. Henri, "Isadora Duncan," 12.

72. See Anne Hollander, *Seeing through Clothes* (New York: Viking Press, 1978).

73. Quoted in Duncan, *Duncan Dancer*, 46.

74. Hortense Kooluris, interview with author, New York City, 9 July 1990. Kooluris began study as a child with Anita Zahn and Erna Lane of the Elizabeth Duncan School. She began working with Irma Duncan at fifteen and went on to study with two other Isadorables, Anna and Maria-Theresa.

75. Henri, "Isadora Duncan," 12.

76. "It was about devouring space," recalls second-generation Duncan dancer Julia Levien about her training. "How to handle space, to be a part of it, but not to be destroyed by it and not to destroy it" (Julia Levien, interview with author, New York City, 10 July 1990). Levien studied with Irma and Anna Duncan.

77. Duncan, *Art*, 99.

78. For a treatment of rhythm in the arts in Germany in the early twentieth century, see Janice Joan Schall, "Rhythm and Art in Germany, 1900–1930" (Ph.D. diss., University of Texas at Austin, 1989). I thank Linda Henderson for referring me to this source.

79. Although many of Duncan's dances—especially the earlier ones—are closely related to their musical scores, some of them are more loosely configured. "There are times in Tchaikovsky's 'Pathétique' symphony," Julia Levien explains, "when we're just standing still and the music is going on and on and on, for 20 phrases, in the most devastating rhythms, and all I'm doing is opening my hands. No way am I following the music" (Levien interview, 1990).

80. Marie Theresa Duncan, "Isadora, the Artist, Daughter of Prometheus," in Abraham Walkowitz, *Isadora Duncan in Her Dances* (Girard, Kans.: Haldeman-Julius Publications, 1945), 5. She was later known as Maria-Theresa Duncan.

81. See Lillian Loewenthal, "Isadora Duncan and Her Relationship to the Music of Chopin," in *Proceedings Society of Dance History Scholars*, comp. Christena L. Schlundt (Riverside, Calif.: Society of Dance History Scholars, 1987), 159–165.

82. Harold Bauer, *Harold Bauer: His Book* (New York: W. W. Norton and Co., 1948), 70–72.

83. Bolton Hall, "Isadora Duncan and Liberty," quoted in *Dionysion*, performance pamphlet, 1914, DC.

84. Susanne K. Langer, *Feeling and Form* (New York: Charles Scribner's Sons, 1953), 175.

85. Lincoln Kirstein, "The Curse of Isadora," *New York Times*, 23 November 1986, sec. II, p. 28.

86. Some dances, particularly some of the later and group works, do offer a more formal spatial structure. The symphonies, according to Julia Levien, are about "cutting space" (Levien interview, 1990).

87. H. T. Parker, *Motion Arrested: Dance Reviews of H. T. Parker*, ed. Olive Holmes (Middletown, Conn.: Wesleyan University Press, 1982), 59.

88. "Triumphs Again," *Philadelphia Telegraph*, 24 November 1908, Isadora Duncan Clippings, DC.

89. W. L. Hubbard, "Isadora Duncan's Dancing High Example of Real Art," *Chicago Tribune*, 6 December 1908.

90. Duncan, *My Life*, 165.

91. Quoted in Millicent Dillon, *After Egypt: Isadora Duncan and Mary Cassatt* (New York: Dutton, 1990), 163–164.

92. "Sister Collapses at News," *New York Times*, 16 September 1927.

93. Duncan, *My Life*, 21.

94. Paul Hertelendy, "Isadora's Childhood," *Dance Magazine* 51, no. 7 (July 1977): 50.

95. Ibid., 49.

96. These exercises were introduced into American Turnvereins after 1865. See Nancy Lee Chalfa Ruyter, *Reformers and Visionaries: The Americanization of the Art of Dance* (New York: Dance Horizons,1978), 86.

97. Arnold Rood Collection, Theatre Museum, Victoria and Albert Museum, London, England.

98. San Francisco Clippings, Performing Arts Library and Museum, San Francisco, California.

99. Several articles suggest that Duncan studied with Marie Bonfanti and Katti Lanner:

   A young dancer named Lola Yberri, who seems to have been genuine in her claim to have known Duncan in New York, reported that "Miss Duncan was a hard worker. She used to take lessons of my teacher, Mme. Bonfanti, up to 5 o'clock in the afternoon, and then teach her own class, such people as Mrs. Stuyvesant

Fish and Miss Belmont being on her list of patrons" ("Wins Plaudits Far from Home," *San Francisco Call*, 25 February 1903, Isadora Duncan Clippings, DC).

Irma Duncan's research turned up this information: "She had her first lesson in San Francisco, then put in a year at a ballet school in New York and afterwards came to Europe to study" ("An American Dancer," *Times (London)*, 16 March 1990, quoted in Irma Duncan, "Isadora Duncan, Pioneer in the Art of Dance," *Bulletin of the New York Public Library*, May 1958, 3).

Duncan herself told an interviewer: "When I was about 12 we left 'Frisco and went east to New York, and there my dancing life began in real earnest, for my father, who was a wealthy banker, suddenly lost all his money through a rash speculation. Something had to be done, and dancing seemed to me the one thing worth doing. But a training of some sort was absolutely necessary, apart from the artistic and intellectual help my parents gave me. So I hit upon a splendid scheme. I started to give lessons myself on an entirely new and unusual principle, and with the dollars I earned paid for my own lessons" (*American Journal*, 3 September 1908, Isadora Duncan Clippings, DC).

According to Augustin Duncan: "She studied every kind of dancing. She studied with Marie Bonfanti—she came over with 'The Black Crook' and taught in New York for years—and with Katti Lanner, who was ballet mistress at the Empire Theater in London, to my knowledge" (Margaret Lloyd, "Fifty Years of 'La Boheme'—The Stage and Art—Brother of a Legend; Augustin Duncan Recalls Earlier Days of Isadora," *Christian Science Monitor*, 16 February 1946, C10).

Duncan told the *New York Daily Tribune*, when she was leaving for London in 1899, that "she will as soon as she reaches London put herself under her old dancing teacher for at least a short term." This points, again, to Katti Lanner ("She Will Dance in London," *New York Daily Tribune*, 7 May 1899, sec. III, p. 5).

British writer Nesta Macdonald discovered evidence that Duncan had toured to England with Daly's company in August 1897 (Nesta Macdonald, "Isadora Reexamined, Part One," *Dance Magazine* 57, no. 7 [July 1977]: 54), and a dance program in the Howard Holtzman Documentation of Isadora Duncan proves that she was there again, presenting her "Done into Dance" repertoire, in July 1898.

100. See Kristina Gintautiene, "The Black Crook: Ballet in the Gilded Age (1866–1876)" (Ph.D. diss., New York University, 1984).

101. "Wins Plaudits Far from Home."

102. See Barbara Barker, *Ballet or Ballyhoo: The American Careers of Maria Bonfanti, Rita Sangalli and Giuseppina Morlacchi* (New York: Dance Horizons, 1984), 223.

103. Ivor Guest, *The Empire Ballet* (London: Society for Theatre Research, 1962). Although Guest suggests that Duncan unsuccessfully auditioned for the Empire Ballet, implying that it happened in 1903, Duncan would not have done so then— she was in Berlin and successful on her own terms.

104. When Duncan made the headlines upon her return to America in 1908, the *Chicago Tribune* ran an article, with much internal evidence of accuracy, that suggested: "Then Mr. Daly, ever quick to recognize subtle talent and the theatrical advantage of it, sent Isadora to Europe to go into artistic training under famous masters of thought expression through adaptation of motion to music" ("Isadora Duncan Returns to Scene of First Triumphs," *Chicago Tribune*, 29 November 1908, Isadora Duncan Clippings, DC).

105. Quoted in Lois Rather, *Lovely Isadora* (Oakland, Calif.: Rather Press, 1976), 40.

106. See Suzanne Shelton, *Divine Dancer: A Biography of Ruth St. Denis* (Garden City, N.Y.: Doubleday and Co., 1981), 12–13; Ann Barzel, "European Dance Teachers in the United States," *Dance Index* 3 (April–May–June 1944): 68–69.

107. "Here's Something Brand New in Dancing Class Methods," *New York Herald*, 9 January 1898, New York Clippings 1785–1939, Performing Arts Library and Museum, San Francisco, California.

108. According to J. C. Trewin, the "contentious young dancer, Isadora Duncan, [was] not very popular with her companions" (J. C. Trewin, *Benson and the Bensonians* [London: Barrie and Rockliff, 1960], 109). Also see Sir Frank Benson, *My Memoirs* (1930; reprint, New York: Benjamin Blom, 1971).

109. *Era*, 24 February 1900, 13. Other reviews of this production ran in the *Times* (London), 23 February 1900, 6; the *World*, 28 February 1900, 24; the *Stage*, 1 March 1900, 15; the *Illustrated London News*, 3 March 1900, 285.

110. Duncan to Ainslie, 8 December 1900, Ainslie Papers.

111. Lori Belilove, letter to author, 8 September 1994.

112. I am indebted to New York–based Duncan dancer Lori Belilove for her private tutorials in Duncan technique.

113. "Russia's Poetess of Art in Motion," *Musical America*, 5 March 1910, 25.

114. "A Last Interview," *New York Dramatic Mirror*, 1913, Bonfanti Scrapbook, DC, quoted in Barker, *Ballet or Ballyhoo*, 221.

115. Valerien Svetloff, "Isadora Duncan," *Dancing Times* 207 (December 1927): 336.

116. Kirstein, "Curse of Isadora."

117. André Levinson, *André Levinson on Dance: Writings from Paris in the Twenties*, ed. Joan Acocella and Lynn Garafola (Hanover, N.H.: University Press of New England, 1991), 48. See also Lynn Garafola, "Politics in Paradise: André Levinson's Classicism," *New Dance Review* 6, no. 3 (Spring 1994): 12–18.

118. Duncan, *Art*, 103.

119. Marcel Mauss, "Techniques of the Body," in *Incorporations*, 455.

120. Levien interview, 1990.

121. A fine Duncan dancer, Belilove trained with Isadorables Irma and Anna Duncan and with leaders of the second generation—Julia Levien, Hortense Kooluris, and Mignon Garland. Belilove is artistic director of Lori Belilove & Company, which performs the Duncan repertory as well as Belilove's Duncan-inspired compositions. In 1979 she founded the Isadora Duncan Foundation for Contemporary Dance, Inc., an educational and sponsoring center for workshops, classes, and public performances of "The Art of Isadora" as performed by Lori Belilove & Company. I am grateful to her for my understanding of Duncan technique.

An earlier exponent of Duncan dancing was Annabelle Gamson, whose performances in the 1970s helped to initiate the current interest in performing the Duncan repertory. For an account of her process, see the videotape *On Dancing Isadora's Dances* (prod. Annabelle Gamson, 1988).

122. Irma Duncan, "Isadora Duncan: Pioneer in the Art of Dance," *Bulletin of the New York Public Library*, May 1958, 8; also see Irma Duncan, *The Technique of Isadora Duncan* (1937; reprint, Brooklyn: Dance Horizons, 1973).

123. Levien interview, 1990.

124. Duncan, "Pioneer," 7.

125. Duncan, "Form and Movement." (Duncan's citation of classical Greek meter is not accurate.) I have cited the original notebook copy, because the edited and published version in *The Art of the Dance* smooths out Duncan's prose and omits

key elements: the emphasis on rhythm; the ingraining of rhythm into an expressive tool; and the progression from line to angle to curve:

> The exercises begin by a simple gymnastic preparation of the muscles to make them strong and flexible; the first dancing steps only begin after these gymnastic exercises are completed. They consist at first of a simple rhythmic walk, learning to walk slowly to the sounds of a simple rhythm, then to walk quicker to the sound of more complicated rhythms, then to run, at first slowly, then to jump lightly at a certain moment of the rhythm.
>
> By means of these exercises the pupils learn to read the notes on the scale of movement as the notes of music are learnt on the scale of sound. Later, these notes can be made to harmonize with the most various and subtle compositions. (Duncan, *Art*, 81–82)

126. Martin Shaw, Gordon Craig's composer-conductor friend, wrote that "she walked with a kind of floating sway from the hips" (Martin F. Shaw, *Up to Now* [London: Oxford University Press, 1929], 59, quoted in *"Your Isadora": The Love Story of Isadora Duncan and Gordon Craig*, ed. Francis Steegmuller [New York: Random House and the New York Public Library, 1974], 123).

127. Duncan, *Duncan Dancer*, 127–128.

128. Marie-Louise de Meeus, "A Star Danced—," *Cornhill* 72 (May 1932): 546.

129. Ibid., 547.

130. The Duncan repertory as it exists today has been reconstructed from those particular dances that the Isadorables either saw or were taught, further mediated by their students, such as Levien and Kooluris. As Kooluris explains, her teachers (Irma, Anna, and Maria-Theresa) "each taught different aspects of the work. . . . It's doubly hard to separate out what exactly is Isadora's because she did different things at different times" ("Decision-Making Dancers," *Ballet Review* 20, no. 4 [Winter 1992–93]: 87). This explains why some of Duncan's dances have become standards and others have disappeared, and why the same dance can look so different when performed by dancers trained in different branches of the Duncan lineage.

131. "Girls in the Gymnasium," *San Francisco Examiner*, 21 October 1893, San Francisco Clippings, Performing Arts Library and Museum, San Francisco, California.

132. "Calisthenics in Boudoirs," *San Francisco Examiner*, 26 May 1895, San Francisco Clippings, Performing Arts Library and Museum, San Francisco, California.

133. Modern American physical education emerged in the mid-nineteenth century. For much of the century it consisted of gymnastics—the Swedish or German system, American innovations, or a combination thereof. See June A. Kennard, "The History of Physical Education," *Signs* 2, no. 4 (1977): 835–842.

134. See Harvey Green, *Fit for America: Health, Fitness, Sport and American Society* (New York: Pantheon Books, 1986).

135. "Isadora Duncan's Dancing," *New York Sun*, 8 September 1908, Isadora Duncan Clippings, DC.

136. For the early response to rhythmic gymnastics, see Charles B. Ingham, "Music and Physical Grace: The New Rhythmic Gymnastics," *Good Housekeeping* 52 (1911): 14–17; "The Synthetic Art of the Super-Dance," *Current Opinion* 55, no. 1 (July 1913): 51–53; Margaret Naumburg, "The Dalcroze Idea: What

Eurhythmics Is and What It Means," *Outlook* 106 (17 January 1914): 127–131; Elise de Merlier, "Jaques-Dalcroze and Eurhythmics," *Musician* 19, no. 9 (September 1914): 575–576.

137. Redfern Mason, "'I Aim to Speak the Language of Humanity,' Says Isadora Duncan," *San Francisco Examiner*, 25 November 1917, Isadora Duncan Collection, Performing Arts Library and Museum, San Francisco, California.

The Eurhythmics of Jaques-Dalcroze, the first book-length explication of the method in English, was published in England (London: Constable and Co.) in 1912 and in America (Boston: Small, Maynard and Co.) in 1913.

Rhythmic gymnastics, which came to be known more commonly as "eurhythmics," was originally designed by Jaques-Dalcroze as a system of teaching rhythm to musicians through body movement. By the time Ida Lenggenhagen was giving demonstrations of rhythmic gymnastics to New York gatherings in 1914, it had developed into something more than just musician training. It had become "a synthetic training of mind and body" (Naumburg, "The Dalcroze Idea," 131)—a way of developing in anyone, musician or not, an inner sense of rhythm and harmony. It had grown into both a theatrical form visualizing classical music (both Jaques-Dalcroze and Duncan produced music-dance-dramas of Gluck's *Orpheus*) and an educational means of developing individual expressiveness in children. In 1914 there were at least three Dalcroze teachers in America: one in Chicago, one at Bryn Mawr College, and one in New York. They taught not only children and lay adults but future professionals as well. The importance of music and expression to the next generation of modern dancers was the influence not only of Duncan but also of such Dalcroze-trained teachers as Lucy Duncan Hall, Marion Kappes, and Elsa Findlay. See Selma Landen Odom, "Chicago, 1913: Eurhythmics Entering American Dance," *American Dalcroze Journal* 11, no. 1 [Fall 1983]: 1, 4, 6).

Since both dancer and composer focused on expression through rhythmic body movement, they were, understandably, seen sometimes as fellow travelers. It irritated Duncan to be associated with rhythmic gymnastics, perhaps not just on aesthetic grounds but also because Jaques-Dalcroze had been critical of her in his 1912 essay "How to Revive Dancing" (reprinted in Emile Jaques-Dalcroze, *Rhythm Music and Education*, trans. Harold F. Rubenstein [London: The Dalcroze Society, 1980], 132–145). Continuing this enmity, Irma Duncan went so far as to charge that Jaques-Dalcroze had gleaned all his ideas from a visit to Grunewald (Duncan, *Duncan Dancer*, 38–39).

While she surely overstated the significance of Duncan to Jaques-Dalcroze, who had been searching for a new understanding of the relationship between music and movement well before his alleged visit to Grunewald, word of Duncan's performances likely gave him encouragement for his ongoing experiments. Jaques-Dalcroze scholar Selma Landen Odom has concluded that "even though he probably had not yet seen her himself, Jaques-Dalcroze was informed about the serious response to Duncan almost from the beginning of her European career, at exactly the time he decided to focus on what movement had to offer to teachers of music" (Selma Landen Odom, "Mouvement du corps dans l'enseignement d'Emile Jaques-Dalcroze," in *La Danse: Art du XXe Siècle?* trans. Selma Landen Odom [Lausanne: Editions Payot, 1990], 129).

For an overview of Jaques-Dalcroze's work and legacy, see Marie-Laure Bachmann, *Dalcroze Today: An Education through and into Music*, trans. David Parlett

(Oxford: Clarendon Press, 1991); Irwin Spector, *Rhythm and Life: The Work of Emile Jaques-Dalcroze* (Stuyvesant, N.Y.: Pendragon Press, 1990).

138. Dudley Sargent, "Modern Dances as Athletic Exercises," *New York Times*, 3 January 1909, sec. 5, p. 7.

139. Lady Kennet, *Self Portrait of an Artist: From the Diaries and Memoirs of Lady Kennet* (London: John Murray, 1949), 44.

140. See Maurice Dumesnil, *An Amazing Journey: Isadora Duncan in South America* (New York: Ives Washburn, 1932).

141. Morris R. Werner, *To Whom It May Concern: The Story of Victor Ilyitch Seroff* (New York: Jonathan Cape and Harrison Smith, 1931), 260.

3. THE NATURAL BODY

1. Isadora Duncan, *The Art of the Dance*, ed. Sheldon Cheney (New York: Theatre Arts, 1928), 126.

2. See Jackson Lears, *No Place of Grace: Antimodernism and the Transformation of American Culture, 1880–1920* (New York: Pantheon Books, 1981), 59–96.

3. Duncan, *Art*, 78.

4. David E. Shi, *The Simple Life: Plain Living and High Thinking in American Culture* (New York: Oxford University Press, 1985), 176, 194.

5. "Triumphs Again," *Philadelphia Telegraph*, 24 November 1908, Isadora Duncan Clippings, Dance Collection, New York Public Library for the Performing Arts (hereafter cited as DC).

6. Between 1865 and 1914, the population tripled, the value created by manufacturing increased nearly twelvefold, and the capital invested in industry multiplied twenty-two times. By 1920, more than half the population, for the first time in the country's history, lived in cities (Carl N. Degler, *Out of Our Past: The Forces That Shaped Modern America*, rev. ed. [New York: Harper Colophon Books, 1970], 237–238, 304).

7. See Lears, *No Place of Grace*; Mark Seltzer, *Bodies and Machines* (New York and London: Routledge, 1992).

8. Kevin Starr, *Americans and the California Dream, 1850–1915* (New York: Oxford University Press, 1973), 417, 418.

9. Entry dated 11 May 1902, folder 141, Irma Duncan Collection of Isadora Duncan Materials, DC.

10. "The California Girl Who Made Athens Gasp by Wearing Classic Grecian Costumes in the Streets and to the Theatres," *San Francisco Chronicle*, 22 November 1903, 8.

11. See Millicent Dillon, *After Egypt: Isadora Duncan and Mary Cassatt* (New York: Dutton, 1990), 162; Duncan, *Art*, 128–129.

12. A program, entitled "The Story of Narcissus: Done into Dance by Isadora Duncan" and performed at Lowther Lodge, London, on 18 July 1898, started with a dance titled *Morgensonne* (Howard Holtzman Documentation of Isadora Duncan).

13. Irma Duncan donated the *Primavera* costume to the DC.

14. Allen Monroe Foster, ". . . Fatherland: Isadora Duncan's Poetic Dances Have Divided Germany into Two Camps," December 1902, Isadora Duncan Clippings, DC.

15. Duncan to Douglas Ainslie, 22 December [1899], Douglas Ainslie Papers, Harry Ransom Humanities Research Center, University of Texas at Austin.

16. Duncan to Ainslie, 11 October 1900, ibid.
17. I have found nothing in the Duncan literature regarding Harrison. Furthermore, according to the archivist in the Newnham College Library at Cambridge, there is nothing connecting Duncan and Harrison in the Jane Ellen Harrison Papers (Elisabeth M. C. van Houts, letter to author, 23 September 1993).
18. Duncan to Ainslie, n.d., Douglas Ainslie Papers.
19. Friedrich Nietzsche, "Attempt at a Self-Criticism," in *The Birth of Tragedy, Or: Hellenism and Pessimism*, trans. Walter Kaufmann (reprint, rev. ed. 1886 [New York: Vintage Books, 1967], 19. Duncan wrote to the Isadorables that *The Birth of Tragedy* was her "Bible" (Duncan, *Art*, 108).
20. Paul Gsell and Auguste Rodin, *Rodin on Art*, trans. Mrs. Romilly Fedden (New York: Horizon Press, 1971), 46–47.
21. After initial resistance, the different organized religions in America eventually made their peace with evolutionism in a variety of ways, mostly without disrupting religious convention. Those more on the left wing, such as Lyman Abbott, Minot J. Savage, James T. Bixby, Francis Ellingwood Abbot, and Octavius B. Frothingham, attempted to construct an evolutionary theology which, like Haeckel's monism, posited God as an immanent force rather than as a remote ruler. Cynthia Eagle Russett, *Darwin in America: The Intellectual Response, 1865–1912* (San Francisco: W. H. Freeman and Co., 1976), 25–45.

    Robert M. Young argues that Darwinism cannot be thought of as an isolated discourse. It was, rather, part of a wider naturalistic movement in psychology, social theory, science, and religion. "The evolutionary debate," he wrote, "was seen by its participants as occurring within natural theology, with no antitheistic overtones, while those who used evolution for other purposes were themselves devoted believers in the secular religion of Progress, albeit a different religion, but one which has retained its appeal for the faithful" (Robert M. Young, *Darwin's Metaphor: Nature's Place in Victorian Culture* [Cambridge: Cambridge University Press, 1985], 21–22).
22. See Richard Hofstadter, *Social Darwinism in American Thought*, rev. ed. (Boston: Beacon Press, 1955).
23. Jacques Barzun, *Darwin, Marx, Wagner: Critique of a Heritage*, rev. 2nd ed. (Garden City, N.Y.: Doubleday Anchor Books, 1958), 65.
24. Jack London, *Martin Eden* (New York: Macmillan Co., 1908), 108. Quoted in Russett, *Darwin in America*, 16.
25. See Russett, *Darwin in America*.
26. Edith Wharton, *A Backward Glance* (New York and London: D. Appleton-Century Co., 1934), 94.
27. See Raymond H. Geselbracht, "Transcendental Renaissance in the Arts: 1890–1920," *New England Quarterly* 48, no. 4 (December 1975): 477.
28. A short essay written by the director of the Haeckel Archives suggests that Duncan read Haeckel's *Natural History of Creation* and probably *The Riddle of the Universe* at the British Museum (folder 34, Allan Ross Macdougall Collection, DC).

    At least two dozen English imprints were made of *The Evolution of Man: A Popular Exposition of the Principal Points of Human Ontogeny and Phylogeny*, beginning in 1874. It was originally published as *Anthropogenie oder Entwicklungsgeschichte des Menschen* (Leipzig: W. Engelmann, 1874). *The Riddle of the Universe at the Close of the Nineteenth Century* was first translated into English in 1900, one year after the original German. *Die welträthsel: Gemeinvertändliche Studien über monistische Philosophie* (Bonn: E. Strauss, 1899).

29. From one of two letters quoted in Allan Ross Macdougall, *Isadora: A Revolutionary in Art and Love* (New York, Edinburgh, Toronto: Thomas Nelson and Sons, 1960), 91. According to Duncan biographer Fredrika Blair, the original letters from Duncan to Haeckel are at the Haeckel Archives in Jena, Germany. Fredrika Blair, *Isadora: Portrait of the Artist as a Woman* (New York: William Morrow, 1986), 415. There is also a letter from Duncan to Haeckel in the Howard Holtzman Documentation of Isadora Duncan collection, which went on sale in 1990. Until the collection is open for inspection, it remains to be confirmed whether this is one of the letters quoted by Macdougall or a previously unknown letter.

30. Ernst Haeckel, *The Riddle of the Universe at the Close of the Nineteenth Century*, trans. Joseph McCabe (New York and London: Harper and Brothers, 1901), 20.

31. Ibid., 344.

32. Not all evolutionists interpreted Darwin's theories as positing an inherent design in nature. (Darwin himself was undecided on this issue.) In the philosophical dispute between chance and design, evolutionists such as Thomas Henry Huxley argued against the idea of a grand design by Divine Providence, while Spencer and Haeckel supported the notion of an underlying design and order. See Russett, *Darwin in America*, 32–36. As for these radically contradictory uses for evolution theory, Robert M. Young points out that Darwin's central concept of "natural selection," which "binds all of life together and defines its relations with the rest of nature, was anthropomorphic, deeply ambiguous, and amenable to all sorts of readings and modifications" (Young, *Darwin's Metaphor*, 125).

33. Duncan, *Art*, 102–103.

34. See Russett, *Darwin in America*.

35. Francis Steegmuller, ed., *"Your Isadora": The Love Story of Isadora Duncan and Gordon Craig* (New York: Random House and the New York Public Library, 1974), 97.

36. Isadora Duncan, *My Life* (New York: Boni and Liveright, 1927), 344.

37. Isadora Duncan, "Like an Ancient Greek Bas-Relief Come to Life She Astonishes Paris," 1901, Isadora Duncan Clippings, DC.

38. Quoted in Macdougall, *Isadora*, 85.

39. After six months, the boys' voices and behavior were deteriorating. Finally, when Duncan was informed that they were escaping at night and frequenting the cafés, she packed them off back to Athens (Duncan, *My Life*, 138–140).

40. "Wriggling into Wealth. Two Dancing Daughters of Sunny Spain, Carmencita and Otero. The Ballet of the Future Will Have Little Use for Legs. They Are Children of Nature, but Their Mother Seems to Have Taught Them How to Dance—They Could Give Delsarte Points on Making Your Body Talk—Poetry of Motion Personified," Performing Arts Library and Museum, San Francisco, California.

41. "Isadora Duncan Raps Maud Allan," *New York Times*, 9 August 1908, sec. 3, p. 3.

42. See Craig Brownell Bowie, "A Survey of Dances and Dancers in Vaudeville" (M.A. thesis, University of Arizona, 1984).

43. Rush, "Isadora Duncan," *Variety*, 2 August 1908, Isadora Duncan Clippings, DC.

44. "It is doubtful," it was reported in 1909, "if a woman ever appeared on a New York stage with more sincere admirers of her own sex in the audience, than has been the case with Isadora Duncan during her appearance as a Greek dancing-girl in her present engagement" (Arthur Mason, "Mistress of the Dance," *Green Book Album* 1 [January 1909]: 139).

45. H. E. Krehbiel, "Miss Duncan's Dancing," *New York Daily Tribune*, 7 November 1908, Isadora Duncan Clippings, DC.

46. "Isadora Duncan's Dance Causes War in St. Louis," *Kansas City Post*, 5 November 1909, Isadora Duncan Clippings, DC.

47. Collections of Greek vases and plaster cast collections of the great statuary circulated in the new urban museums of the late nineteenth century. Even before seeing the British Museum, Duncan herself may have seen San Francisco's brand new collection of Greek vases in the California Midwinter Exposition Memorial Museum, which opened in March 1895. (See *Guide to the Halls and Galleries of the California Midwinter Exposition Memorial Museum*, vol. 1 [San Francisco: H. S. Crocker Co., 1895].) In New York, she may have seen the plaster casts at the Metropolitan Museum of Art.

48. See Elizabeth Ewing, *Dress and Undress: A History of Women's Underwear* (London: B. T. Batsford, 1978), 114–115.

49. "On with the Dance, Isadora's War Cry" [*New York World*, 1922], Isadora Duncan Clippings, DC.

50. Julia Levien, interview with author, New York City, 10 July 1990. Furthermore, writes Levien:

> Those *tea*-dipped undershirts were of silk-jersey (it was *pre*-nylon days). We fashioned them ourselves into a sort of leg-less leotard by just sewing the bottom and cutting the sides high enough not to show. (We also wore briefs underneath this leotard.) The tunic was *pinned* to the shoulders. The complicated elastic harness was also pinned to this, to keep it from riding around and keeping the drapes in place. We always travelled with bundles of little gold safety pins. . . .
>
> However, it is interesting that when we went to have our photos taken by Arnold Genthe (Isadora's favorite photographer) we did not use anything underneath!—He thought the undergarments spoiled the line of the body. This of course added to the legend that we wore nothing under the tunic! (Julia Levien, letter to author, 17 January 1994)

51. Although the removal of underarm hair did not become popular until the late teens, and the removal of leg hair even later, female performers were removing body hair before 1914. It was the sleeveless dancing dresses of the teens that popularized the removal of underarm hair. See Christine Hope, "Caucasian Female Body Hair and American Culture," *Journal of American Culture* 5 (Spring 1982): 93–99. I thank Irene Castle biographer Susan Cook for referring me to this source.

52. Levien interview, 1990.

53. "Miss Duncan's Vivid Dances," *New York Times*, 17 November 1909, 11.

54. Deborah Jowitt, "The Impact of Greek Art on the Style and Persona of Isadora Duncan," *Proceedings Society of Dance History Scholars*, comp. Christena L. Schlundt (Riverside, Calif.: Society of Dance History Scholars, 1987), 199.

55. Maurice Emmanuel's *The Antique Greek Dance after Sculptured and Painted Figures*, trans. Harriet Jean Beauley (1895; reprint, London: John Lane Co., 1916), had been a popular French book at the turn of the century, and by 1916 it had been translated into English. It may well have been one of the dance books that Duncan pored over in the Paris Opera library in 1901. A scholar, Emmanuel

embarked on essentially the same project as Duncan: to reconstruct the movement style of the figures on Greek vases. With profuse illustrations and diagrams, he traced the antique images through to contemporary ballet. He argued, at least as convincingly as Duncan, that much, and perhaps most, of the turned-out ballet vocabulary that Duncan labeled artificial was practiced by those Nature-loving Greeks. The Franco-Russian balletomane critic André Levinson seized upon Emmanuel's material as a way to vindicate classical ballet, when he insisted that it was "high time that the prejudices which range the antique Hellede upon the side of the Duncans and the Dalcrozes in their combat against the art of the ballet, be eliminated, for it is a presumption founded upon a misconception" (André Levinson, "Some Commonplaces on the Dance," *Broom* 4, no. 1 [December 1922]: 17).

56. Ruth St. Denis and, to a lesser extent, Loie Fuller and Maud Allan also pioneered modern dance. Unlike Duncan, however, St. Denis often performed in vaudeville venues. Fuller and Allan spent most of their careers in Europe, as did Duncan, but had much less of an impact in America.

57. Lawrence W. Levine, *Highbrow/Lowbrow: The Emergence of Cultural Hierarchy in America* (Cambridge, Mass., and London: Harvard University Press, 1988), 132.

58. Ibid., 146.

59. Pierre Bourdieu, *Distinction: A Social Critique of the Judgement of Taste*, trans. Richard Nice (Cambridge, Mass.: Harvard University Press, 1984), 11.

60. Ibid., 6.

61. Isadora Duncan, "Dancing in Relation to Religion and Love," *Theatre Arts Monthly* 11 (October 1927): 593.

62. Duncan, *Art*, 118.

63. *The Metropolitan Museum of Art Twenty-fifth Annual Report of the Trustees of the Association* (New York: Metropolitan Museum of Art, 1895), 23.

64. Ibid., 26.

65. Duncan, *Art*, 92.

66. Maurice Dumesnil, *An Amazing Journey: Isadora Duncan in South America* (New York: Ives Washburn, 1932), 153.

67. Duncan, *Art*, 126.

68. Henry F. May, *The End of American Innocence: A Study of the First Years of Our Own Time, 1912–1917* (London: Jonathan Cape, 1960), 333–334.

69. Max Eastman, *Love and Revolution: My Journey through an Epic* (New York: Random House, 1964), 6.

70. "Bodily hexis is political mythology realized, *em-bodied*, turned into a permanent disposition, a durable way of standing, speaking, walking, and thereby of feeling and thinking" (Pierre Bourdieu, *The Logic of Practice*, ed. Richard Nice [Stanford, Calif.: Stanford University Press, 1990], 69–70). See Bourdieu, *Distinction*, 169–225.

71. Dance in the American cultural field shifted with the tours of Anna Pavlova in 1910 and Diaghilev's Ballets Russes in 1916 and 1917. As ballet took a foothold, and the display of technique came to displace "Nature" as the generally accepted basis of theatrical dancing, Duncan's claim to naiveté worked against her.

72. Macdougall, *Isadora*, 222. Like many other tidbits of "documented" Duncan lore, this may be apocryphal. In this case, however, the aphorism rings very true.

73. "The agitated ripples that Isadora Duncan started have widened and divided until now there are many different schools of free dancing," reported the *Woman Citizen*

in 1926. "One of the most popular, whose appeal and influence is national, is the school of Florence Fleming Noyes." She had four schools in New York City and two summer camps in Cobalt, Connecticut (Mildred Adams, "The Rhythmic Way to Beauty," *Woman Citizen* 11 [October 1926]: 27).

74. "Isadora Duncan and Poet Husband Detained on Liner," *New York Times*, 2 October 1922, 3.

4. THE EXPRESSIVE BODY

1. Susanne K. Langer, *Feeling and Form* (New York: Charles Scribner's Sons, 1953), 177; Katharine Everett Gilbert, "Mind and Medium in the Modern Dance," *Journal of Aesthetics and Art Criticism* 1 (Spring 1941): 110.

2. Lincoln Kirstein, "The Curse of Isadora," *New York Times*, 23 November 1986, sec. II, pp. 1, 28.

3. Theodore Dreiser, *Sister Carrie* (1900; reprint, New York: Bantam, 1988), 385.

4. Jackson Lears, *No Place of Grace: Antimodernism and the Transformation of American Culture, 1880–1920* (New York: Pantheon Books, 1981), 32.

5. For an extensive theory on the relationship of the body and subject in dance, see Susan Leigh Foster, *Reading Dancing: Bodies and Subjects in Contemporary American Dance* (Berkeley: University of California Press, 1986). My ideas about Duncan's expressive body as one of outward flow and force were inspired by Bruce A. McConachie's paper presented to the 1992 annual conference of the Association of Theatre in Higher Education, "Metaphors We Act By: Kinesthetics, Cognitive Psychology, and Historical Cultures." This paper subsequently was expanded and published: Bruce A. McConachie, "Metaphors We Act By: Kinesthetics, Cognitive Psychology, and Historical Structures," *Journal of Dramatic Theory and Criticism* 7, no. 2 (Spring 1993): 25–46.

6. Margherita Duncan, "Isadora," in Isadora Duncan, *The Art of the Dance*, ed. Sheldon Cheney (New York: Theatre Arts, 1928), 17.

7. Program, "Rubaiyat of Omar Khayyam: Done into Dance by Isadora Duncan," Newport, Rhode Island, 8 September 1898, Isadora Duncan Programs and Announcements, Dance Collection, New York Public Library for the Performing Arts (hereafter cited as DC).

8. Kristeva uses the term to emphasize the constant fluidity of the self-in-process (Julia Kristeva, *Revolution in Poetic Language*, trans. Margaret Waller [New York: Columbia University Press, 1984]).

9. W. R. Titterton, "Classical Dancing in England," *T. P.'s Magazine* [May 1911], Isadora Duncan Clippings, DC.

10. Eric Homberger, *American Writers and Radical Politics, 1900–39: Equivocal Commitments* (New York: St. Martin's Press, 1986), 190.

11. John Sloan, *John Sloan's New York Scene from the Diaries, Notes and Correspondence, 1906–1913*, ed. Bruce St. John (New York: Harper and Row, 1965), 352.

12. Arthur Frank Wertheim, *The New York Little Renaissance: Iconoclasm, Modernism, and Nationalism, 1908–1917* (New York: New York University Press, 1976), 7.

13. Charles H. Caffin, "Henri Matisse and Isadora Duncan," *Camera Work* 25 (January 1909): 19.

14. See Natalia Rene, "Isadora Duncan and Constantin Stanislavsky," *Dance Magazine* 37, no. 7 (July 1963): 40–43; Natalia Roslavleva, "Stanislvaski and the Ballet," *Dance Perspectives* 23 (Spring 1965).

15. Quoted in Selma Jeanne Cohen, ed., *Doris Humphrey: An Artist First* (Middletown, Conn.: Wesleyan University Press, 1972), 75. For a discussion of the expressive body and subject in early modern dance, see Foster, *Reading Dancing*.

16. Van Wyck Brooks, *America's Coming-of-Age* (Garden City, N.Y.: Doubleday Anchor Books, 1958), 62.

17. Quoted in Harold Aspiz, *Walt Whitman and the Body Beautiful* (Urbana: University of Illinois Press, 1980), 133.

18. Walt Whitman, *Leaves of Grass* (1892; reprint, New York: Bantam, 1983), 76–77.

19. Ibid., 1.

20. See Walt Whitman, "Personalism," *Galaxy* 5, no. 5 (May 1868): 540–547.

21. "Dramatic Expression," Steele MacKaye Papers, Dartmouth College Library, Hanover, New Hampshire.

22. From the preface to the bulletin of MacKaye's "School of Expression" (New York, 1877). Quoted in Claude L. Shaver, "The Delsarte System of Expression as Seen through the Notes of Steele MacKaye" (Ph.D. diss., University of Wisconsin, 1937), 40.

23. For information about MacKaye, see Shaver, *Delsarte System*; Garff B. Wilson, *A History of American Acting* (Bloomington: Indiana University Press, 1966), 99–103.

24. Bliss Carman, *The Making of Personality* (Boston: L. C. Page and Co., 1908), 104–126.

25. Evelyn Allen Aitchison, "Statue-Posing," *Werner's Magazine* 22, no. 6 (February 1899): 434.

26. Genevieve Stebbins, *Delsarte System of Expression* (1902; reprint, New York: Dance Horizons, 1977), 444. Stebbins published the first American book on Delsarte, in 1885; her series of Delsarte matinees stretched from the early 1880s into the next decade. See Suzanne Shelton, "The Influence of Genevieve Stebbins on the Early Career of Ruth St. Denis," in *Essays in Dance Research from the Fifth CORD Conference*, ed. Diane Woodruff (New York: Congress on Research in Dance, 1978), 33–49.

27. See Jack W. McCullough, *Living Pictures on the New York Stage* (Ann Arbor, Mich.: UMI Research Press, 1983).

28. Elsie M. Wilbor, *Delsarte Recitation Book* (1890; reprint, New York: Edgar S. Werner, 1893), 377.

29. See McCullough, *Living Pictures*.

30. "Bodily Responsiveness: An Interview with Mrs. Emily M. Bishop, a Pioneer in the 'Psychologic' Training of the Body for Health and for Self-Expression," *Werner's Magazine* 23, no. 2 (April 1899): 89.

31. Eugene Field, "The Doings of Delsarte," *Argonaut* 30, no. 11 (14 March 1892):12.

32. Gwyneth King Roe Papers, State Historical Society of Wisconsin, Madison.

33. Mara L. Pratt, *The New Calisthenics* (Boston and New York: Educational Publishing Co., 1889), 1.

34. Mrs. H. R. Haweis, *The Art of Beauty* (Franklin Square, N.Y.: Harper and Brothers, 1878), 6.

35. Brochure, "Lectures and Lecture-Lessons by Henriette [*sic*] Hovey (Mrs. Richard Hovey) Pupil and Formerly Assistant of Gustave Delsarte," Richard Hovey Papers, Dartmouth College Library.

36. "A Craze for Delsarte," *New York World*, 16 August 1891, Richard Hovey Papers, Dartmouth College Library.

37. Richard Hovey Papers.

38. Mary Perry King, *Comfort and Exercise: An Essay toward Normal Conduct* (Boston: Small, Maynard and Co., 1900), 12.
39. Ibid., 51.
40. Richard Hovey Papers.
41. Carman, *Personality*, 19.
42. See Warren I. Sussman, "'Personality' and the Making of Twentieth-Century Culture," in *Culture as History: The Transformation of American Society in the Twentieth Century* (New York: Pantheon Books, 1984), 271–285.
43. "Emotional Expression," *New York Herald*, 20 February 1898.
44. There are at least three threads connecting Duncan to Delsarte: (1) Her lover, Gordon Craig, recalled seeing a Delsarte book that Duncan owned, even though Delsarte never wrote a book himself (Francis Steegmuller, ed., *"Your Isadora": The Love Story of Isadora Duncan and Gordon Craig* [New York: Random House and the New York Public Library, 1974], 363). (2) According to Allan Ross Macdougall, a friend and biographer of Duncan, the dancer told one of her later secretaries, Walter Shaw, that she had "Professor of Delsarte" printed on her professional cards during her early years in San Francisco (Allan Ross Macdougall, *Isadora: A Revolutionary in Art and Love* [New York: Thomas Nelson and Sons, 1960], 31). (3) According to Millicent Dillon, when Duncan was teaching dance in San Francisco, "her classes were billed as 'Instruction in the Dance and Delsarte.' (An entry in the San Francisco City Directory of that year shows Delsarte instruction being given at their Sutter-Van Ness address.)" (Millicent Dillon, *After Egypt: Isadora Duncan and Mary Cassatt* [New York: Dutton, 1990], 164).
45. See E. M. Booth, *Outlines of the Delsarte System of Expression, Arranged for Use of Classes*, 3rd ed. (Iowa City: Republican Co., 1890).
46. See John Stokes, Michael R. Booth, and Susan Bassnett, *Bernhardt, Terry, Duse: The Actress in Her Time* (Cambridge, England: Cambridge University Press, 1988).
47. Duncan, *Art*, 100.
48. "Isadora Duncan's Dancing," *New York Sun*, 8 September 1908, Isadora Duncan Clippings, DC.
49. Robert Goldwater, *Symbolism* (New York: Harper and Row, 1979), 4–5.
50. Ibid., 6.
51. Arthur Symons, *Studies in Seven Arts* (1906; reprint, New York: E. P. Dutton and Co., 1924), 30.
52. Paul Gsell and Auguste Rodin, *Rodin on Art*, trans. Mrs. Romilly Fedden (New York: Horizon Press, 1971), 33.
53. Irma Duncan, *Duncan Dancer: An Autobiography* (Middletown, Conn.: Wesleyan University Press, 1966), 170.
54. Duncan, *Art*, 131.
55. Quoted in Gordon McVay, *Isadora and Esenin* (Ann Arbor, Mich.: Ardis Publishers, 1980), 18.
56. Quoted in Ilya Ilyich Schneider, *Isadora Duncan: The Russian Years* (New York: Da Capo Press, 1968), 113.
57. McVay, *Isadora and Esenin*, 88.
58. Maurice Magnus, "Gordon Craig and His Art," 1907, 28, Edward Gordon Craig Papers, Harry Ransom Humanities Research Center, Austin, Texas.
59. Duncan, *Art*, 102.

60. Ibid., 103.

61. William James, *The Principles of Psychology*, vols. 1 and 2 (New York: Henry Holt and Co., 1890). Emotions, he explained, are constituted by physiological reflex actions to outside stimuli; therefore, the number and types of emotions are unlimited, manifested differently in each individual. Perhaps in response to the Delsarte craze, he pointedly concluded that no classification or set of emotional expressions is more true and natural than any other.

62. Duncan, *Art*, 52.

63. Ibid.

64. Loie Fuller, *Fifteen Years of a Dancer's Life* (1913; reprint, New York: Dance Horizons, [1978]), 70.

65. "American Dancing Girl the New Sensation in Paris," *World*, 16 December 1900, Isadora Duncan Clippings, DC; "The New Art of Expressing Thoughts and Emotions in Dancing," *San Francisco Call Magazine*, 3 March 1907, pt. 2, p. 6.

66. Allen Monroe Foster, ". . . Fatherland; Isadora Duncan's Poetic Dances Have Divided Germany into Two Camps," 1902, Isadora Duncan Clippings, DC.

67. Redfern Mason, folder 166, Irma Duncan Collection of Isadora Duncan Materials, DC.

68. See Carl Dahlhaus, *Between Romanticism and Modernism*, trans. Mary Whittall (Berkeley: University of California Press, 1980).

69. Nelson Goodman, *Languages of Art* (Indianapolis: Hackett Publishing Co., 1976).

70. Steegmuller, *"Your Isadora,"* 172, 175.

71. Jean d'Udine, "Isadora Duncan," *Le Courrier musical* 7, no. 10 (15 May 1904): 340. Translated and quoted in Selma Landen Odom, "Mouvement du corps dans l'enseignement d'Emile Jaques-Dalcroze," in *La Danse Art du XXe Siècle?* (Lausanne: Editions Payot, 1990), 129. Translated by Selma Landen Odom.

72. H. T. Parker, *Motion Arrested: Dance Reviews of H. T. Parker*, ed. Olive Holmes (Middletown, Conn.: Wesleyan University Press, 1982), 69–70.

73. For an excellent history of Duncan's choreography from a musical perspective, see Diane Milhan Pruett, "A Study of the Relationship of Isadora Duncan to the Musical Composers and Mentors Who Influenced Her Musical Selections for Choreography" (Ph.D. diss., University of Wisconsin–Madison, 1978).

74. Paul Hertelendy, "Isadora's Childhood: Clearing Away the Clouds," *Dance Magazine* 51, no. 7 (July 1977): 49.

75. Duncan, *Art*, 107.

76. Schopenhauer considered music apart from the other arts, including drama, insofar as it transcended the mere representation of a particular state or emotion to get to the universal essence, or Will, of a state or emotion. Despite the fact that he invoked Schopenhauer, Wagner, in *Opera and Drama*, argued that in opera, music should provide a subordinate service, as an expressive means to the dramatic end. See Dahlhaus, *Romanticism and Modernism*, 19–39, 106–119.

77. Friedrich Nietzsche, *The Birth of Tragedy*, trans. Walter Kaufmann (1886; reprint, New York: Vintage Books, 1967), 103.

78. Redfern Mason, "'I Aim to Speak the Language of Humanity,' Says Isadora Duncan," *San Francisco Examiner*, 25 November 1917, Isadora Duncan Collection, Performing Arts Library and Museum, San Francisco, California.

79. Dahlhaus, *Romanticism and Modernism*, 5.

80. Walter Pater, *The Renaissance: Studies in Art and Poetry* (1873; reprint, Chicago: Pandora Books, 1977), 135.

81. "Isadora Duncan's Dancing," *New York Sun*, [5] September 1908, Isadora Duncan Clippings, DC.

82. Symons, *Seven Arts*, 382.

83. A copy of the bill is in the Billy Rose Theatre Collection, New York Public Library for the Performing Arts.

84. Shaemas O'Sheel, "Isadora Duncan, Priestess," *Poet Lore* 21, no. 6 (November–December 1910): 482.

85. Folder 166, Irma Duncan Papers, DC.

86. Morris R. Werner, *To Whom It May Concern: The Story of Victor Ilyitch Seroff* (New York: Jonathan Cape and Harrison Smith, 1931), 246.

87. Maude Durrant, "Isadora Duncan: The San Francisco Girl Whose Twinkling Heels Have Captivated Europe," *San Francisco Chronicle Magazine*, 2 August 1903, 3.

88. See Nesta Macdonald, "Isadora Reexamined: Lesser-Known Aspects of the Great Dancer's Life, 1877–1900," *Dance Magazine* 57, no. 7 (July 1977): 62.

89. In 1905 she reconstituted an edited and expanded version of her "Dance Idylls" program from the New Gallery. It featured a minuet by Jean-Philippe Rameau; music from Fabritio Caroso's treatise *Nobiltà di Dame* (1600), for *Primavera*; a musette by François Couperin; a tambourin by Rameau; music from Cesare Negri's treatise *Le Gratie d'Amore* (1602) for *Angel with a Viol*; a musette by Rameau; music by Jacopo Peri, for *Narcissus*; music by Attilio Ariosti, for *Pan and Echo*; music by Giovanni Picchi, for *Bacchus and Ariadne*.

90. Although almost all of the concert and opera music that Duncan used prior to Beethoven's Symphony no. 7 in A Major was dance music, there were rare exceptions. Very early, for example, she used Mendelssohn's "Song without Words." Her "Chopin-Abend" program also included nondance music.

91. Carl Van Vechten, *The Dance Writings of Carl Van Vechten*, ed. Paul Padgette (New York: Dance Horizons, 1974), 17.

92. Ibid., 18.

93. "Miss Duncan Dances Wagner," *New York Sun* [February 1911], Isadora Duncan Clippings, DC.

94. Ibid.

95. "Isadora Duncan, Teacher" [*New York American*, 1915], *New York Journal-American* Morgue, Harry Ransom Humanities Research Center, Austin, Texas.

96. Isadora Duncan, *My Life* (New York: Boni and Liveright, 1927), 151.

97. The original, translated by Jurgen Streeck: "Der Meister hat einen fehler gemacht, eben so grosse wie seine Genie . . . Die Musik-Drama, das ist doch ein unsinn" (ibid., 151).

98. As the *New York Times* described it:

> The orchestra played the first movement before the rise of the curtain, and with the second Miss Duncan began her dance. The first part of her dance followed the shadings of the music and might be described as a series of pictures portraying the alternating feelings from woe to gayety, which the dancer interpreted as the composer's meaning. With the rollicking scherzo of the final "presto" movement, however, subtlety was cast aside, and the dance became frankly joyous. ("Miss Duncan Scores in New Dances," *New York Times*, 29 August 1908, 9)

99. Gertrude Norman, "Isadora Duncan and Her Greek Barefoot Dances," *Theatre Magazine* [February 1905], Isadora Duncan Clippings, DC.

100. "Isadora Duncan's Dancing," *New York Sun*, 1908, Isadora Duncan Clippings, DC.

101. "Boston Is Bacchic Says Miss Duncan," *Boston Sunday Herald*, 28 November 1909, Isadora Duncan Clippings, DC.

102. V. Svetlov, "An Evening with Isadora Duncan," *Dance News* 31, no. 3 (November 1957): 7. Reprinted from *Petersburgskaya gazeta*, 9 January 1913.

103. For example, see Van Vechten, *Dance Writings*, 16.

104. Duncan, *Art*, 84.

105. For an analysis of Duncan's tour in the Netherlands, see Lillian Loewenthal, "Isadora Duncan in the Netherlands," *Dance Chronicle* 3, no. 3 (1979–80): 227–253. For a detailed chronology of Duncan's repertoire and musical selections, see Pruett, "Musical Composers and Mentors."

106. For another, schematic description of *Iphigenia in Aulis*, see Caroline and Charles H. Caffin, *Dancing and Dancers of Today: The Modern Revival of Dancing as an Art* (reprint, 1912; New York: Da Capo Press, 1978), 54–56.

107. Folder 166, Irma Duncan Papers, DC.

108. Program note for *Orpheus* [1909], Isadora Duncan Clippings, DC.

109. Duncan also used the Isadorables, her adopted students, as a more literal chorus. That, however, is the subject of another book.

110. Duncan, *Art*, 87.

111. Typescript, folder 149, Irma Duncan Papers, DC.

112. Program, 23 March 1911, Plays and Player Scrapbook 2, Chicago Theatre Collection, Chicago Public Library.

113. Van Vechten, *Dance Writings*, 21–22.

114. Redfern Mason, "Miss Duncan at Her Best in 'Orfeo,'" *San Francisco Examiner*, 3 December 1917, 6.

115. Caffin and Caffin, *Dancing and Dancers*, 61.

116. Hiram Kelly Moderwell, "Dancing Sophocles," *New York Times*, 28 March 1915, sec. 7, p. 5.

117. Duncan was friends with poet, playwright, and pageantry movement advocate Percy MacKaye, who was Steele MacKaye's son. It was most likely out of personal friendship rather than admiration for pageantry (she disdained amateurs) that Duncan agreed to a cameo appearance in his *Caliban* pageant in 1916. On pageantry, see David Glassberg, *American Historical Pageantry: The Uses of Tradition in the Early Twentieth Century* (Chapel Hill: University of North Carolina Press, 1990); Naima Prevots, *American Pageantry: A Movement for Art and Democracy* (Ann Arbor, Mich.: UMI Research Press, 1990); Dorothy J. Olsson, "Arcadian Idylls: Dances of Early Twentieth-Century American Pageantry" (Ph.D. diss., New York University, 1992); Martin S. Tackel, "Women and American Pageantry" (Ph.D. diss., City University of New York, 1982).

118. Witter Bynner, *Iphigenia in Tauris* (New York: Mitchell Kennerley, 1915).

119. At the eleventh hour, as Duncan was trying to leave the country, her own *deus ex machina* descended to square the bills. According to the *New York Telegraph*, "wealthy art lovers, headed by Frank A. Vanderlip, president of the National City Bank, came to her rescue and $3,000 in cash was raised to meet the most pressing bills. The balance was taken care of by notes, guaranteed by responsible parties. So close to the hour of departure were the arrangements completed that the final papers were signed by Miss Duncan on the pier under the direction of her attorney" ("Isadora Duncan Sails for Naples," *New York Telegraph*, 10 May 1915, Isadora Duncan Clippings, DC).

120. Isadora Duncan to Gilbert Murray, 4 September 1911, Ms. Gilbert Murray 18, folio 213; Isadora Duncan to Gilbert Murray, 28 October 1911, Ms. Gilbert Murray 19, folio 33, Gilbert Murray Papers, Bodleian Library, Oxford University. Also see Harry C. Payne, "Modernizing the Ancients: The Reconstruction of Ritual Drama, 1870–1920," *Proceedings of the American Philosophical Society* 122, no. 3 (9 June 1978): 182–192.

121. Margaret Wycherly, "As I Knew Them," folder 37, Allan Ross Macdougall Collection, DC.

122. "Isadora Duncan in 'Oedipus Rex,'" *New York Times*, 17 April 1915, 11.

123. Sigmund Spaete, "Duncan Players Give Sophocles' 'Oedipus,'" *New York Mail*, 17 April 1915, Isadora Duncan Clippings, DC.

124. "Isadora Duncan by Sophocles," *New York Telegraph*, 17 April 1915, Isadora Duncan Clippings, DC.

125. "Isadora Duncan in 'Oedipus Rex,'" 11.

126. Mary Fanton Roberts, "Isadora—The Dancer," *Denishawn Magazine* 1, no. 4 (Summer 1925): 10.

127. H. T. Parker, "Isadora's Plight: The Sorry End of Mistaken Ventures," *Boston Evening Transcript*, 9 May 1915, Isadora Duncan Clippings, DC.

128. Sewell Stokes, *Isadora Duncan: An Intimate Portrait* (London and New York: Brentano's, 1928), 84.

129. *Isadora Duncan Technique and Choreography* (New York: Dance Films Association, 1979). This video features reconstructions performed by the Isadora Duncan Centenary Dance Company.

5. THE FEMALE BODY

1. Louis C. Fraina, "Lydia Kyasht—Spirit of Beauty," *Modern Dance Magazine*, April 1914, 12.

2. Arthur Hornblow, "Dancing as a Fine Art," *Munsey's* 16, no. 6 (March 1897): 741. Also see Camille Hardy, "Ballet Girls and Broilers: The Development of the American Chorus Girl, 1895–1910," *Ballet Review* 8, no. 1 (1980): 96–127; Derek and Julia Parker, *The Natural History of the Chorus Girl* (Indianapolis and New York: Bobbs-Merrill, 1975).

3. See Robert C. Allen, *Horrible Prettiness: Burlesque and American Culture* (Chapel Hill: University of North Carolina Press, 1991); Marilyn A. Stolzman Moses, "Lydia Thompson and the 'British Blondes' in the United States" (Ph.D. diss., University of Oregon, 1978).

4. Quoted in Robert J. Wills, Jr., "The Riddle of Olive Logan: A Biographical Profile" (Ph.D. diss., Case Western Reserve University, 1971), 129.

5. Ibid., 135.

6. See "Cultural Feminism," in Josephine Donovan, *Feminist Theory: The Intellectual Traditions of American Feminism* (New York: Frederick Ungar Publishing Co., 1985), 31–63.

7. Abba Goold Woolson, *Woman in American Society* (Boston: Roberts Brothers, 1873), 136.

8. Victoria Claflin Woodhull and Tennessee C. Claflin, *The Human Body the Temple of God; or, The Philosophy of Sociology* (London: Hyde Park Gate, 1890), v.

9. Quoted in the St. Louis, Missouri *Globe-Democrat*, 2 February 1876. Reprinted in Woodhull and Claflin, *The Human Body*, 507.

10. J. C. Croly, "The Woman's Club Movement," in Lydia Hoyt Farmer, ed., *The National Exposition Souvenir: What America Owes to Women* (Buffalo and Chicago: Charles Wells Moulton, 1893), 305–317.

11. May Wright Sewall, ed., *The World's Congress of Representative Women*, vol. 1 (Chicago and New York: Rand, McNally and Co., 1894), 162.

12. Floyd Dell, *Women as World Builders: Studies in Modern Feminism* (1913; reprint, Westport, Conn.: Hyperion Press, 1976), 44.

13. Fraina, "Lydia Kyasht," 13.

14. See Nancy F. Cott, *The Grounding of Modern Feminism* (New Haven, Conn.: Yale University Press, 1987).

15. Janet Vale, "Interviewing Isadora," *New York Morning Telegraph*, 14 February 1915, 5. When Duncan married Sergei Esenin in the Soviet Union in 1922, they both adopted a double surname, adding the other's to their own (Folder 171, Irma Duncan Papers, Dance Collection, New York Public Library for the Performing Arts [hereafter cited as DC]).

16. Amy Wellington to Mary Fanton Roberts, 9 November [19??], Mary Fanton Roberts Collection of Isadora Duncan Materials, Theatre Collection, Museum of the City of New York.

17. Vale, "Interviewing Isadora," 5. Duncan seems to have believed that Ida Sniffen Walters was pregnant, but there is no mention of a pregnancy in the extensive coverage by the *New York Times*.

18. Isadora Duncan, *My Life* (New York: Boni and Liveright, 1927), 18.

19. "No Wickedness in Ida Rogers," *New York Evening Sun*, 12 January 1915, DC.

20. Mona Caird's articles, published in magazines such as *North American Review, Westminster Review, Fortnightly Review*, and *Nineteenth Century*, were reprinted in a volume titled *The Morality of Marriage and Other Essays on the Status and Destiny of Woman* (London: George Redway, 1897), 1. Sociologist Thorstein Veblen took up this same idea of marriage as property and tied it to economics in his essay "The Barbarian Status of Women," *American Journal of Sociology* 4, no. 4 (January 1899): 503–514.

21. See "The New Morality," in Richard J. Evans, *The Feminist Movement in Germany, 1894–1933* (London: Sage Publications, 1976), 115–143.

22. Edward Gordon Craig Papers, Harry Ransom Humanities Research Center, University of Texas at Austin. Among the other names in the address book for 1903–1907 were Ernst Haeckel, Karl Federn, and Douglas Ainslie.

23. Duncan, *My Life*, 17.

24. For a contemporary comparison of the Anglo-American and the German/Scandinavian approaches to Feminism, see Katharine Anthony, *Feminism in Germany and Scandinavia* (New York: Henry Holt and Co., 1915).

25. See Evans, *Feminist Movement*, 117. Although today some understand Nietzsche as a misogynist, and others as a proto-Nazi, many people at that time understood him as exhorting a romantic individualism that urged everyone to live beyond the strictures of bourgeois existence. Helene Stocker, one of the founders of the Mutterschutz movement, was deeply influenced by Nietzsche, and argued that he had taught women to be spiritually independent.

26. Ibid., 138. Also see Ann Taylor Allen, *Feminism and Motherhood in Germany, 1800–1914* (New Brunswick, N.J.: Rutgers University Press, 1991).

27. Francis Steegmuller, ed., *"Your Isadora": The Love Story of Isadora Duncan and Gordon Craig* (New York: Random House and the New York Public Library, 1974), 119–120.

28. Ibid., 205.
29. Carroll Smith-Rosenberg, "The Hysterical Woman: Sex Roles and Role Conflict in 19th-Century America," *Social Research* 39, no. 4 (Winter 1972): 652–678.
30. Duncan, *My Life*, 208.
31. Steegmuller, *"Your Isadora,"* 206.
32. Ibid., 185.
33. Ibid., 192.
34. Ibid., 202.
35. Ibid., 205.
36. Ibid., 86.
37. Ibid., 79–80.
38. Duncan, *My Life*, 245.
39. Isadora Duncan, *Der Tanz der Zukunft* (Leipzig: Eugen Diederichs, 1903), 23.
40. Duncan, *My Life*, 241–242.
41. Actually, Duncan had started working with the image of the mother very early in her career, well before her identification as the mourning mother. In 1901, for example, she danced Gretchaninoff's "Berceuse," in which she pretends to lean, while kneeling, over the cradle of a child.
42. Irma Duncan wrote: "The only boy pupil she had in my time was called Jean and of Italian parentage in her school in France. He remained for a couple of years in the school and then returned to his parents. I believe he subsequently danced in the French Ballet at the Opera in Paris. He also knew none of Isadora's dances only what he was taught to do as a child" (Irma Duncan to Mignon Garland, 20 June 1971, folder 112, Irma Duncan Papers, DC).

Although Isadora believed that no school of the dance was complete without both boys and girls, she felt ill-equipped to provide the model of strength required by the boys. She wrote in a notebook:

It is now many years since the idea first began to dance in me of the possibility of raising young girls in such an atmosphere surrounded by Beautiful form & that by holding before them always the ideal form they would gradually grow to a personification of it in their own Bodies—and thus by the continuous practice of beautiful movement in coincident of that form would become perfect Beings in form & movement—It is this idea which for many years I fostered as a sort of pattern of the Ideal Dance School—Though such a School could not be deemed complete without the male & female element together still I felt for my part capable only of forming such a school for girls—as I believe for the stronger or male element it would need a man as conductor—(Collection of Isadora Duncan Materials, Theatre Collection, Museum of the City of New York)

43. "Isadora is teaching young boys now" (Irma Duncan diary, 16 December 1921, DC).
44. Irma Duncan and Allan Ross Macdougall, *Isadora Duncan's Russian Days and Her Last Years in France* (New York: Covici-Friede, 1929), 276.
45. Duncan, *My Life*, 345. She also recalled that upon discovering that the lover of a young man she was trying to help was male, "I was not as shocked as some people might have been. I believe the highest love is a purely spiritual flame which is not necessarily dependent on sex" (Duncan, *My Life*, 285). Not incidentally, I think, Duncan was writing these passages at the same time she was having her

affair with de Acosta, who was helping her broker her memoirs. Millicent Dillon unearthed and published the erotic letters from Duncan to de Acosta, deposited in the de Acosta Archives in the Rosenbach Museum and Library in Philadelphia (Millicent Dillon, *After Egypt: Isadora Duncan and Mary Cassatt* [New York: Dutton, 1990], 350–351). For an account of de Acosta's affairs with actresses Greta Garbo, Eva Le Gallienne, and Marlene Dietrich, among others, see Hugo Vickers, *Loving Garbo: The Story of Greta Garbo, Cecil Beaton and Mercedes de Acosta* (London: Jonathan Cape, 1994).

46. Mrs. H. R. Haweis, *The Art of Beauty* (Franklin Square, N.Y.: Harper and Brothers, 1878), 26.

47. Collection of Isadora Duncan Materials, Theatre Collection, Museum of the City of New York. Interestingly enough, this section was marked "skip" and was not included in the published version.

48. Although this excerpt sounds as if Duncan is asserting an essentialist definition of Woman as knowing through the body rather than through the mind, another version of this essay makes clear that Duncan is merely asserting experience as an alternately valid means of understanding, beside the intellectual. See Isadora Duncan, "The Dance and Its Inspiration: Written in the Form of an Old Greek Dialogue," *Touchstone* 2, no. 1 (October 1917): 6, 13–15.

49. Duncan, *Art*, 66–67.

50. See Henry Adams, "Primitive Rights of Women," in Adams, *Historical Essays* (New York: Charles Scribners' Sons, 1891), 1–41; David R. Contosta, "Henry Adams on the Role of Woman," *New Scholar* 4, no. 2 (1974): 181–190.

51. Charles Henry Meltzer, *New York American*. Quoted in Duncan program, 23 February [1911], Boston Opera House, Harry Ransom Humanities Research Center, University of Texas at Austin.

52. S. H., "Visions of the Nude," *Camera Work* 31 (July 1910): 30–31.

53. See Christian A. Peterson, "American Arts and Crafts: The Photograph Beautiful, 1895–1915," *History of Photography* 16, no. 3 (Autumn 1992): 189–234.

54. J. Nilsen Laurvik, "Mrs. Annie W. Brigman—A Comment," *Camera Work* 25 (January 1909): 47. See also Theresa Thau Heyman, *Anne Brigman* (Oakland, Calif.: The Oakland Museum, 1974).

55. Historian Ann Douglas argues that northeastern clergyman and middle-class women came to prominent influence in the realm of secular culture during the Victorian era (Ann Douglas, *The Feminization of American Culture* [New York: Anchor Press Doubleday, 1988]). On the patronage and leadership of women in pageantry and the visual arts in the mid- to late nineteenth and early twentieth century, see Martin S. Tackel, "Women and American Pageantry, 1908 to 1918" (Ph.D. diss., City University of New York, 1982), and Kathleen D. McCarthy, *Women's Culture: American Philanthropy and Art, 1830–1930* (Chicago: University of Chicago Press, 1991).

56. By the time that expression calcified into its own academic convention, it had become a matter of mastery and been coded as masculine. Thus, after women pioneered modern dance, the form went mainstream with a generation that featured significantly more male choreographers.

57. Carl Van Vechten, *The Writings of Carl Van Vechten*, ed. Paul Padgette (New York: Dance Horizons, 1974), 24.

58. Martin F. Shaw, *Up to Now* (London: Oxford University Press, 1929), 72.

59. "The Vulgarization of Salome," *Current Literature* 45, no. 4 (October 1908): 440.

60. W. L. Hubbard, "Girl's Art Dance Airy As Her Garb," *Chicago Daily Tribune*, 1 December 1908, Chicago Theatre Collection, Chicago Public Library.

61. The public was ripe for indignation, in no small part because Duncan's American debut came in the midst of an epidemic of Salome acts—no fewer than twenty-four in vaudeville in October 1908. See "The Vulgarization of Salome," 437.

62. Before Duncan had left for Europe, in 1899, when women were still covered neck to ankle, the dancer was baring her arms in performance. At that point she was still wearing pink stockings and dancing slippers. Her costumes—not yet fashioned after the Greek chiton—were described as filmy or draping.

By the time the dancer returned to the U.S. in 1908, she wore Greek-style tunics, leaving her legs and feet bare as well. Duncan's garments, which hung loosely from the shoulders, were not a complete shock to her audiences, for women were already wearing (in their homes) loose, high-waisted Empire- or Directoire-style tea gowns, which marked the transition from the narrow-waisted, S-curved silhouette of the Edwardians to the modern sheath, with its verticality and relatively unconstricted waist.

Although Duncan echoed the nineteenth-century dress-reform advocates' cry that "the unnatural can never be beautiful," I do not see her as triumphant where the mid-nineteenth-century dress-reform advocates had failed. Duncan's impact on American fashion had less to do with the dress-reform movement than with the emergence of a modern ideal of female beauty and fashion. Duncan's reappearances, 1908–1911, coincided with a significant shift in "look," from an emphasis on a slim waist and full, matronly mono-bosom to a slender and sinuous body type, draped in neo-Directoire gowns or, later on, ensconced in the narrow hobble skirt. The new look was associated with the French designer Paul Poiret, who credited Duncan as his inspiration.

For an excellent history of fashion in this period, including a chapter on the complexities of "the corset controversy," see Valerie Steele, *Fashion and Eroticism: Ideals of Feminine Beauty from the Victorian Era to the Jazz Age* (New York and Oxford: Oxford University Press, 1985).

63. See Mark Gabor, *The Pin-up: A Modest History* (New York: Bell Publishing Co., 1972).

64. Roland Barthes, "Striptease," in *A Barthes Reader*, ed. Susan Sontag (New York: Hill and Wang, 1982), 88.

65. Steele, *Fashion and Eroticism*, 172–186.

66. Abigail Solomon-Godeau, "The Legs of the Countess," *October* 39 (Winter 1986): 104.

67. For a detailed theoretical analysis, see Ann Daly, "Dance History and Feminist Theory: Reconsidering Isadora Duncan and the Male Gaze," in *Gender in Performance: The Presentation of Difference in the Performing Arts*, ed. Laurence Senelick (Hanover and London: University Press of New England, 1992).

68. Floyd Dell, "Who Said That Beauty Passes Like a Dream?" *The Masses* 8, no. 12 (October 1916): 27.

69. "What Modern Women Want," *Modern Dance Magazine*, January 1914, 11.

70. Shaemas O'Sheel, "Isadora Duncan, Priestess," *Poet Lore* 21, no. 6 (November December 1910): 481.

6. THE BODY POLITIC

1. Max Eastman, *Heroes I Have Known* (New York: Simon and Schuster, 1942), 86.
2. Irma Duncan and Allan Ross Macdougall, *Isadora Duncan's Russian Days and Her Last Years in France* (New York: Covici-Friede, 1929), 171. In her last, penurious years in Europe, she found that it was much easier to stall payment at the high-class hotels.
3. Merle Armitage, "Isadora Duncan," Mary Fanton Roberts Collection of Isadora Duncan Materials, Theatre Collection, Museum of the City of New York.
4. "No Wickedness in Ida Rogers," *New York Evening Sun*, 12 January 1915, Isadora Duncan Clippings, Dance Collection, New York Public Library for the Performing Arts (hereafter cited as DC).
5. "This artistic ferment has been called The Confident Years, The Rebellion, The Liberation, The Joyous Season, The League of Youth, and The New Paganism" (Arthur Frank Wertheim, *The New York Little Renaissance: Iconoclasm, Modernism, and Nationalism in American Culture, 1908–1917* [New York: New York University Press, 1976], xi). Edward Abrahams calls it "the lyrical left" (Edward Abrahams, *The Lyrical Left: Randolph Bourne, Alfred Stieglitz and the Origins of Cultural Radicalism in America* [Charlottesville: University of Virginia Press, 1986]).
6. Adele Heller and Lois Rudnick, "Introduction," in *1915, The Cultural Moment: The New Politics, the New Woman, the New Psychology, the New Art, and New Theatre in America*, ed. Adele Heller and Lois Rudnick (New Brunswick, N.J.: Rutgers University Press, 1991), 3.
7. Abrahams, *Lyrical Left*, 6.
8. Mabel Dodge Luhan, *Movers and Shakers* (1936; reprint, Albuquerque: University of New Mexico Press, 1985), 83.
9. Irving Howe, "To *The Masses*—With Love and Envy," in *Echoes of Revolt: The Masses, 1911–1917*, ed. William L. O'Neill (Chicago: Quadrangle Books, 1966), 5.
10. Floyd Dell, *Love in Greenwich Village* (New York: George H. Doran Co., 1926), 27.
11. Robert Henri, "The New York Exhibition of Independent Artists," *Craftsman* 18, no. 2 (May 1910): 161.
12. Max Eastman, *Enjoyment of Living* (New York: Harper and Brothers, 1948), 399.
13. Luhan, *Movers and Shakers*, 333.
14. Emma Goldman, *Living My Life*, vol. 1 (New York: Alfred Knopf, 1931), 56.
15. The full list of the committee, published in *Dionysion* 1, no. 1 (1915), is Herbert Adams, Jacob Adler, John Alexander, Louis K. Anspacher, Gertrude Atherton, George Grey Barnard, George Bellows, Karl Bitter, Gutzon Borglum, Witter Bynner, John Collier, Will Levington Comfort, Julia Culp, Walter Damrosch, Randall Davey, Arthur B. Davies, Paul Dougherty, Theodore Dreiser, John Drew, Max Eastman, Abastenia St. L. Eberle, Barry Faulkner, James Fraser, Elizabeth Freeman, John Hemming Fry, Elena Gerhardt, Sara Greene, Bolton Hall, Walter Hampden, Bert Hansen, Robert Henri, Alfred Hertz, Mrs. Frederick C. Howe, Charles Rann Kennedy, Kathryn Kidder, Isidore Konti, Fola LaFollette, Walter Lippmann, Percy MacKaye, Paul Manship, Edith Wynne Mathison, Charles Henry Meltzer, Hiram K. Moderwell, Luis Mora, Dr. Moskowitz, Lloyd Osbourne, Ernest Peixotto, Van Deering Perrine, Mary Fanton Roberts, W. Carman Roberts, Henrietta Rodman, Janet Scudder, John Sloan, Ellen Terry, Charles Hanson Towne, John Butler Yates [*sic*].

16. Thomas Bender, *New York Intellect: A History of Intellectual Life in New York City, from 1750 to the Beginnings of Our Own Time* (New York: Alfred A. Knopf, 1987), 241–242.
17. Quoted in Wertheim, *New York Little Renaissance*, 178.
18. Abrahams, *Lyrical Left*, 24. Abrahams makes a distinction between the conservatives such as Herbert Croly and the *New Republic* writers, with their static vision of an orderly society founded upon the principles of corporate bureacracy, and the cultural radicals, who emphasized individuality, spontaneity, and expression.
19. Mary Fanton Roberts, "The Dance of the People," *Craftsman* 22, no. 2 (May 1912): 196.
20. Eastman, *Enjoyment*, 420.
21. Howe, "To *The Masses*," 5.
22. H. G. Wells, "First and Last Things," quoted in "On Beauty," *Camera Work* 27 (July 1909): 17.
23. During the war, Duncan was in the United States November 1914 to May 1915 and September 1916 to early 1918.
24. Her lover, the sewing machine heir Paris Singer, offered to make a gift of Madison Square Garden to her in 1917, but she sabotaged that opportunity with an outburst of temperament similar to the one that ruined her 1915 meeting with New York City mayor John Purroy Mitchel, which was set up by Mabel Dodge, Walter Lippmann, and John Collier to gain her an armory for a new school. After the disaster with the mayor, Lippmann wrote Dodge:

    I'm utterly disgusted. If this is Greece and Joy and the Aegean Isles and the Influence of Music, I don't want anything to do with it. It's a nasty, absurd mess, and she is obviously the last person who ought to be running a school. I want you to let me off the committee; you can tell the others I'm too busy. (Quoted in Luhan, *Movers and Shakers*, 331)

25. Isadora Duncan, "Oh! Shame on America!" *Louisville Herald*, March 1915, Isadora Duncan Clippings, DC.
26. Even when Duncan offered affordable ten-cent seats to the general public during her Dionysion month at the Century Theatre in April 1915, she was able to do so only because Otto H. Kahn, partner in the brokerage house of Goldschmidt, Kahn, and Teutsch and a powerful patron of the arts who served as chairman of the board of directors of the Metropolitan Opera, had procured the theater for her.
27. Duncan, "Shame on America!"
28. For an account of this tour, see Maurice Dumesnil, *An Amazing Journey: Isadora Duncan in South America* (New York: Ives Washburn, 1932).
29. Either some reviewers found it inappropriate to mention the nudity or the other reviewers conflated Duncan's performance with the bare-breasted images of Marianne that she was invoking.
30. Carl Van Vechten, *The Dance Writings of Carl Van Vechten*, ed. Paul Padgette (New York: Dance Horizons, 1974), 25.
31. The Nike of Samothrace, another heroic classical image used in the French past (and one of Duncan's own favorites), was also being recycled by the Parisian avant-garde: "After the start of the war in 1914 it [classicism] always referred to a new national sense of self-identity" (Kenneth E. Silver, *Esprit de Corps: The Art of the Parisian Avant-Garde and the First World War, 1914–1925* [Princeton:

Princeton University Press, 1989], 100). I thank Lynn Garafola for directing me to this source.

32. Quoted in "Isadora Duncan Dances the Marseillaise," *Current Literature*, January 1917, Isadora Duncan Clippings, DC.

33. "'Does the Spirit of France Mean Anything to America?'" *New York Tribune* [1915], Isadora Duncan Clippings, DC.

34. Allan Ross Macdougall and Irma Duncan, *Isadora Duncan's Russian Days and Her Last Years in France* (Covici-Friede, 1929), 267. Quoted in Kay Bardsley, "Reanimations of Duncan Masterworks," in *Dance Reconstructed: Conference Proceedings* (New Brunswick, N.J.: Rutgers State University, 1993), 198.

Duncan's impulse toward the allegorization of human Will had manifested itself much earlier. *Death and the Maiden* (c. 1902), for example, depicted the dancer in an ultimately fatal encounter with a menacing external force. She repeatedly danced forward and backward on a diagonal, the dynamic development of her movements demonstrating the struggle against the enervating force of Fate that faced her at the end of her pathway. As Karl Federn described it in 1903:

> She has a dance without music, horrible and moving: "Death and the Maiden." The maid dances joyously in the meadow, the whole youthful life rejoices in her half-childlike movements—then she is frightened, becomes motionless, and looks to the side; a shudder passes over her— but in the next moment it is forgotten and again she joyfully leaps and jumps at blossoms and fruits. Then—again!—as it is announced in Maeterlinck's "Intruse"—somewhere the scythe must become whetted. She stands, she raises herself on tiptoe, her hands become motion-less—coldness seems to flow through her limbs, her widened eyes look with deepest fear to the other side, and it overwhelms the spectator. But now she moves again—life still triumphs, her pleasure has become only more painful, her dance more hurried, more anxious. Everyone in the hall senses the arrival of the destroyer—as her fingers convulsively stretch and bend and the horror of impending death weaves around her! Once again quivering and quaking the earlier dance—and as under fiercely complaining struggle she plunges to the floor. (Karl Federn, "Einleitung," in Isadora Duncan, *Der Tanz der Zukunft* [Leipzig: Eugen Diederichs, 1903], 9)

35. "War Depicted in Series of Dances," *New York Telegraph*, 7 March 1917, Isadora Duncan Clippings, DC.

36. Folder 5, Isadora Duncan programs and announcements, DC.

37. Here again, Duncan is drawing upon a French patriotic tradition, one that reaches back to 1849, when the great French actress Rachel enacted a live allegory of the mythical nationalist goddess Marianne, singing the "Marseillaise," wearing a classical dress, and wrapping herself in the French flag. Red, the color of Duncan's robe, was the color of Marianne's Phrygian cap.

38. "Isadora Duncan Dances," 7 March 1917, Isadora Duncan Clippings, DC.

39. "Music and Musicians: Isadora Duncan Dances World Struggle with 'Star Spangled Banner' Climax," *New York Sun*, 7 March 1917, Isadora Duncan Clippings, DC.

40. Henry F. May, *The End of Innocence: A Study of the First Years of Our Own Time, 1912–1917* (London: Jonathan Cape, 1960), 371.

41. Ibid., 363.

42. Joseph Freeman, *An American Testament: A Narrative of Rebels and Romantics* (New York: Octagon Books, 1973), 95.

43. See Maurice Agulhon, *Marianne into Battle: Republican Imagery and Symbolism in France, 1789–1880*, trans. Janet Lloyd (Cambridge: Cambridge University Press, 1979). On the image of the Statue of Liberty in war posters, see George M. Dembo, "The Statue of Liberty in Posters: Creation of an American Icon," *P.S.: The Quarterly Journal of the Poster Society*, Winter 1985–86, 18–21; Wendy Shadwell, "The Statue of Liberty: A Century in the Graphic Arts," *Imprint* 10 (Spring 1985): 20–27; Donald E. Kloster and Edward C. Ezell, "American Posters and the First World War," *AB Bookman's Weekly* 79 (29 June 1987): 2879–2884.

44. The discourse of French patriotism was circulated in a variety of ways. The brokerage house of Otto Kahn, the philanthropist who supported Duncan's 1915 Dionysion season at the Century Opera House, underwrote huge loans to the Allies. Images of wealthy American expatriate women such as Edith Wharton and Gertrude Stein driving ambulances and nursing the wounded in Paris were published in American magazines including *Vanity Fair*. And at the Metropolitan Opera House, some conductors, such as Pierre Monteux, refused to conduct German music.

45. Quoted in "Isadora Duncan Dances the Marseillaise," *Current Literature*, January 1917, Isadora Duncan Clippings, DC.

46. Isadora Duncan, *My Life* (New York: Boni and Liveright, 1927), 334. The music and lyrics of the "Marseillaise," originally called "The War Hymn of the Army of the Rhine," had been composed by Captain Claude-Joseph Rouget de Lisle in 1792, in order to inspire French troops under siege by Prussian soldiers in Strasbourg. It caught on, and when soldiers sang it on their march from Marseilles to Paris several months later, it was given its present name. It was adopted as the French national anthem in 1795.

47. Van Vechten, *Dance Writings*, 28.

48. Ibid., 27.

49. Margherita Duncan, "Isadora," in Isadora Duncan, *The Art of the Dance*, ed. Sheldon Cheney (New York: Theatre Arts, 1928), 20.

50. Rene Fauchois, untitled poem printed in dress rehearsal program, 21 November 1916, Metropolitan Opera House, Isadora Duncan Ephemera, University of California at Los Angeles Research Library. Translation by Neda Doany.

51. "Music and Musicians."

52. Also featuring Duncan's five pupils, the program included dances to Beethoven's Symphony no. 7; Schubert's Unfinished Symphony; works by Chopin, Schubert, Brahms; the "Marche Lorraine"; and the "Marseillaise."

53. Duncan, *My Life*, 162.

54. Ibid., 334.

55. Ibid., 334–335.

56. Van Vechten, *Dance Writings*, 25–26.

57. Bender, *New York Intellect*, 246.

58. Duncan, *Art*, 109.

59. Ibid., 111.

60. "Isadora Duncan Off Will Never Return," *New York Times*, 4 February 1923, 15.

61. For extended accounts of Duncan's time in the Soviet Union, see Duncan and Macdougall, *Russian Days*; Gordon McVay, *Isadora and Esenin* (Ann Arbor, Mich.: Ardis Publishers, 1980); Ilya Ilyich Schneider, *Isadora Duncan: The Russian Years*

(New York: Da Capo Press, 1968). For an account of the revolutionary dances she composed there for her students, see Ann Daly, "The Continuing Beauty of the Curve: Isadora Duncan and Her Last Compositions," *Ballett International* 13, no. 8 (August 1990): 10–15.

62. Isadora Duncan, *Isadora Speaks*, ed. Franklin Rosemont (San Francisco: City Lights Books, 1981), 63.

63. Ibid., 75.

64. Betty Van Benthuysen, "Which Is Right?" *San Francisco Chronicle Sunday Magazine*, 26 March 1922.

65. Quoted in Schneider, *Isadora Duncan*, 37.

66. Eugene Lyons, "An Interview with Isadora Duncan," *Daily Worker*, 10 February 1923, 4.

67. Ibid.

68. Sol Hurok, *Impresario* (New York: Random House, 1946), 98.

69. See Theodore Draper, *The Roots of American Communism* (New York: Viking Press, 1957); Peter G. Filene, *Americans and the Soviet Experiment, 1917–1933* (Cambridge, Mass.: Harvard University Press, 1967); Julian F. Jaffe, *Crusade against Radicalism: New York during the Red Scare, 1914–1924* (Port Washington, N.Y., and London: Kennikat Press, 1972); Robert K. Murray, *Red Scare: A Study in National Hysteria, 1919–1920* (Minneapolis: University of Minnesota Press, 1955); David A. Shannon, *Between the Wars: America, 1919–1941*, 2nd ed. (Boston: Houghton Mifflin Co., 1979).

70. "Isadora Duncan and Poet Husband Detained on Liner," *New York Times*, 2 October 1922, 1.

71. "Admit Miss Duncan after 2-Hour Quiz," *New York Times*, 3 October 1922, 12. According to Hurok, the media flap sold out three performances in twenty-four hours (Hurok, *Impresario*, 101).

72. For a glimpse of how Duncan looked at this time, see a film clip of Duncan and Esenin culled from the outtakes of the Fox Movietone News Collection. The clip appears to have been taken upon their arrival in the U.S. (DC).

73. H. T. Parker, *Motion Arrested: Dance Reviews of H. T. Parker*, ed. Olive Holmes (Middletown, Conn.: Wesleyan University Press, 1982), 69.

74. Most of her repertoire during the last American tour was familiar: dances to Tchaikovksy's Symphony No. 6 ("Pathétique") and "Marche Slav"; Beethoven's Symphony no. 7; Schubert's "Ave Maria," "Marche Militaire," and Unfinished Symphony; selections from the Brahms waltzes; and Wagner's "Liebestod" from *Tristan and Isolde* and "Bacchanale" from *Tannhäuser*. New to her American audiences were two other Wagner works ("Siegfried's Funeral March" from *Die Götterdämmerung* and "Ride of the Valkyries" from *Die Walküre*); four by Alexander Scriabin (Sonata no. 4 and three études); and two by Franz Liszt ("Bénédiction de Dieu dans la solitude," no. 3, and "Funérailles," no. 7, from "Harmonies poétiques et religieuses").

75. Duncan, *Art*, 121.

76. Quoted in Walter Terry, *Isadora Duncan: Her Life, Her Art, Her Legacy* (New York: Dodd, Mead and Co., 1963), 157.

77. "Reflections of John Joseph Martin," c. 1967, 29–30, Oral History Program, University of California, Los Angeles, Research Library. British music critic Ernest Newman said that Duncan's "Ride of the Valkyries" illustrated her "secret," which seemed to him to be in the cooperation of every cell of her brain

and every movement of her face and limbs. "So perfectly does the machine work that, paradoxically, we can sometimes see it working when it is quite still" (Ernest Newman, "The World of Music: Isadora Duncan," *Sunday Times*, 17 April 1921, Mary Fanton Roberts Papers, Archives of American Art, Detroit, Michigan). In a moment of immobility,

> she gave us an incredible suggestion of the very ecstasy of movement: something in the rapt face, I imagine, carried on the previous joy of the wild flight through the air. The sudden cessation of physical motion had the overwhelming effect that Beethoven and Wagner now and then make, not with their music, but by a pause in it. (Ibid.)

78. "Miss Duncan's Farewell," *New York Times*, 15 November 1922, 22.
79. "Miss Duncan Dances Again," *New York Times*, 16 November 1922, 26.
80. Henry Levine, "Boston Bars Isadora Duncan," *Musical America* 37, no. 1 (28 October 1922): 2.
81. "On with the Dance, Isadora's War Cry," *World*, 1922, Isadora Duncan Clippings, DC.
82. "US Probe Ordered," *San Francisco Examiner*, 24 October 1922, 10.
83. Brom Weber, ed., *The Letters of Hart Crane 1916–1932* (New York: Hermitage House, 1952), 109.
84. Hurok, *Impresario*, 118.
85. "Isadora Duncan Soviet Dancer," *San Francisco Examiner*, 16 October 1921, 9.
86. Shannon, *Between the Wars*, 33.
87. A. J. Lorenz, "Isadora Denies She's Nude; Skirt Is 'Glued' to Form," *San Francisco Examiner*, 25 October 1922, 5.
88. " 'America Makes Me Sick: Nauseates Me,' " *San Francisco Examiner Magazine*, 4 March 1923, 9.
89. "Girls Repudiate Isadora Duncan," *New York Telegraph*, May 1923, Isadora Duncan Clippings, DC.
90. The *New York Times* reported the decision:

> "Had Isadora Duncan's marriage taken place subsequent to the passage of the Cable Women's Separate Citizenship bill," the department's announcement said, "she would have retained her American citizenship, but since she lost it prior to Sept. 22, 1922, she cannot become an American citizen again without filing a petition in the manner provided for any other alien, and must prove herself to be a person of good moral character attached to the principles of the Constitution of the United States, and that she is not a disbeliever in or opposed to organized government or a member of or affiliated with any organization or body of persons teaching disbelief in organized government, et cetera." ("Holds Isadora Duncan Lost Her Citizenship," *New York Times*, 10 March 1923, 14. Also see "Davis Would Take Citizenship Away from Isadora Duncan," *New York Times*, 27 February 1923, 21)

Apparently Duncan knew about the rules regarding loss of citizenship for American women who married foreigners (Lyons, "Interview"), but apparently she also knew about the Cable Women's Separate Citizenship Bill. According to the *New York Times*'s account of her arrival in early October 1922, "The dancer said that she would apply under the recent law enacted for the restoration of her citizenship lost by marrying the young Russian" ("Isadora Duncan and Poet Husband Detained on Liner," 3).

7. EPILOGUE

1. Sol Hurok, *Impresario* (New York: Random House, 1946), 90.
2. Walter Lippmann, "Free Time and Extra Money," *Woman's Home Companion* 4 (1933), quoted in Ronald Steel, *Walter Lippmann and the American Century* (Boston and Toronto: Little, Brown and Co., 1980), 258.
3. Sean Dennis Cashman, *America in the Twenties and Thirties: The Olympian Age of Franklin Delano Roosevelt* (New York and London: New York University Press, 1989), 59.
4. Harold E. Stearns, ed., *Civilization in the United States* (New York: Harcourt, Brace and Co., 1922), vii.
5. Margaret C. Anderson, "Isadore [*sic*] Duncan's Misfortune," *Little Review* 3, no. 10 (April 1917): 5, 7.
6. Ibid., 5.
7. Ibid., 7.
8. Ibid.
9. Eugene Lyons, "An Interview with Isadora Duncan," *Daily Worker*, 10 February 1923, 4.
10. Robert M. Crunden, *Ministers of Reform: The Progressives' Achievement in American Civilization, 1889–1920* (New York: Basic Books, 1982).
11. Isadora Duncan, *My Life* (New York: Boni and Liveright, 1927), 152.
12. Ibid., 63–64.
13. Lois W. Banner, *American Beauty* (Chicago and London: University of Chicago Press, 1983), 271–273.
14. See "The Flapper," *Smart Set* 45, no. 2 (February 1915): 1–2; Valerie Steele, *Fashion and Eroticism: Ideals of Feminine Beauty from the Victorian Era to the Jazz Age* (New York and Oxford: Oxford University Press, 1985), 237; Sara M. Evans, *Born for Liberty: A History of Women in America* (New York: Free Press, 1989), 176.
15. Evans, *Born for Liberty*, 178–179.
16. George Landy, "Dancer's Path Leads to Cinema Land," *American Dancer* 1, no. 5 (November 1927): 11.
17. Gilbert Seldes, *The Seven Lively Arts* (New York: Harper and Brothers, 1924), 318.
18. *New York World*, quoted in "Isadora Duncan's Artistic Credo," *Literary Digest* 95 (8 October 1927): 29.
19. Duncan, *My Life*, 340.
20. "The Library: Two Enterprising Ladies," *American Mercury* 14, no. 56 (August 1928): 507.
21. She begins that paragraph explicitly: "I call my dance American rather than classic. By American I mean belonging to this country essentially" (Isadora Duncan, *The Art of the Dance*, ed. Sheldon Cheney [New York: Theatre Arts, 1928], 133).
22. Duncan, *My Life*, 343.
23. Ibid., 341.
24. Ibid., 342.
25. Ernest A. Breisach, *American Progressive History: An Experiment in Modernization* (Chicago and London: University of Chicago Press, 1993), 21–28. See Frederick J. Turner, "The Significance of the Frontier in American History," in Turner, *The Frontier in American History* (1893; reprint, New York: Henry Holt and Co., 1920), 1–38.
26. Crunden, *Ministers of Reform*, 74.
27. Duncan, *My Life*, 340, 341.

28. See Bruce Kellner, *Carl Van Vechten and the Irreverent Decades* (Norman: University of Oklahoma Press, 1968). Van Vechten wrote a controversial novel based on his Harlem experiences. See *Nigger Heaven* (New York: Alfred A. Knopf, 1926).
29. Claude McKay, *A Long Way from Home* (New York: Lee Furman, 1937), 212.
30. See Beverly Armstrong Chapman, "New Dance in New York, 1911–1915" (M.A. thesis, American University, 1977); Lewis A. Erenberg, *Steppin' Out: New York Nightlife and the Transformation of American Culture, 1890–1930* (Chicago and London: University of Chicago Press, 1981); Marshall and Jean Stearns, *Jazz Dance: The Story of American Vernacular Dance* (New York: Schirmer Books, 1968). For a class and gender analysis, see Kathy Peiss, *Cheap Amusements: Working Women and Leisure in Turn-of-the-Century New York* (Philadelphia: Temple University Press, 1986). For a race analysis, see David Nasaw, *Going Out: The Rise and Fall of Public Amusements* (New York: Basic Books, 1993).
31. Duncan, *My Life*, 340.
32. Ibid., 342.
33. Ibid., 340.
34. Ibid.
35. Isadora Duncan, "Dancing In Relation to Religion and Love," *Theatre Arts Monthly* 11 (August 1927): 591.
36. Ibid.
37. Duncan, *Art of the Dance*, 100.
38. Duncan, "Religion and Love," 590.
39. Wilbur C. Abbott, *The New Barbarians* (Boston: Little, Brown, and Co., 1925), 226.
40. Ibid., 8–9.
41. Ibid., 224.
42. Andre Siegfried, *America Comes of Age* (New York: Harcourt, Brace and Co., 1927), 141.
43. I thank Lynn Garafola for making this point. On the treatment of the Chinese immigrants in California, see Sucheng Chan, *This Bittersweet Soil: The Chinese in California Agriculture, 1860–1910* (Berkeley: University of California Press, 1986); Sucheng Chan, ed., *Entry Denied: Exclusion and the Chinese Community in America, 1882–1943* (Philadelphia: Temple University Press, 1991); Alan M. Kraut, *Silent Travelers: Germs, Genes, and the "Immigrant Menace"* (New York: Basic Books, 1994). Duncan's good friend Arnold Genthe made a photographic record of San Francisco's Old Chinatown from 1895 to 1906. See Arnold Genthe, *Genthe's Photographs of San Francisco's Old Chinatown* (New York: Dover Publications, 1984).
44. On race and *The Masses*, see Adele Heller and Lois Rudnick, eds., *1915, The Cultural Moment: The New Politics, the New Woman, the New Psychology, the New Art, and New Theatre in America* (New Brunswick, N.J.: Rutgers University Press, 1991), 42. On race and the settlement house movement, see Elisabeth Lasch-Quinn, *Black Neighbors: Race and the Limits of Reform in the American Settlement House Movement, 1890–1945* (Chapel Hill and London: University of North Carolina Press, 1993). On eugenics, see Donald K. Pickens, *Eugenics and the Progressives* (Nashville: Vanderbilt University Press, 1968). On eugenics and the birth control movement, see Linda Gordon, *Woman's Body, Woman's Right: Birth Control in America* (New York: Penguin Books, 1977).

While Duncan's interest in health, morality, and education certainly appears to be informed by the eugenics discourse, she never overtly promulgated "race purity." Elizabeth Duncan's school, however, under the influence of musician Max Merz, did emphasize German *körperkultur*, a physical culture practice that stressed racial hygiene. See Irma Duncan, *Duncan Dancer* (Middletown, Conn.: Wesleyan University Press, 1970), 107, 110, 127.

45. Toni Morrison, *Playing in the Dark: Whiteness and the Literary Imagination* (Cambridge, Mass.: Harvard University Press, 1992), 6.
46. Ibid., 17.
47. Duncan, *My Life*, 78, 255.
48. Morrison, *Playing in the Dark*, 7.
49. Duncan, *My Life*, 19.
50. Ted Shawn, *The American Ballet* (New York: Henry Holt and Co., 1926), 7–8, 22.
51. See Mr. and Mrs. Vernon Castle, *Modern Dancing* (New York: Harper and Brothers, 1914).
52. Isadora Duncan to Irma Duncan, 10 June 1924, Tashkent to Moscow, folder 17, Irma Duncan Collection of Isadora Duncan Materials, Dance Collection, New York Public Library for the Performing Arts.
53. I thank both Lynn Garafola and Robert M. Crunden for their thoughts on this point, in separate conversations.

INDEX

Abbott, Wilbur C., 218
Abrahams, Edward, 180–81, 252n5, 253n18
Ainslie, Douglas, 29, 74, 93
Aitchison, Evelyn Allen, 242n25
Allan, Maud, 60, 61
Allen, Robert C., 227n18, 247n3
Anderson, Margaret, 208–209, 258n5
Anspacher, Louis, 150
Apollo, 93, 95, 144
Armitage, Merle, 180, 252n3
Art, 12, 17, 20; expression in, 132, 134–35; Greek, 93–97, 100–103
The Art of the Dance, 17, 233n125
Aspiz, Harold, 242n17
Atherton, Gertrude, 14, 129, 226n51
Atwell, John E., 229n37
Avant-garde movement, 121–22
Ave Maria (1914), 185

Bach, Johann Sebastian, 143
Bachmann, Marie-Laure, 235n137
Baker, George M., 125
Balanchine, George, 67

Ballet, 24, 26–27, 34–35, 68–69, 75–77
Ballroom dancing, 25
Banner, Lois W., 258n13
Barker, Barbara, 232n102
Barthes, Roland, 175, 251n64
Barzun, Jacques, 98
Battersea, Lady, 24, 227n10
Bauer, Harold, 66, 231n82
Beauty, xiii, 4, 10; of the body, 30, 171; and human goodness, 36; and Nature, 32, 99; in the physical culture movement, 128
Beethoven, Ludwig van, 140, 143, 145, 245n90, 245n98
Beland, Elizabeth, 227n8
Belilove, Lori, 75, 78, 79, 233n112, 233n121
Bender, Thomas, 196–97, 253n16
Benson, F. R., 68, 72
Bishop, Emily, 127
The Black Crook, 158–59
Blair, Fredrika, xiii, 222n6
Blue Danube Waltz program, 62, 140, 145

Body, 3–5, 20, 171; in aesthetic theory, 30–31; dancing girl's, 156–60, 162; Duncan's development of, 77–81, 170–72; expressive, 120; form and movement of, 33–34; in Nature, 11, 19, 99, 172–73; positioning of, 74–75; soul's connection to, 31–32
Bok, Edward, 90
Bonfanti, Marie, 68–71, 76, 231n99
Booth, E. M., 243n45
Botticelli, Sandro, 91, 92, 139
Bourdieu, Pierre, xiii, 3–4, 7, 17, 112, 115, 222n1, 223n2, 223n14, 240n59
Bourne, Randolph, 182
Bow, Clara, 214
Boynton, Florence Treadwell, 68, 225n39
Breisach, Ernest A., 258n25
Brigman, Anne, 4, 173
Brooks, Van Wyck, 121, 122, 182, 242n16
Buchanan, Dr. Joseph Rodes, 122
Burgess, Gelett, 14, 225n48
Bynner, Witter, 246n118

Caffin, Charles H., 42, 122, 241n13
Caird, Mona, 164, 248n20
California, influence of, 8, 11–14, 91–92
Carman, Bliss, 129–30, 242n24
Cashman, Sean Dennis, 258n3
Castle, Irene, 209, 211, 214, 220
Cayvan, Georgia, 161
Chan, Sucheng, 259n43
Chapman, Beverly Armstrong, 259n30
Children: dancing as character formation for, 27, 227n21, 228n22. See also Duncan, Deirdre; Duncan, Patrick
Chopin, Frédéric, 66–67, 142–43, 245n90
"Chopin-Abend" program, 6, 245n90
Choreography, 6–7, 74–75, 142, 231n79, 231n86, 244n73
Christensen, Lew, 220
Claflin, Tennessee C., 161, 247n8
Clará, José, 42–43, 46–47
Clark, Mabel, 59
Class hierarchy, 111–16
Cohen, Selma Jeanne, 242n15
Coleman, Bud, 221n1
Cook, Susan, 239n51
Coolbrith, Ina, 12, 13, 28, 225n43
Costumes: Greek-inspired, 109; reform of, 74, 176, 251n62
Couperin, François, 143
Craig, Gordon, 8, 17, 29, 100, 139, 223n20, 243n44; Duncan's affair with, 135–36, 165–67, 224n33

Crane, Hart, 202
Croly, Herbert, 182, 228n30, 253n18
Croly, J. C., 248n10
Crunden, Robert M., 209, 216, 224n27, 260n53
Culture, 9–10, 224n32; and class hierarchy, 111–13; dancing as, 19, 110–11; and the female body, 172–73; and Nature, 90–92, 112, 172–73

Dahlhaus, Carl, 141, 244n68
Daly, Augustin, 68, 71–73, 232n104
Damrosch, Walter, 62, 107, 143–44
Dance: Duncan's theories of, 27–36; form and movement in, 33–34; gesture in, 18, 64, 66–67, 144; Greek-inspired, 100–110; as high culture, 19, 110–11; participated in Nature, 31; scholarly study of, 24–25; as socially progressive, 35–36; as soul's expression, 31–32; springs from music, 139–40, 142, 144–45; in successive movements, 34–35; wave movements in, 35, 99; Will expressed through, 32–33, 68
"Dance Idylls" program, 146, 245n89
"The Dance of the Future," 27, 29–36, 163
Darwin, Charles, 16, 29, 34, 100, 123, 228n34, 238n32. See also Evolutionism
de Acosta, Mercedes, 170, 250n45
Death and the Maiden program, 254n34
Degler, Carl N., 224n29
Dell, Floyd, 7, 162, 176, 181, 187, 223n16, 248n12
Delsarte, François, 123–24, 242n26, 243n44
Delsartism, American, 4, 123–31, 135
Descartes, René, 29
Després, Suzanne, 137
Desti, Mary, 226n55
Dillon, Millicent, 225n39, 231n91, 236n11, 243n44, 250n45
Dionysus, 95, 144; Dionysion season, 150–53, 184, 246n119
Dodge, Mabel, 180, 181–82, 252n8
Dodworth, Allen, 25–26, 227n15
Dolmetsch, Arnold, 142
"Done into Dance" program, 2
Donovan, Josephine, 247n6
Douglas, Ann, 250n55
Douglas, Mary, 3, 222n1, 223n13
Dreiser, Theodore, 120, 241n3
Dress reform, 30–31, 74, 176, 251n62
d'Udine, Jean, 140, 244n71

Dumesnil, Maurice, 240*n*66
Duncan, Anna (Isadorable), 78, 226*n*55, 230*n*74, 233*n*121
Duncan, Augustin (brother), 120, 150–52
Duncan, Deirdre (daughter), 100, 165–69, 188, 224*n*33
Duncan, Elizabeth (sister), 27–28, 68, 81, 228*n*27, 259*n*44
Duncan, Irma (Isadorable), 18, 36, 78, 134, 150–51, 226*n*55, 226*n*57; on Duncan's technique, 80; as teacher, 81–82, 230*n*74, 233*n*121
Duncan, Isadora: ballet lessons, 68–71, 231*n*99; childhood, 11–14; choreography by, 74–75, 142, 231*n*79, 231*n*86, 244*n*73; dance education of, 68–74; her dance schools, 81, 115–16, 145, 168, 184, 187–88, 196–98, 203, 249*n*42, 253*n*24; dance techniques, 64–68, 77–81, 170–72, 233*n*125; dance theories, 27–36; on Delsartism, 131, 135, 243*n*44; drawings of, 39, 42–47; dress reform by, 30–31, 74, 176, 251*n*62; exiles of, 16, 185, 203–204, 257*n*90; expression theory, 136–39; expressive movements of, 64–68, 120–21; in film, xi, 221*n*1, 222*n*4, 226*n*55; as mother, 165–69, 249*n*41; and music, 139–44; and nationalism, 20, 185–95; origins of her dancing, 24–27, 226*n*5; photographs of, xi, 39–41, 43, 47–59; physical characteristics of, 36–37, 173–77; and politics, 178–83; presence of, 38–39; racialism of, 90, 112–14, 217–19; and the Russian revolution, 195–97; in the Soviet Union, 15–16, 197–98, 255*n*61; as symbolist, 137–38; theatrical performances, 71–74
—Programs: Beethoven's Symphony no. 7 in A Major (1904), 62, 143, 145, 245*n*98; Blue Danube Waltz (1902), 62, 140, 145; "Chopin-Abend" (c. 1904), 6, 245*n*90; "Dance Idylls" (1900–c. 1903), 146, 245*n*89; Death and the Maiden (c. 1902), 254*n*34; "Done into Dance" (1898), 2; Iphigenia (1905–1915), 15; Iphigenia in Aulis (1905–1915), 62, 107, 108, 139, 146–48, 150; Iphigenia in Tauris (c. 1914–1915), 62, 107, 146–48, 150; Liebestod (1911), 143–44, 194; Marche Slav (1917), 196; Marseillaise (1914), 15, 139, 185–87, 189–91, 193–94, 253*n*29, 254*n*37, 255*n*46; Moment Musicale (1908), 62;

Oedipus Rex (1915), 15, 151; Orpheus (1900–1915), 15, 62, 107, 146, 148–50, 170; Pan and Echo (1903), 170; Pathétique (Beethoven, c. 1904), 140, 145; Pathétique (Tchaikovsky, 1916), 153, 188, 193, 200, 202, 231*n*79; La Primavera (c. 1898–1909), 92–94, 139; Siegfried's Funeral March (1918), 140, 153; Suite in D (1911), 143
—Tours in America: first tours (1908, 1909, 1911), 14–15, 59–68, 103–10, 142–44; second tours (1914–1918), 15, 139, 185–87, 189–91, 193–94, 253*n*29, 254*n*37; last tour (1922–23), 15, 198–203, 256*n*74
—Writings: Art of the Dance, 17, 233*n*125; "The Dance of the Future," 27, 29, 33, 163; "Form and Movement," 33–34; My Life, 11, 13, 17, 20, 215–16, 219–29; Your Isadora, 17
Duncan, Joseph C. (father), 11, 13, 111, 225*n*43, 225*n*44
Duncan, Marie Therese (Isadorable; aka Maria-Theresa), 18, 66, 226*n*56, 230*n*74, 231*n*80
Duncan, Mary Dora Gray (mother), 11, 92
Duncan, Patrick (son), 24, 100, 168–69, 188
Duncan, Raymond (brother), 69
Durrant, Maude, 245*n*87
Duse, Eleonora, 38, 131–32, 133, 135, 153

Eastman, Max, 16, 180, 181, 183, 226*n*52, 240*n*69
Ellis, Havelock, 164
Emerson, Ralph Waldo, 98
Empire Ballet, 71, 232*n*103
Esenin, Sergei, 15, 135, 196, 210, 248*n*15
Evolutionism, 24–25, 98–100, 162, 237*n*21, 238*n*32; and dance theory, 29
Ewing, Elizabeth, 239*n*48
Expression, 122; in art, 132, 134–35; groups, 125–26; and politics, 180–83; in theater, 131–32

Falck, Edward, 150
Fashion, reform in. See Dress reform
Fauchois, René, 194
Federn, Karl, 8, 95, 223*n*19, 254*n*34
Female body. See Body
Feminism, 162–64; German, 164–65, 248*n*24

Field, Eugene, 242*n*31
Flappers, 206, 209, 212, 214
Follen, Charles, 83
Force, bodily, 5–8, 223*n*17
Form: corresponding to movement, 33–34
"Form and Movement," 33–34
Foster, Susan L., 227*n*16, 241*n*5
Fraina, Louis C., 162, 182, 247*n*1
France, Anatole, 187
Franck, César, 153, 194
Frazer, James George, 25
Freeman, Helen, 150, 151
Freeman, Joseph, 255*n*42
Freud, Sigmund, 120
Froebel, Friedrich, 27, 228*n*22
Frohman, Charles, 59–62, 103, 107
Fuller, Loie, 62, 103, 106, 137, 244*n*64
Fuller-Maitland, John Alexander, 142
Funérailles (1918), 153, 186

Gabor, Mark, 251*n*63
Gamson, Annabelle, 233*n*121
Garafola, Lynn, 233*n*117, 254*n*31, 259*n*43, 260*n*53
Garland, Mignon, 233*n*121
Geertz, Clifford, xv, 222*n*7
The Geisha program, 72
Genée, Adeline, 63, 84–85
Genthe, Arnold, 39–41, 230*n*64, 239*n*50
Geselbracht, Raymond H., 237*n*27
Gesture, 18, 64, 144; virtual, 66–67
Gilbert, Katharine Everett, 118–19
Gilman, Charlotte Perkins, 163
Gintautiene, Kristina, 232*n*100
Glassberg, David, 246*n*117
Gluck, Christoph Willibald, 107, 143, 146–48
Goldman, Emma, 182
Goldwater, Robert, 132, 134, 243*n*49
Goodman, Nelson, 139, 244*n*69
Gorky, Maxim, 135
Gorman, Margaret, 209, 213
Graff, Ellen, 224*n*35
Graham, Martha, 194, 220
Graham, Patricia Albjerg, 228*n*30
Grandjouan, Jules, 42, 45
Greeks, influence of, 16–17, 29, 100–103, 112–14, 178, 215; and art, 93–97; the Dionysion season, 150–53, 184, 246*n*119; and the female body, 170; the Greek chorus, 15, 145–47; and Nature, 90–92
Grove, Mrs. Lilly, 25, 227*n*13

Guest, Ivor, 230*n*70
Guinn, James Miller, 225*n*42
Gymnastics, 82–87, 124, 235*n*137

Haeckel, Ernst, 4, 13, 29, 91, 237*n*28, 238*n*29, 238*n*32; natural theology of, 98–99, 114
Hall, Bolton, 66, 67, 231*n*83
Halley, William, 225*n*42
Hardy, Camille, 230*n*70
Harris, George Jr., 150
Harrison, Jane Ellen, 93, 237*n*17
Haweis, Mrs. H. R., 170, 250*n*46
Hayman, Philip, 26
Heller, Adele, 180, 252*n*6
Henderson, Linda, 230*n*78
Henri, Robert, 17, 39, 64, 121, 181, 230*n*63
Henry V performances, 72
Hertelendy, Paul, 69, 228*n*29, 231*n*94, 244*n*74
Heyman, Therese Thau, 250*n*54
Hill, Eunice, 59
Hitchcock, Edward, 83
Hofstadter, Richard, 237*n*22
Homberger, Eric, 241*n*10
Hornblow, Arthur, 247*n*2
Hovey, Henrietta Russell, 128–29
Howard, Eric, 224*n*31
Hubbard, W. L., 67, 231*n*89, 251*n*60
Humphrey, Doris, 122
Hurok, Sol, 198, 206, 256*n*71
Huxley, Thomas Henry, 238*n*32

"I See America Dancing," 20, 215–16, 219–20
Iphigenia in Aulis program, 15, 62, 107, 108, 139, 146–48, 150
Iphigenia in Tauris program, 62, 107, 146–48, 150
Isadorables, 18, 34, 36, 230*n*74, 246*n*109. *See also* Duncan, Anna; Duncan, Irma; Duncan, Marie Theresa

Jahren, Neal, 229*n*47
James, William, 4, 136, 244*n*61
Jaques-Dalcroze, Emile, 65, 84–85, 235*n*137
Jazz, critique of, 7, 114–15, 217, 219–20
Jensen, Joan M., 225*n*38
Johnson, Mark, xiii, 5, 223*n*5
Johnston, Frances, 173
Jones, Howard Mumford, 8, 224*n*22
Jowitt, Deborah, xiii, 110, 222*n*6, 239*n*54

Kahn, Otto, 151, 185, 255*n*44
Kandinsky, Wassily, 42, 65
Keats, John, 91
Kellermann, Annette, 209, 213
Kellner, Bruce, 259*n*28
Kendall, Elizabeth, xiii, 222*n*6
Kern, Stephen, 228*n*23
Key, Ellen, 164–65
Kinel, Lola, 135
King, Mary Perry, 129, 243*n*38
Kingsley, Charles, 107
Kirstein, Lincoln, 77, 119, 231*n*85, 241*n*2
Kooluris, Hortense, 64, 82, 230*n*74, 233*n*121
Kozodoy, Ruth, 221*n*2
Krehbiel, H. E., 107
Kristeva, Julia, xiii–xiv, 7, 121, 176, 223*n*12, 241*n*8

Langer, Susanne K., 66–67, 118, 231*n*84, 241*n*1
Lanner, Katti, 68, 69, 71, 231*n*99
Laurvik, J. Nilsen, 173, 250*n*54
Lears, Jackson, 120, 236*n*2, 241*n*4
Lecomte, Valentine, 42, 44
Levien, Julia, 82, 223*n*11, 233*n*121, 239*n*50; on Duncan's choreography, 6, 231*n*79, 231*n*86; on modern dance techniques, 78, 230*n*76; *Mother* performance, 153–54
Levine, Lawrence W., 111, 112, 240*n*57
Levinson, André, 8, 75–77, 224*n*21, 233*n*117
Liebestod program, 143–44, 194
Lippmann, Walter, 207–208, 253*n*24
Liszt, Franz, 153
Living statues, 125–26
Loewenthal, Lillian, 231*n*81, 246*n*105
Logan, Olive, 159
London, Jack, 98, 237*n*24
Loring, Eugene, 220
Lothrop, Gloria Ricci, 225*n*38
Lully, Jean Baptiste, 142
Lunacharsky, Anatoly, 197–98, 203

Macdonald, Nesta, 245*n*88
Macdougall, Allan Ross, xiii, 222*n*6, 226*n*5, 230*n*62, 243*n*44
MacKaye, Percy, 152, 246*n*117
MacKaye, Steele, 123, 124, 242*n*23, 246*n*117
Maeterlinck, Maurice, 137
Manners, 25–26
Marche Slav performance, 196

Marlowe, Julia, 161
Marriage, feminist criticism of, 163–65
Marseillaise programs, 15, 139, 185–87, 189–91, 193–94, 253*n*29, 254*n*37, 255*n*46
Marsh, Lucile, 36, 229*n*58
Martin, Theodore Penny, 228*n*30
Marwedel, Emma, 227*n*21
Marwig, Carl, 72
Mason, Redfern, 137
Mastbaum, Jay, 69
Matisse, Henri, 42, 121–22
Mauss, Marcel, 77, 222*n*5, 222*n*1
May, Henry F., 114, 187, 224*n*29, 240*n*68, 254*n*40
McConachie, Bruce A., 241*n*5
McCullough, Jack W., 242*n*27
McKay, Claude, 217
McVay, Gordon, 255*n*61
The Meg Merrilies performances, 72
Mencken, Ada Isaacs, 159
Mencken, H. L., 121, 215
Mendelssohn, Felix, 2, 142, 245*n*90
A Midsummer Night's Dream performances, 72–74
Miss Pygmalion performances, 72
Modern dances, 217. *See also* Ragtime
Moderwell, Hiram Kelly, 150, 246*n*116
Modjeska, Helen, 161
Moment Musicale program, 62
Monteverdi, Claudio, 143
Montez, Lola, 159
Morality: dancing and, 9–10, 25–26; the New Morality, 164–65, 248*n*21
Morris, Clara, 161
Morrison, Toni, xiii, 219, 223*n*15
Mother (1924), 153–54
Motherhood, voluntary, 163–65
Movement: corresponding to form, 33–34
Much Ado about Nothing performances, 72
Muir, John, 90
Mulford, Harry, 225*n*45
Mumford, Lewis, 9, 121, 224*n*28
Munro-Fraser, J. P., 225*n*42
Murray, Gilbert, 151
Music, 139–44; dance born of, 139–40, 142, 144–45; and emotion, 138, 244*n*76; neoromantic, 141. *See also* Rhythm
Muybridge, Eadweard, 8
My Life, 11, 13, 17; " I See America Dancing," 20, 215–16, 219–20

Nathan, Marvin R., 225*n*50
Nationalism, 20, 185–95
Nature, xiii, 4, 75; in Art, 134; Beauty in, 32; and Culture, 89–92, 112, 172–73; dancing and, 31, 112, 134; Dionysian, 95; Duncan's identification with, 88, 91–92; in evolutionism, 98–100; and the female body, 11, 19, 99, 172–73; the Greeks and, 90–92, 100–103; and social control, 90; and Truth, 98, 99; wave movements in, 35, 99
Neurasthenia, 166
Nevin, Ethelbert, 2, 142
New Morality, 164–65, 248*n*21
Newman, Ernest, 256*n*77
Nietzsche, Friedrich, 16, 17, 91, 113, 144, 229*n*35, 229*n*37, 237*n*19; on the body, 31; and the Dionysian, 95; and feminism, 165; on music, 138, 140–41; and the Superman, 29–30; and the Will, 6, 32, 228*n*34; his Zarathustra, 10, 39, 40
Nikolenko, Ivan, 226*n*55
Norman, Gertrude, 245*n*99
Nude, 19, 109, 172–73

Oakland Turnverein, 68, 69
Odom, Selma Landen, 235*n*137
Oedipus Rex program, 15, 151
Oliphant, James, 227*n*6
Olsson, Dorothy J., 246*n*117
Orpheus program, 15, 62, 107, 146, 148–50, 170
O'Sheel, Shaemas, 4, 142, 177, 223*n*3

Pan and Echo program, 170
Pantomimes, Delsartrean, 125
Parker, H. T., 67, 140, 152–53, 231*n*87, 247*n*127
Pater, Walter, 141, 244*n*80
Pathétique (Beethoven) program, 140, 145
Pathétique (Tchaikovsky) program, 153, 188, 193, 200, 202, 231*n*79
Pathognomy, 122–23
Pavlova, Anna, 75, 76, 185, 240*n*71
Physical Culture movement, 26, 83, 123, 127–31, 259*n*44
Plato, 16, 140, 178
Poletaev, N. G., 135
Politics: Duncan's, 178–83; of the Village radicals, 180–83, 187
Porter, Bruce, 14
Pratt, Mara L., 242*n*33
Presence, 38–39

La Primavera performances, 92–94, 139
Primitivism, rejection of, 112–14
Progressivism, 9–10, 224*n*27
Pruett, Diane Milhan, 244*n*73, 246*n*105

Racialism, 90, 112–14, 217–19
Ragtime, critique of, 7, 114–15, 217
Rameau, Jean-Philippe, 143, 245*n*89
Rather, Lois, 232*n*105
Rédemption (1916), 153, 185, 194–95
Redgrave, Vanessa, 221*n*1
Rene, Natalia, 241*n*14
Revolutionary (1924), 186, 220
Rhythm, 65–66, 230*n*78, 231*n*79, 233*n*125
Roberts, Mary Fanton, 152, 182–83, 247*n*125
Rodin, Auguste, 17, 29, 42, 91, 95, 121, 134–35
Roslavleva, Natalia, 241*n*14
Rousseau, Jean-Jacques, 29
Rudnick, Lois Palken, 180, 252*n*6
Russell, Ken, 221*n*1
Russian revolution, 195–97
Ruyter, Nancy Chalfa, xiii, 222*n*6

St. Denis, Ruth, 103, 105, 125
Sargent, Dr. Dudley A., 83, 129
Sargent, Margherita, 120, 150, 151, 241*n*6
Sause, Judson, 227*n*17
Savada, Elias, 226*n*55
Schall, Janice Joan, 230*n*78
Schlereth, Thomas J., 9, 224*n*25
Schloss, Jacob, 43, 47–59
Schneider, Ilya Ilyich, 255*n*61
Schools, dance, 168, 249*n*42; efforts to establish in America, 115–16, 184, 187–88, 253*n*24; in Moscow, 196–98, 203
Schopenhauer, Arthur, 6, 32–33, 141, 244*n*76
Schubert, Franz, 188
Schwartz, Hillel, 8–9, 223*n*17, 224*n*23
Science. *See* Evolutionism
Scriabin, A. N., 153–54
Seldes, George, 226*n*3
Seldes, Gilbert, 214
Self, xiii, 4, 68, 136–37; in the physical culture movement, 26, 130–31
Shapiro, Michael Steven, 228*n*22
Shaver, Claude L., 242*n*22
Shaw, Martin, 174
Shawn, Ted, 219–20, 260*n*50
Shelley, Percy Bysshe, 17, 88, 91

2891

Shelton, Suzanne, 233n106
Sherman, Martin, 221n2
Shi, David, 90, 236n4
Siegfried, Andre, 218, 259n42
Siegfried's Funeral March program, 140, 153
Singer, Paris, 168, 184, 253n24
Skirt dancing, 24, 227n7
Sloan, John, 121, 183, 241n11
Smith-Rosenberg, Carroll, 166, 249n29
Social dancing, 24, 25–26, 64, 120
Solomon-Godeau, Abigail, 176, 251n66
Soul, 4, 31–32, 68
Spaete, Sigmund, 247n123
Spencer, Herbert, 25, 65, 98, 227n12
Spicer, Alice, 226n55
Stanislavsky, Constantin, 122
Starr, Kevin, 91, 225n36, 236n8
Statue posing, 125–26
Stearns, Harold E., 258n4
Stebbins, Genevieve, 123, 125, 242n26
Steegmuller, Francis, 222n6, 224n33, 238n35, 248n27
Steel, Ronald, 258n2
Steele, Valerie, 176, 251n62
Steichen, Edward, 222n4
Stein, Gertrude, 9, 224n26
Stickley, Gustav, 90
Stieglitz, Alfred, 172–73, 180, 183
Stokes, John, 243n46
Stokes, Sewell, 38, 153, 247n128
Strauss, Richard, 62, 140, 142, 145
Suffragism, 163, 180
Sussman, Warren I., 243n42
Svetloff, Valerien, 77, 145
Symons, Arthur, 134, 141–42, 243n51

Tackel, Martin S., 246n117, 250n55
Tamiris, Helen, 116, 200, 220
Tchaikovsky, Peter I.: *Marche Slav*, 196; *Pathétique*, 153, 188, 193, 200, 202, 231n79
Techniques, body, 222n5; gymnastic, 82–87; in modern dance, 77–82, 230n16, 233n125
The Tempest performances, 72
Terry, Ellen, 131–32, 133, 214, 224n33
Theater, expression in, 131–32
Theology, natural, 98–100
Thompson, Lydia, 159–60
Thoreau, Henry David, 98
Tilden, Douglas, 225n49
Torque, 8–9, 223n17
Trewin, J. C., 233n108

Truth, 4, 10, 98–99
Turner, Frederick Jackson, 216, 258n25
Turnvereins, 68, 69, 83
Tylor, E. B., 25

Vale, Janet, 248n15
Van Vechten, Carl, 143, 174, 245n91; and jazz, 217, 259n28; on *Marche Slav*, 196; on *Orpheus*, 149; on *Rédemption*, 194
Vance, Lee J., 227n14
Veblen, Thorstein, 90, 248n20
Vickers, Hugo, 250n45
Village radicals, 180–83, 187

Wagner, Richard, 29, 141, 144, 200; *Liebestod*, 143–44; *Siegfried's Funeral March*, 140, 153
Walkowitz, Abraham, 39, 42–43
Walters, Ida Sniffen, 163
Wave movements, 35, 99
Wells, H. G., 187
Werner, Morris R., 245n86
Wertheim, Arthur Frank, 180, 241n12, 252n5
Wharton, Edith, 22, 98, 226n1, 237n26
Whiteford, Sarah, 150, 151
Whitman, Walt, 4, 10–11, 28, 31, 122–23, 182, 197, 224n33
Wilbor, Elsie M., 242n28
Will, 6, 32–33, 68, 228n34, 229n47, 244n76, 254n34
Williams, William Carlos, 121
Winckelmann, Johann Joachim, 91, 93
Woman movement, 159–63
Woodhull, Victoria C., 159, 161, 247n8
Woolson, Abba Goold, 159–61, 247n7
World War I, 183–95, 253n23
Wycherly, Margaret, 151

Yacco, Sada, 65
Yberri, Lola, 71, 231n99
Young, Robert M., 237n21, 238n32
Young, Rose, 163
Your Isadora, 17

Zarathustra, 10, 30, 39, 40

Ann Daly
is
Assistant Professor
in the
Department
of Theatre
and Dance
at the University
of Texas
at Austin.